Uncertain Justice

The Constitution Project
50 F Street, N.W., Suite 1070
Washington, D.C. 20001
202-662-4240
info@constitutionproject.org
www.constitutionproject.org

UNCERTAIN JUSTICE
Politics and America's Courts

THE REPORTS OF THE TASK FORCES OF CITIZENS FOR INDEPENDENT COURTS

Thomas O. Sargentich, Reporter for the
TASK FORCE ON FEDERAL JUDICIAL SELECTION

Paul D. Carrington and Barbara E. Reed, Reporters for the
TASK FORCE ON SELECTING STATE COURT JUDGES

Charles Gardner Geyh, Reporter for the
TASK FORCE ON THE DISTINCTION BETWEEN
INTIMIDATION AND LEGITIMATE CRITICISM OF JUDGES

Erwin Chemerinsky, Reporter for the
TASK FORCE ON THE ROLE OF THE LEGISLATURE IN
SETTING THE POWER AND JURISDICTION OF THE COURTS

A Publication of CITIZENS FOR INDEPENDENT COURTS,
an Initiative of the CONSTITUTION PROJECT

Uncertain Justice: Politics and America's Courts was created by Citizens
for Independent Courts when it was a project of The Century Foundation.

2000 ◆ THE CENTURY FOUNDATION PRESS ◆ New York

Library of Congress Cataloging-in-Publication Data

Uncertain justice : politics and America's courts : the reports of the task forces of Citizens for Independent Courts.
    p. cm.
"A publication of Citizens for Independent Courts, an initiative of the Constitution Project."
Includes bibliographical references and index.
  ISBN 0-87078-448-X (pbk.)
1. Judicial process—United States. 2. Judges—Selection and appointment—United States. 3. Law reform—United States. 4. Law and politics—United States. I. Citizens for Independent Courts. II. Constitution Project. III. Century Foundation.
  KF8775 .U52 2000
  347.73'1—dc21
                                                              00-008494

For information about this report or any other work of the Constitution Project, please contact:

> The Constitution Project
> 50 F Street, N.W., Suite 1070
> Washington, D.C. 20001
> 202-662-4240
> info@constitutionproject.org
> www.constitutionproject.org

Nothing written here is to be construed as necessarily reflecting the views of The Century Foundation or as an attempt to aid or hinder the passage of any bill before Congress.

Contents

FOREWORD

The complete independence of the courts of justice is peculiarly essential in a limited Constitution.
          —Alexander Hamilton, *The Federalist* No. 78.

From its beginning, our system of constitutional democracy has depended on the independence of the judiciary. Judges are able to protect the basic rights of individuals and decide cases fairly only when they are free to make decisions according to the law, without regard to political or public pressure. Similarly, the judiciary can maintain the checks and balances essential to preserving a healthy separation of powers only when it is able to resist overreaching by the political branches. Indeed, the cornerstone of American liberty is the power of the courts to protect the rights of the people from the momentary excesses of political and popular majorities.

In recent years, as part of the polarization and posturing that increasingly characterize our national and state politics, threats to the independence of the judiciary have become more commonplace. Attacks on judges for unpopular decisions, even when those decisions are a good faith and reasonable interpretation of the law, have become rampant. Politicians, both federal and state, are responding to unpopular decisions and litigants by attempting to restrict the powers of the courts over certain kinds of cases. Longstanding ethical rules, limiting the kinds of issues judges may discuss in public, are being breached in pursuit of electoral goals. Efforts to politicize the judicial selection process are increasing around the country, and campaign contributions by litigants and their lawyers are escalating.

It was to address such threats that Citizens for Independent Courts (CFIC) was formed in June 1998 by the Constitution Project, with major funding and support from The Century Foundation, the Open Society Institute, and the Deer Creek Foundation. Citizens for Independent Courts is a bipartisan committee of prominent and influential businesspeople, scholars, former public officials, and other Americans, and it promotes public education on the importance of our courts as protectors of Americans' essential constitutional freedoms.

CFIC's blue-ribbon committee serves as a unique, bipartisan voice in debates over judicial independence. It is chaired by two distinguished Americans of very different political views: the Honorable Mickey Edwards, former congressman (R-OK) and chair of the House of Representatives Republican Policy Committee, and now John Quincy Adams Lecturer in Legislative Politics at the John F. Kennedy School of Government at Harvard University; and the Honorable Lloyd N. Cutler, a prominent Washington lawyer and White House counsel to Presidents Jimmy Carter and Bill Clinton. CFIC has also created separate committees of distinguished individuals in the academic and business communities.

As part of the effort to change the nature of the public debate on judicial independence to a more sober and informed one, CFIC formed task forces from among the members of its committees to develop consensus recommendations in four key areas. These task forces were guided in their work by reporters with significant and relevant expertise, and benefited enormously from the diverse experiences and philosophies of their members.

1. Task Force on Federal Judicial Selection
Reporter: Professor Thomas O. Sargentich of the American University Washington College of Law

In recent years, the White House and the Senate have battled over delays in the nomination and confirmation process for federal judges, each blaming the other for vacancies on the federal bench that have existed, in some cases, for several years. To determine objectively for the first time whether there is a pattern of increasing delay in the federal judicial selection process, and where responsibility lies for any delay, this task force gathered and analyzed data from 1977 through 1998, the period covering the presidencies of Jimmy Carter, Ronald Reagan, George Bush, and Bill Clinton through the sixth year of his administration. These data have never before been collected in a comprehensive manner, and are published here for the first time. In light of its findings, the task force developed recommendations for expediting the nomination and confirmation process so that vacancies can be filled more expeditiously. In addition, the task force's recommendations address the thorny issue of the ideology of nominees and what role it should play in the decision-making process of both the White House and the Senate.

2. TASK FORCE ON SELECTING STATE COURT JUDGES
Reporters: Professor Paul D. Carrington of the Duke University School of Law; Barbara E. Reed, Associate Executive Director of the Fund for Modern Courts

The vast majority of judicial decisions are made in state courts. Unfortunately, electoral politics have played an increasingly significant role in judicial selection in many of these states. Thirty-nine states have some form of judicial elections; 77 percent of all judges of trial courts of general jurisdiction and 53 percent of all appellate judges face contestable elections. State judges are frequently targeted for defeat because of unpopular decisions they have rendered, with no regard for whether the judges acted impartially, in good faith, and in accordance with the law. Campaign contributions by litigants and their lawyers create the appearance, if not the reality, of conflicts of interest. The task force developed specific recommendations, focusing particularly on the role of money in judicial campaigns, that states can adopt to improve the way in which judges are selected.

3. TASK FORCE ON THE DISTINCTION BETWEEN INTIMIDATION AND LEGITIMATE CRITICISM OF JUDGES
Reporter: Professor Charles Gardner Geyh of the Indiana University School of Law

Independence of the judiciary does not mean that judges should be shielded from criticism. From the earliest years of the Republic, controversial decisions of the courts have engendered opposition from across the ideological spectrum. Criticism of judges and their decisions is protected by the First Amendment and is, in the words of Justice Felix Frankfurter, "a practice familiar in the long history of Anglo-American litigation." However, when criticism becomes political intimidation—such as threatening federal judges with impeachment because they make politically unpopular decisions—it may undermine the integrity and impartiality of judicial decision-making. This task force has developed recommendations, consistent with the First Amendment, for responding to criticism that threatens independence.

4. TASK FORCE ON THE ROLE OF THE LEGISLATURE IN SETTING THE POWER AND JURISDICTION OF THE COURTS
Reporter: Professor Erwin Chemerinsky of the University of Southern California Law School

Limits on the powers of the federal courts have, throughout history, been a legislative response to unpopular court decisions. In recent years, Congress has limited dramatically the federal courts' powers to vindicate federal rights in, for example, immigration, *habeas corpus*, and prison litigation cases. Governors and state legislators around the country are responding to unpopular court decisions—and even to lawsuits—by proposing similar laws to limit the courts' powers. This task force examined whether such limits are constitutional and, even if constitutional, whether they are sound public policy. The task force's recommendations should be useful for Congress and the state legislatures when they consider whether to enact such limits.

*   *   *

At the heart of the recommendations of each of CFIC's task forces is the concept of self-restraint. The actions and statements of political, civic, and other opinion leaders and members of the public may be legally or constitutionally permissible, but they may also be inconsistent with the effective and sound functioning of our democratic system. We have much to lose if Americans do not exercise self-restraint and instead choose short-term political gain at the expense of our judicial system. The independence of our judiciary is, as Chief Justice Rehnquist has described it, "one of the crown jewels of our system of government today." Emerging democracies around the world look to our judiciary as a model. They understand that without independent courts, the rights and liberties of all citizens are at risk. It is a truth that, too often, Americans themselves take for granted. Citizens for Independent Courts hopes that its recommendations serve to remind us all of that truth and of the risks of our current course.

Acknowledgments

The preparation and publication of these task force reports were supported in part by a grant from the Open Society Institute (OSI). The Constitution Project gratefully acknowledges the support and assistance of OSI, the Deer Creek Foundation, and The Century Foundation.

The Constitution Project wishes to thank several people for their assistance in preparing these reports: Russell Davis and the law firm of Wilmer, Cutler & Pickering for cite-checking two of the reports; Lisa Dewey, Amy Potter, and the law firm of Piper & Marbury for preparing Appendix A to *Defending Justice*; and Edward W. Madeira, Jr., Daniel M. Schaffzin, and the law firm of Pepper Hamilton for preparing Appendix B to that report. The Project is grateful to Harold Spaeth and Wendy Martinek of Michigan State University's Program for Law and Judicial Politics for their critical work in compiling the database on judicial vacancies and the charts in *Justice Held Hostage*. The Project especially wishes to thank the five task force reporters, Paul D. Carrington, Erwin Chemerinsky, Charles Gardner Geyh, Barbara E. Reed, and Thomas O. Sargentich, whose extensive commitment, effort, and expertise made these reports possible.

JUSTICE HELD HOSTAGE
POLITICS AND SELECTING FEDERAL JUDGES

THE REPORT OF THE CITIZENS FOR INDEPENDENT COURTS
TASK FORCE ON FEDERAL JUDICIAL SELECTION

MEMBERS OF THE TASK FORCE*

REPORTER

Thomas O. Sargentich, Professor of Law, American University Washington College of Law

MEMBERS

Jan Witold Baran, Esq., Partner, Wiley, Rein & Fielding; former General Counsel, Republican National Committee

Daniel S. Cheever, Jr., President, Simmons College

Norman Dorsen, Stokes Professor of Law, New York University School of Law

Irene R. Emsellem, Senior Legislative Counsel, American Bar Association

Michael J. Gerhardt, Professor of Law, College of William and Mary, Marshall-Wythe School of Law; Dean Emeritus, Case Western Reserve University, Franklin T. Backus School of Law

---

* Affiliations of members listed for purposes of identification only. The views expressed in this report do not necessarily reflect the views of the institutions with which the members are affiliated.

Tracy Hahn-Burkett, Esq., Legislative Counsel, People for the American Way Foundation

James L. Huffman, Dean, Lewis and Clark Law School

Lawrence J. Korb, Ph.D., Vice President / Maurice R. Greenberg Chair and Director of Studies, Council on Foreign Relations; former Director, Center for Public Policy Education, The Brookings Institution

Steven C. Markoff, Chairman and CEO, A-Mark Financial Corporation

John J. McMackin, Jr., Esq., Partner, Williams & Jensen, P.C.

Elliot M. Mincberg, Esq., Vice President, General Counsel, and Legal Director, People for the American Way Foundation

Burt Neuborne, Legal Director, Brennan Center for Justice; John Norton Pomeroy Professor of Law, New York University School of Law

Charles Nihan, Professor of Law, American University Washington College of Law

The Honorable William A. Norris, former Judge, U.S. Court of Appeals for the Ninth Circuit

The Honorable James L. Oakes, Senior Judge, U.S. Court of Appeals for the Second Circuit

Bernard Petrie, Esq., former Member, California Judicial Nominees Evaluation Commission

Thomas R. Plough, Ph.D., Professor and President, Assumption College

Lynn Rhinehart, Esq., Associate General Counsel, AFL-CIO

Walter Rieman, Esq., Partner, Paul, Weiss, Rifkind, Wharton & Garrison

The Honorable William D. Ruckelshaus, Administrator, Environmental Protection Agency, Nixon and Reagan administrations

The Honorable William S. Sessions, Director, Federal Bureau of Investigation, Bush administration; former Chief Judge, U.S. District Court for the Western District of Texas

Jerome J. Shestack, Esq., former President, American Bar Association

Michael E. Solimine, Professor of Law, University of Cincinnati College of Law

The Honorable Harold R. Tyler, Jr., Deputy Attorney General, Ford administration; former Judge, U.S. District Court for the Southern District of New York; Co-Chairman, Miller Commission on Judicial Selection

Robert A. Van Kirk, Esq., Williams & Connolly; Acting Deputy Assistant Attorney General, U.S. Department of Justice (1996–1997); Office of Counsel to the President (1995–1996)

Ronald H. Weich, Esq., Partner, Zuckerman, Spaeder, Goldstein, Taylor & Kolker, L.L.P.; former Chief Counsel to Senator Edward M. Kennedy, Senate Judiciary Committee

Stephen Wermiel, Associate Director, Program on Law and Government, American University Washington College of Law; former Supreme Court Reporter, the *Wall Street Journal*

TASK FORCE RECOMMENDATIONS

RECOMMENDATIONS FOR EXECUTIVE AND LEGISLATIVE BRANCH REVIEWERS ON IDEOLOGY IN FEDERAL JUDICIAL SELECTION

1. Candidates for judgeships should be committed to deciding cases based on the law and facts of particular cases, without the intrusion of any rigid ideological precommitments to certain results or approaches to the law.

2. Reviewers should investigate a candidate's experience, qualifications, temperament, character, and general views of the law and of the judicial role. Selecting a federal judge is not just a matter of picking a legal technician, for a person's judgments may well reflect one's broad values and commitments.

3. Reviewers must refrain from asking candidates for particular precommitments about unresolved cases or issues that may come before them as judges.

4. The limit on questions seeking precommitments should be applied by reviewers in a common-sense fashion. In particular, this limit should not be allowed to prevent a fully deliberative investigation into the backgrounds, qualifications, and judicial philosophies of candidates for judgeships.

5. The limit on questions seeking precommitments should be respected equally by the president and other executive branch reviewers as well as by senators and other legislative branch reviewers, despite differences in the roles played by the two branches in the appointment process.

6. The limit on questions seeking precommitments should apply with respect to candidates for courts at all levels of the federal judiciary.

7. Reviewers seeking to assess a candidate's views should exercise caution when evaluating a person's current or former clients, memberships, and writings or speeches.

8. The value of judicial independence is consistent with pursuing diversity on the federal bench.

9. The value of judicial independence is consistent with active involvement by bar associations in the selection process.

RECOMMENDATIONS FOR EXECUTIVE AND LEGISLATIVE BRANCHES ON DELAY IN FEDERAL JUDICIAL SELECTION

1. The president and other executive branch officials should make it a high priority to choose nominees for federal judgeships in a more expeditious manner.

2. The president and other executive branch officials should routinely engage in advance planning for possible vacancies on the federal bench. Such advance planning should include developing lists of available, qualified candidates for judgeships, while coordinating early in the process with concerned senators.

3. Senators and other legislative branch officials should make it a high priority to take final action on nominees in a more expeditious manner.

4. Once a nomination is made, the Senate process should proceed expeditiously to a committee hearing, committee review and voting, and floor consideration and voting. The Task Force is especially concerned about the use of holds by individual senators that have the effect of preventing collective deliberation about and voting on candidates, either in committee or on the Senate floor. Respect for the views of individual senators, while vital, should not be allowed to undermine collective decision-making in an open, deliberative process.

5. Both executive and legislative branch officials should avoid engaging in delays to obtain strategic advantage during the judicial selection process.

6. Both executive and legislative branch officials should devote adequate staff resources to the task of reviewing candidates for federal judgeships so that the process is not delayed due to lack of staff.

7. Both executive and legislative branch officials should make decisions about a candidate in light of the person's own merits. Such decisions should not be linked with unrelated business that is the subject of bargaining between the legislative and executive branches of government.

8. The Task Force endorses as aspirational ideals the time-related goals set forth in the Miller Center Report, the most recent prior study of delay in federal judicial selection. The goals are the following: nominations within 180 days of vacancies and confirmations within 60 days of nominations—for an average total of 240 days, or about eight months. By endorsing these goals, the Task Force underscores the need for executive and legislative branch officials to make strong commitments to reversing the trend of increasing delay in federal judicial selection.

9. Public records that provide reliable and meaningful information about the federal judicial selection process should be maintained, regularly updated, and made easily accessible to all persons wishing to study such issues as delay in the process. It is the responsibility of executive and legislative branch officials to see that these steps are taken as soon as possible.

10. The data on judicial appointments show that the average number of days between nomination and final action for women is greater than the number of days for men. (Adequate data on race of nominees were not available.) We recommend that the responsible officials address this matter to assure that candidates for judgeships are not treated differently based on their gender.

REPORT OF THE TASK FORCE ON FEDERAL JUDICIAL SELECTION

INTRODUCTION

This report of Citizens for Independent Courts' Task Force on Federal Judicial Selection follows a distinguished line of recent blue-ribbon studies of the federal courts and federal judicial selection in particular."[1] It is striking that, despite the earlier reports' powerful calls for reform, very little has changed in the federal judicial selection process.[2] Indeed, there is scant evidence that officials in charge of judicial selection have taken seriously the critiques that have been offered.[3] The Task Force strongly believes that the pattern of inaction must be broken.

In particular, executive and legislative branch officials responsible for judicial selection—the president, the chair and members of the Senate Committee on the Judiciary, the Senate majority leader, and others—have a pressing responsibility both to moderate the role of partisan ideology and to reverse the trend of increasing delay in order to promote the independence of the federal courts. The purpose of our report is not to criticize or second-guess any particular administration or Congress. Rather, we suggest what we consider, after careful deliberation, to be in the best interests of the Constitution, the constitutional actors, and the public, which relies on the federal courts to resolve important disputes. We call upon present and future officials in the executive and legislative branches to react publicly to the proposals we put forward, for such an open dialogue would benefit the process and the public.

After discussing the background of our central concerns about moderating the role of partisan ideology and decreasing delay in federal judicial selection, we will consider each matter in turn.

I. Background: Contemporary Conflicts about Federal Judicial Selection

In the last few years, a number of senators have complained that at least some of President Clinton's judicial nominees have been unduly activist in their orientation toward judging. Critics of the Senate have argued that legislative branch actors have been unacceptably partisan in their opposition to the administration's nominees. Others have claimed that President Clinton has nominated excessively conservative judges largely in response to political pressures. These controversies have not been confined to official actors, for private interest groups also have been deeply involved in the judicial selection process.

Moreover, conflicts have arisen concerning the increasing amount of time consumed by the selection process. Some have charged that the Senate's leadership has indulged in strategies of delay in order to support partisan views. Others have alleged that the president has shown insufficient attention to the problem of filling judicial vacancies in an expeditious manner.[4]

What the country has recently witnessed, therefore, is heightened partisan wrangling about judicial selection.[5] In the Task Force's view, it is time to lower the temperature of the debate considerably. The responsible officials need to move away from a perspective of short-term political advantage toward a longer-term effort to improve the process in the name of good government.

One should bear in mind that current debates are not entirely new. Indeed, this decade's partisan conflicts about judicial appointments are reminiscent of those of the last decade. During the 1980s, Republicans assailed Democratic opposition to President Reagan's nominations, notably including that of Robert Bork to the Supreme Court in 1987. During the 1990s, Democrats have decried the Republican Senate's handling of President

Clinton's nominees, especially after power in Congress shifted away from the Democrats in 1995.

We encourage executive and legislative branch officials responsible for federal judicial selection to move beyond the stalemate created by these partisan charges and countercharges. The highly political "blame game" does not serve the values of judicial quality, impartiality, and independence that the involved actors should promote.[6]

The nomination and confirmation of federal judges requires careful, on-the-merits deliberation by the executive and legislative branches, separately as well as together. The political branches have the important constitutional responsibility thoughtfully to review the backgrounds, qualifications, and judicial philosophies of persons considered for the federal bench. At the same time, the selection process needs to show greater respect for the principle of judicial independence, which is among the most fundamental underpinnings of constitutionalism in the United States. The core of judicial independence is decisional independence, which is the principle that judges must be free to make decisions independently, without regard to outside pressure or any obligation other than to the governing law.

Decisional independence is protected by the "good behavior" clause of Article III of the U.S. Constitution, which guarantees federal judges continued tenure during good behavior.[7] This protection frees judges to make decisions without having to face elections or other challenges to their tenure resulting from unpopular decisions. Once in office, federal judges can retain their positions for life, subject only to possible removal following impeachment and conviction for "treason, bribery, and other high crimes and misdemeanors."[8] In addition, the Constitution guarantees that federal judges are to receive a compensation that shall not be diminished during their continuance in office.[9]

Chief Justice Rehnquist has stated that the independent judiciary is one of the "crown jewels" of the nation's system of government.[10] Certainly, judicial independence is an essential ingredient of the protection of individual liberty and equality in our constitutional system.[11] Moreover, the independent judiciary checks the legislative and executive branches of the federal government, thereby helping to maintain our constitutional commitments both to separation of powers at the national level and to federalism in nation-state relations.

The Task Force seeks to focus public attention on the need for the key actors in the executive and legislative branches to respect judicial independence by moderating the role of partisan ideology and decreasing the delay involved in judicial appointments. In the Task Force's view, the major way to address concerns about ideology and delay is for the leading actors to exercise leadership and self-restraint. At bottom, the Task Force's recommendations are designed to encourage such behavior.

II. IDEOLOGY IN FEDERAL JUDICIAL SELECTION

A. GENERAL CONSIDERATIONS

1. *What is ideology in this context?* The first step in discussing ideology in federal judicial selection is to be clear about the meaning of the word itself. *Ideology* has two major, opposed usages in the context of judging.[12]

At one end of the spectrum, the word carries a pejorative meaning. It refers to fixed or rigid ideological commitments to certain results whatever the facts or law of a case. These commitments are often connected to partisan differences. It is unacceptable for judges to be ideological in this sense, for that would undermine their independence and legitimacy. A fixed or rigidly ideological approach to judging contradicts the ideal of the rule of law.[13] This ideal requires that judges follow established legal norms in light of the facts of particular cases, without being led to results by arbitrary ideological factors.[14]

At the other end of the spectrum, the word *ideology* has a much broader, nonpejorative meaning. It refers to "the origin and nature of ideas,"[15] to "the doctrines, opinions, or ways of thinking of an individual" and "the body of ideas on which a particular political, economic, or social system is based."[16] In this usage, ideology plays a role in everyone's thinking about legal issues, including that of judges. Ideology in this broad sense includes a person's views about justice, about key values like liberty and equality, about basic institutional relations like judicial deference to legislatures, and about core constitutional concepts like separation of powers, federalism, and judicial review itself.

2. *Given ideology's dual meaning, what are the main obligations of the reviewers of candidates for federal judgeships?* The Task Force believes that the discussion of ideology in judicial selection can be significantly clarified by distinguishing the word's two meanings. When invoking the first, pejorative meaning, it is appropriate to condemn ideology as inconsistent with our ideals of fair, rule-governed behavior by courts.

Yet when the second, broadly descriptive meaning is used, it is appropriate to encourage reviewers to investigate the ideology of candidates for federal judgeships. In our postrealist age, we know that legal materials may well be somewhat indeterminate or conflicting, and that judges often invoke background normative notions in deciding how to rule.[17] Accordingly, it is both appropriate and important for reviewers to ask questions designed to flesh out a candidate's underlying philosophical and normative commitments. These could include, but would not necessarily be limited to, questions about a candidate's general attitudes about justice, about reasoning from precedent, about major constitutional values such as liberty and equality, and about leading cases in our legal culture.

3. What should be the central limit on questions asked of candidates for federal judgeships?

There needs to be a definite limit on questions asked of candidates in order to preserve judicial independence. This limit relates to questions that go beyond general inquiries into a candidate's broad views about judging or a candidate's knowledge of leading cases. In particular, a reviewer might ask a candidate how he or she would vote on an unresolved case or issue that could come before him or her as a judge.[18] Such a request for a particularized precommitment should be regarded as wholly inappropriate. One should not ask a candidate to prejudge a matter that might come before him or her as a judge.[19] If such a question is nonetheless asked, we urge that a candidate decline to answer it on the ground that it seeks an inappropriate precommitment.

Political officials should not pressure candidates to make precommitments because such pressure directly undermines the principle of decisional independence. Judges need to be free to decide matters that come before them based on the facts and law of the case, without being worried about commitments made during the selection process.

In addition, members of the public, including litigants, need to have full confidence in the impartiality of courts. Such confidence is eroded if a candidate for a federal judgeship prejudges a case or issue during the process of judicial selection. Moreover, efforts to seek pre-commitments by reviewing officials in either the legislative or executive branch of government merely encourage officials in the other branch to undertake similar efforts. This dynamic can generate a vicious cycle, further undermining the principle of an independent judiciary.[20]

B. Particular recommendations for legislative and executive branch reviewers

1. Candidates for judgeships should be committed to deciding cases based on the law and facts of particular cases, without the intrusion of any rigid ideological precommitments to certain results or approaches to the law.

Recall the first meaning of *ideology* discussed above: a candidate for a federal judgeship should not be, nor be asked to participate in a process that is, ideological in a rigid or partisan sense.[21] To the contrary, candidates for judgeships should be dedicated to deciding cases in light of their understanding of the applicable law and facts. A judge should be professionally qualified, intelligent, impartial, committed to equal justice under law, and possessed of a judicial temperament that examines all sides of a case before rendering a decision.[22]

2. Reviewers should investigate a candidate's experience, qualifications, temperament, character, and general views of the law and of the judicial role. Selecting a federal judge is not just a matter of picking a legal technician, for a person's judgments may well reflect one's broad values and commitments.

Recall the second meaning of *ideology* discussed above: it is appropriate for reviewers to probe a candidate's general normative views and assumptions that make up ideology in the broad, non-pejorative sense.[23] After all, federal judges should be expected to have background understandings about law and society, and about justice and fairness, that can become important when they are called on to make difficult decisions. In addition, candidates for judgeships may have highly developed understandings of a judge's role, of precedent, of leading cases, and of other aspects of the legal system that can be significant in reaching judgments in hard cases. Reviewers should investigate such broad understandings in order fully to consider a candidate for a life-tenured position on the federal bench.

3. Reviewers must refrain from asking candidates for particular precommitments about unresolved cases or issues that may come before them as judges.

Although questioning directed at a candidate's general views is appropriate, an important line must not be crossed. A reviewer should not ask a candidate how he or she would vote on an unresolved case or issue if that matter were to come before him or her as a judge. Moreover, a candidate should decline to answer a question that, in his or her judgment, calls for an unacceptable precommitment.

There is, of course, no guarantee that a reviewer and a candidate will agree about whether a particular question calls for an unacceptable precommitment.[24] If a candidate and a reviewer disagree, that fact itself would be a good subject for dialogue between the candidate and reviewer. Such a dialogue could be revealing about the candidate's general judicial philosophy. In any event, both reviewers and candidates should be alert to the importance of protecting judicial independence throughout the process.

4. The limit on questions seeking precommitments should be applied by reviewers in a common-sense fashion. In particular, this limit should not be allowed to prevent a fully deliberative investigation into the backgrounds, qualifications, and judicial philosophies of candidates for judgeships.

Our recommendation against questions seeking precommitments does not mean that we imagine that a profitable interchange would consist of a bland inquiry into the judicial equivalent of "name, rank, and serial number." In order for there to be a fully deliberative process, executive and legislative branch reviewers need to be able to conduct a probing inquiry into a candidate's background, qualifications, and judicial philosophy.

Nor do we believe that a simplistic bright line can be drawn in advance between sensitive probing of a candidate's qualifications and general views, on the one hand, and inappropriate efforts to seek particular precommitments as to unresolved cases or issues, on the other hand. In each situation, the facts and the context in which a question is asked will matter a great deal. One important variable involves the generality of a given question: the more general the question, the less likely will be the need to state how one would decide an unresolved issue or case. Another important issue concerns whether the question involves settled, well-established legal principles, or whether the question deals with yet-to-be-decided matters. If a question concerns an unresolved matter, there is a greater risk of precommitment. Again, there is no simple matrix or rule that can clearly identify in advance the range of acceptable, as opposed to unacceptable, questions.

Two hypothetical examples may help to illustrate the distinction, although we underscore that they do not exhaust the possibilities. Let us assume that a recent Supreme Court opinion is being heatedly criticized by some politicians and citizens. Assume that a reviewer asks a judicial candidate how he or she would apply that opinion in deciding a specific controversial issue that is governed by the opinion. In this context, the question seeks an inappropriate precommitment. In contrast, let us assume that a reviewer asks whether a candidate supports the basic holding against segregated public schools in *Brown v. Board of Education*.[25] The purpose of the question, the reviewer states, is to determine whether the candidate accepts the consensus view that *Brown* was an important milestone in U.S. constitutional law. This question does not seek a particularized precommitment as to an unresolved case or issue. The point to be stressed is that participants in the judicial selection process must keep in mind the core obligation to respect the values of judicial impartiality and independence.

5. The limit on questions seeking precommitments should be respected equally by the president and other executive branch reviewers as well as by senators and other legislative branch reviewers, despite differences in the roles played by the two branches in the appointment process.

All executive and legislative branch reviewers, and especially the president and senators, should respect judicial independence by not asking candidates for precommitments about unresolved cases or issues. Placing such responsibility equally on the president and senators is not meant to deny that there are significant differences in their roles in the appointment process. The president is responsible for choosing a nominee, whereas the Senate gives its advice and consent in reviewing the nominee.[26] Also, it is easier to monitor the questions asked by senators during public confirmation hearings than it is to monitor the questions asked by presidents, for executive branch interviews with candidates are not public.[27] Despite the differences in the roles and activities of the branches, however, both the president and the Senate share the obligation to respect the independence of the third branch of government.

6. The limit on questions seeking precommitments should apply with respect to candidates for courts at all levels of the federal judiciary.

The principle of avoiding questions seeking particular precommitments as to unresolved cases or issues should be followed with candidates for appellate as well as trial courts. To be sure, appellate judges perform some functions that differ from those of trial judges. Nevertheless, the principle against questions seeking precommitments must apply to candidates for judgeships at all levels of the federal judiciary—at the district court, court of appeals, and Supreme Court levels.

7. Reviewers seeking to assess a candidate's views should exercise caution when evaluating a person's current or former clients, memberships, and writings or speeches.

There are ways to assess a candidate's orientations other than by asking intrusive questions about how the candidate would vote with respect to unresolved cases or issues. A common method is to assess a candidate's professional background, including his or her experiences as a lawyer, memberships in legal and nonlegal groups, and writings or speeches. Questions about such matters are appropriate, although caution should be exercised in drawing conclusions about a candidate's beliefs based simply on such factors.

With respect to clients, it is a cardinal principle of our adversary system that unpopular or controversial persons, like others, may need lawyers, and that the lawyers for such clients should not be assumed personally to embrace the positions they advanced as advocates.

With respect to memberships, it is inappropriate merely to assume that a lawyer embraces all of the views advanced by organizations with which the lawyer is associated. Candidates should be free to distinguish their views from those of organizations with which they have professional or other ties. In a given case, much may depend on the nature of the organization and the character of the candidate's role in it. Moreover, it is wholly inappropriate to condemn a candidate for participating in organizations serving the public interest. Attacks on public-service activities tend to discourage publicly-minded candidates from seeking judgeships. In the interest of seeking diversity on the bench and of encouraging volunteer and pro bono service, the process should encourage public-service activities by candidates, assuming that the groups with which candidates participate lie within the broad mainstream of views debated widely in American law and society.

In addition, we endorse the notion that judicial candidates should resign from clubs that intentionally discriminate on the basis of race, color, religion, sex, disability, or national origin. We understand that the practice of the Senate Committee on the Judiciary has been to enforce this norm, pursuant to a 1990 committee resolution that, among other things, excludes from coverage fraternities and sororities as well as religious or ethnic heritage organizations.

With respect to writings or speeches, it is appropriate for a reviewer to ask whether they express a view that the candidate would consider binding or influential in a future context of judging. Some writing, such as by law professors, may be intended to provoke debate by going beyond current understandings of the law. The selection process should not discourage such writing, for it is an important means by which the law evolves. It is reasonable for a candidate to explain, if it is true, that his or her earlier pronouncements do not reflect current views or, even if they do, that they do not reflect how he or she would decide a case as a judge. Of course, a reviewer is free to assess the credibility of any statement distinguishing or disclaiming previously stated views. Reviewers need to have confidence that a candidate can set aside his or her own views and decide cases in light of the applicable law and facts, and should not automatically assume that the candidate cannot or will not do so.

With respect to prior decisions by a judge who is a candidate for another judicial appointment, executive and legislative branch reviewers should not punish a judge for a controversial decision. Judges need to decide cases on their own merits without regard to the popularity of a ruling under the law.

8. *The value of judicial independence is consistent with pursuing diversity on the federal bench.*

The value of judicial independence is consistent with seeking a federal judiciary that reflects diversity on many fronts, including general views of judging as well as such factors as ethnicity, race, gender, sexual orientation, professional background, and geographic origin. Having people with different views and backgrounds on the bench enriches the judiciary.

9. The value of judicial independence is consistent with active involvement by bar associations in the selection process.

In the past, the participation by bar associations in judicial selection has drawn some criticism from both liberals and conservatives. In our view, professional, on-the-merits assessments of judicial candidates by bar associations can contribute significantly to the selection process. At the same time, in order to prevent delay, bar associations need to act expeditiously in sharing their assessments with relevant officials, and they should refrain from making their own political assessments of candidates.

III. Delay in Federal Judicial Selection

A. General Considerations

Over many years, there has been generally increasing delay in the processes of nominating and confirming federal judges. In particular, since Jimmy Carter was president, the average numbers of days from vacancy to nomination and from nomination to confirmation or other final action have grown. (See Appendix, Table 1, pp. 40–41.) From 1977 to 1998, the mean number of days from vacancy to nomination was 277; for the same period, the mean number of days from nomination to confirmation or other final action was 100. In these years, the greater increase in delay occurred during the interval from nomination to confirmation or other final action. During his first six years in office, President Clinton took an average of 75 more days to nominate a candidate for the federal judiciary than President Carter took. During the 105th Congress of 1997–98, the Senate took an average of 163 more days to act on a nomination (or to let it expire) than the Senate did in the 95th Congress of 1977–78.

Such increasing delay is an important problem for at least three key reasons. First, delay in filling vacancies on the federal bench slows the process of delivering justice in the United States. The "consumers" of the courts—the litigants with personal stakes in pending cases—are directly affected by delay in selecting judges. Second, the judicial branch is negatively affected by having to perform with less than a full complement of authorized judges. As Chief Justice Rehnquist has underscored in recent years, the institutional costs of increasing delay are considerable.[28] Third, the two political branches have a constitutional responsibility to select judges for the third branch of government in an expeditious and efficient manner. The failure to do so risks eroding the public's respect for governmental institutions.

The Task Force believes that officials in the executive and legislative branches must commit themselves more actively to counteracting the tendency toward greater delay in judicial selection. To be sure, some time is consumed by virtue of there being a more complicated selection process involving larger numbers of judgeships.[29] Nevertheless, we believe that if both branches make greater commitments of time and effort to address delay, significant improvements could result. Both the president and the Senate need to work together with appropriate self-restraint, as required by the system of checks and balances, to address the problem of increasing delay in selecting federal judges.

To track delay, information on vacancies and the process of filling them must be readily available. However, the Task Force has been disturbed to learn about the lack of easily available and meaningful data concerning the judicial selection process. Surprising as it has been to us, the Task Force has had to walk a long road involving our independent research, data gathering, and data analysis with the assistance of specialized scholars.[30] We were unable to find an authoritative public source with comprehensive, easily understood data about delay in judicial selection, for such records have either not been kept or are not easily or publicly accessible. We strongly urge that a set of public records providing reliable and meaningful information about the judicial selection process be maintained, regularly updated, and made easily accessible, such as on the World Wide Web.

B. PARTICULAR RECOMMENDATIONS FOR THE EXECUTIVE AND LEGISLATIVE BRANCHES

1. The president and other executive branch officials should make it a high priority to choose nominees for federal judgeships in a more expeditious manner.

Statistics show that most of the time expended in judicial selection occurs during the period from vacancy to nomination. There are many factors contributing to this delay. Still, the president should undertake a major and ongoing commitment to reducing delay in judicial nominations.

2. The president and other involved executive branch officials should routinely engage in advance planning for possible vacancies on the federal bench. Such advance planning should include developing lists of available, qualified candidates for judgeships, while coordinating early in the process with concerned senators.

3. Senators and other legislative branch officials should make it a high priority to take final action on nominees in a more expeditious manner.

The data also show increasing delay over time in the period from nomination to confirmation of federal judges. We believe that the Senate leadership should make a major and ongoing commitment to address the increasing delay in judicial selection.

4. Once a nomination is made, the Senate process should proceed expeditiously to a committee hearing, committee review and voting, and floor consideration and voting. The Task Force is especially concerned about the use of holds by individual senators that have the effect of preventing collective deliberation about and voting on candidates, either in committee or on the Senate floor. Respect for the views of individual senators, while vital, should not be allowed to undermine collective decision-making in an open, deliberative process.

5. Both executive and legislative branch officials should avoid engaging in delays to obtain strategic advantage during the judicial selection process.

6. Both executive and legislative branch officials should devote adequate staff resources to the task of reviewing candidates for federal judgeships so that the process is not delayed due to lack of staff.

7. Both executive and legislative branch officials should make decisions about a candidate in light of the person's own merits. Such decisions should not be linked with unrelated business that is the subject of bargaining between the legislative and executive branches of government.

8. The Task Force endorses as aspirational ideals the time-related goals set forth in the Miller Center Report, the most recent prior study of delay in federal judicial selection. The goals are the following: nominations within 180 days of vacancies and confirmations within 60 days of nominations—for an average total of 240 days, or about eight months. By endorsing these goals, the Task Force underscores the need for executive and legislative officials to make strong commitments to reversing the trend of increasing delay in federal judicial selection.

We acknowledge that the eight-month guideline, as an average from vacancy to confirmation, represents a substantial reduction in the period of time that the process has actually consumed in recent years. We also recognize that the suggested guideline will be useful only if responsible officials take it seriously. As an initial matter, the key step is to begin moving in the direction of this guideline rather than, as has been happening, away from it.

9. Public records that provide reliable and meaningful information about the federal judicial selection process should be maintained, regularly updated, and made easily accessible to all persons wishing to study such issues as delay in the process. It is the responsibility of executive and legislative branch officials to see that these steps are taken as soon as possible.

10. The data on judicial appointments show that the average number of days between nomination and final action for women is greater than the number of days for men. (Adequate data on race of nominees were not available.) We recommend that the responsible officials address this matter to assure that candidates for judgeships are not treated differently based on their gender.

The Task Force is concerned that all responsible officials involved in federal judicial selection commit themselves to assuring that candidates are treated equally and fairly, without regard to gender or race. The data suggest that, on average, female candidates have taken a longer time to proceed from nomination to final action than have male candidates. (See Appendix, Figures 12–14, pages 63–67.) The Task Force urges the responsible officials to address this issue and to report on efforts made to eliminate any appearance of unevenness in the treatment of female candidates.

The Task Force was unable to obtain similarly complete information about minority candidates. Information about minority candidates during the 105th Congress shows that unsuccessful minority candidates confronted a longer period of time, on average, from nomination to final action than unsuccessful white candidates. (See Appendix, Figures 15 and 16, pages 69 and 70.) Although these data are limited to the 105th Congress, they suggest that the involved officials should redouble efforts to treat candidates evenly without regard to race.

IV. CONCLUSION: A CALL FOR GREATER LEADERSHIP AND SELF-RESTRAINT BY EXECUTIVE AND LEGISLATIVE BRANCH OFFICIALS INVOLVED IN FEDERAL JUDICIAL SELECTION

Reform of federal judicial selection requires greater leadership and self-restraint by the officials who control the process, the president and members of the Senate. Such behavior is needed specifically to moderate the role of partisan ideology and to reverse the trend of increasing delay in judicial selection.

It should be underscored that self-restraint by our leaders is a major constituent of a well-functioning system of separation of powers and checks and balances. Under our Constitution, the legislative, executive, and judicial powers are vested in separate institutions. Such separation implies interdependence, for the branches must work with each other in order for the government to work. As Justice Robert Jackson noted in the steel seizure case, effective government under the U.S. Constitution presupposes "separateness but interdependence, autonomy but reciprocity" among the branches of government.[31] This interdependence of separate institutions sharing power requires self-restraint at the most basic level. Without it, the balance needed for a reasonably well-functioning government is threatened.

In the end, the president and the Senate must devote immediate and sustained attention to both moderating the role of partisan ideology and reversing the trend of increasing delay in the process of selecting qualified, impartial, and independent federal judges.

NOTES

1. *See, e.g.,* American Bar Association Commission on Separation of Powers and Judicial Independence, *An Independent Judiciary* (Washington, D.C.: American Bar Association, 1997); Miller Center Commission on the Selection of Federal Judges, *Improving the Process of Appointing Federal Judges* (Charlottesville: University of Virginia, Miller Center of Public Affairs, 1996) (hereinafter Miller Center Report); Judicial Conference of the United States, *Long-Range Plan for the Federal Courts* (1995) (hereinafter Long-Range Plan); Association of the Bar of the City of New York, *Report of the Ad Hoc Committee on the Senate Confirmation Process* (New York: Association of the Bar of the City of New York, 1992). For a recent discussion of normative controversies in current debates about the federal courts as civil justice providers, *see* Robert G. Vaughn, *Normative Controversies Underlying Contemporary Debates about Civil Justice Reform: A Way of Talking about Bureaucracy and the Future of the Federal Courts,* 76 Denver U. L. Rev. 217 (1998).

2. When we speak of the "federal judicial selection process," we are referring comprehensively to the nomination, confirmation, and appointment of federal judges.

3. *See, e.g.,* Miller Center Report.

4. Although we are not undertaking to analyze the causes of recent partisan conflicts about judicial selection, some would suggest that tensions between the branches of government become more partisan in situations of divided government. These are situations when the presidency is controlled by one of the major political parties and Congress, and in particular the Senate, is controlled by the other major political party. For discussion of divided government—which has been relatively common since the Eisenhower administration—*see* Morris P. Fiorina, *Divided Government* (New York: Macmillan, 1992); David Mayhew, *Divided We Govern* (New Haven: Yale University Press, 1991); Gary W. Cox and Samuel Kernell, eds., *The Politics of Divided Government* (Boulder, Colo.: Westview Press, 1991). For a discussion of federal judicial selection in the context of divided government, *see* Carl Tobias, *Federal Judicial Selection in a Time of Divided Government,* 47 Emory L.J. 527 (1998).

5. Moreover, the judicial selection process has become more complicated over several decades as a result of, among other things, greater activity by the Senate in reviewing presidential nominees.

"Lest there be any doubt about the deepening and expansive consideration of judicial nominees. . . , ponder these bits of information: in 1922, . . .

President Warren G. Harding nominated George Sutherland, and the Senate confirmed the candidate within hours; in 1953, the Senate confirmed Earl Warren to be chief justice without questioning him; and before the 1981 confirmation hearing of Sandra Day O'Connor, no radio or television network had ever broadcast from the hearing room" (Robert A. Katzmann, *Courts and Congress* [Washington, D.C.: Brookings Institution, 1997], p. 9).

6. The Task Force does not seek to assign blame for the problems we have identified, but rather seeks to encourage an active effort by responsible governmental officials to address issues in the public interest. There is too much at stake to permit indulgence in finger pointing rather than problem solving.

7. U.S. Constitution, art. III, sec. 1.

8. U.S. Constitution, art. II, sec. 4.

9. U.S. Constitution, art. III, sec. 1.

10. Chief Justice William H. Rehnquist, Keynote Address, *Symposium on the Future of the Federal Courts,* 46 Am. U. L. Rev. 267, 274 (1996).

11. Alexander Hamilton quoted Montesquieu approvingly for the proposition that "there is no liberty if the power of judging be not separated from the legislative and executive powers" (*The Federalist* No. 78 [New York: New American Library, 1961], p. 466).

12. For discussions of ideology, *see, e.g.,* Judith N. Shklar, ed., *Political Theory and Ideology* (New York: Macmillan, 1966).

13. By "rule of law," we are referring to the notion that authoritative legal materials can and should both guide the use of executive discretion and serve as the basis of judicial checks on agencies, even though the materials' meaning and implications in particular cases may be contested. For a discussion of the rule of law, *see, e.g.,* Richard H. Fallon, Jr., *"The Rule of Law" as a Concept in Constitutional Discourse,* 97 Colum. L. Rev. 1 (1997).

14. Concern about rigid or partisan ideology was expressed in the Miller Center Report, p. 12: "Just as candidates should put aside their partisan political views when appointed to the bench, so too should they put aside ideology. To retain either is to betray dedication to the process of impartial judging. Men and women qualified by training and experience to be judges generally do not wish to and do not indulge in partisan or ideological approaches to their work. The rare exception should not be taken as the norm."

15. *Webster's Third New International Dictionary of the English Language, Unabridged* (Springfield, Mass.: G & C Merriam, 1976).

16. *Webster's New World Dictionary of American English,* 3d ed. (New York: Webster's New World, 1988), p. 670.

17. For instance, H. L. A. Hart speaks of the law's "open texture" that demands an interpreter's judgment, rather than formalistic rule-following.

Herbert Lionel Adolphus Hart, *The Concept of Law* (Oxford: Clarendon Press, 1961), pp. 120–32. Ronald Dworkin, in a different way, stresses the need for judges to turn to underlying policies and principles in deciding hard cases. Ronald Dworkin, *Taking Rights Seriously* (Cambridge, Mass.: Harvard University Press, 1977), pp. 14–130; Ronald Dworkin, *A Matter of Principle* (Cambridge, Mass.: Harvard University Press, 1985), pp. 9–71; Ronald Dworkin, *Law's Empire* (Cambridge, Mass.: Harvard University Press, 1986), pp. 1–86. The distinction between narrow rules and broad standards or principles, the latter of which may seem quite open-ended, is well-recognized in the law. *See, e.g.,* Louis Kaplow, *Rules Versus Standards: An Economic Analysis,* 42 Duke L.J. 557 (1992); Antonin Scalia, *The Rule of Law as a Law of Rules,* 56 U. Chi. L. Rev. 1175 (1989); Kathleen M. Sullivan, *The Supreme Court, 1991 Term—Foreword: The Justices of Rules and Standards,* 106 Harv. L. Rev. 22 (1992).

18. We recognize that, in a given instance, there may be debate about whether a matter is truly "unresolved." If there is a plausible basis for considering it so, the matter should be treated carefully in order to protect judicial independence.

19. *See* Katzmann, *Courts and Congress,* p. 41 ("To compel a nominee to prejudge issues runs counter to the norms of judicial decisionmaking").

20. It bears noting that there are ways to find out a person's views other than by inappropriately asking for precommitments. One might, for example, look at what a person has done in his or her career, although caution should be exercised in assuming either that past history necessarily demonstrates what a person will do as a judge, or that a person will not change his or her views. (*See* Recommendation II.B.7, p. 19.) This cautionary lesson is confirmed by the experience of President Lincoln in filling the vacancy on the Supreme Court left by Roger Taney. Lincoln is reported to have said: "[W]e wish for a Chief Justice who will sustain what has been done in regard to emancipation and the legal tenders. We cannot ask a man what he will do, and if we should, and he should answer us, we should despise him for it. Therefore we must take a man whose opinions are known" (George S. Boutwell, *Reminiscences of Sixty Years in Public Affairs* [New York: 1902], p. 29). Lincoln nominated as chief justice his secretary of the treasury, Salmon P. Chase, who, among other things, had helped to draft and shepherd the Legal Tender (or greenback) legislation through Congress. Contrary to Lincoln's expectations, Chief Justice Chase wrote the opinion declaring the Legal Tender legislation unconstitutional. As Chief Justice William Rehnquist has noted: "Chief Justice Chase's vote in the Legal Tender Cases is a textbook example of the proposition that one may look at a legal question differently as a judge from the way one did as a member of

the executive branch." William H. Rehnquist, *The Supreme Court: How It Was, How It Is* (New York: Morrow, 1987), p. 241.

21. *Cf.* Katzmann, *Courts and Congress,* p. 43 ("What should be out of bounds is any effort to make the appointment process part of a politicized agenda, in which the judiciary becomes a pawn in often highly charged battles between groups and partisans").

22. While we are not seeking to establish a complete list of the desirable characteristics of judges, we endorse the listing in Henry Abraham's introduction to his book on Supreme Court appointments: "One, demonstrated judicial temperament. Two, professional expertise and competence. Three, absolute personal as well as professional integrity. Four, an able, agile, lucid mind. Five, appropriate professional educational background or training. Six, the ability to communicate clearly, both orally and in writing, especially the latter" (Henry J. Abraham, *Justices and Presidents: A Political History of Appointments to the Supreme Court,* 3d ed. [New York, Oxford University Press, 1992], p. 4). Sheldon Goldman has also developed an excellent list of desirable judicial characteristics: "1. Neutrality as to the Parties in Litigation. 2. Fair-mindedness. 3. Being Well Versed in the Law. 4. Ability to Think and Write Logically and Lucidly. 5. Personal Integrity. 6. Good Physical and Mental Health. 7. Judicial Temperament. 8. Ability to Handle Judicial Power Sensibly" (Sheldon Goldman, *Picking Federal Judges: Lower Court Selection from Roosevelt through Reagan* [New Haven: Yale University Press, 1987]).

23. *See* Katzmann, *Courts and Congress,* p. 10 ("[I]t is appropriate to consider a nominee's core values, perspectives about the law and the role of the Court, and approaches to judging . . ."), and p. 38 ("It is consistent with the norms of judicial independence and proper for senators to learn of a nominee's perspectives").

24. In fact, there may be wide ground for disagreement. *See* Katzmann, *Courts and Congress,* p. 19 (noting that nominees "may draw the line in different ways and may not always adhere to the standards they set for themselves," whereas senators "will commonly express their frustration about the responsiveness of those being questioned, about what they believe are the highly selective and subjective criteria by which nominees determine whether to answer queries").

25. 347 U.S. 483 (1954).

26. U.S. Constitution, art. II, sec. 2. For a discussion of the appointment process in general, *see* Michael J. Gerhardt, *Toward a Comprehensive Understanding of the Federal Appointments Process,* 21 Harv. J.L. & Pub. Pol'y 467 (1998).

27. Nor are senators' discussions with candidates outside the hearing room on the public record.

28. *See* William H. Rehnquist, *The 1997 Year-End Report on the Federal Judiciary* (Jan. 1, 1998).

29. For a study of federal judicial selection at the lower court level from the time of President Roosevelt to that of President Reagan, *see* Sheldon Goldman, *Picking Federal Judges.* Professor Goldman also has published a series of articles about judicial selection in the journal of the American Judicature Society. *See* Sheldon Goldman, *Reagan's Judicial Legacy: Completing the Puzzle and Summing Up,* 72 Judicature 318 (April/May 1989); Sheldon Goldman, *The Bush Imprint on the Judiciary: Carrying on a Tradition,* 74 Judicature 294 (April/May 1991); Sheldon Goldman, *Bush's Judicial Legacy: The Final Imprint,* 76 Judicature 282 (April/May 1993); Sheldon Goldman, *Judicial Selection under Clinton: A Midterm Examination,* 78 Judicature 276 (May/June 1995); Sheldon Goldman and Elliot Slotnick, *Clinton's First Term Judiciary: Many Bridges to Cross,* 80 Judicature 254 (June 1997); Sheldon Goldman and Elliot Slotnick, *Clinton's Second Term Judiciary: Picking Judges under Fire,* 82 Judicature 264 (May/June 1999). *See also* Gordon Bermant, Jeffrey A. Hennemuth, and A. Fletcher Mangum, *Judicial Vacancies: An Examination of the Problem and Possible Solutions,* 14 Miss. C.L. Rev. 319 (1994).

30. We are grateful for the assistance of Professor Harold Spaeth and Wendy L. Martinek, Ph.D. candidate and senior research assistant of the Program for Law and Judicial Politics at Michigan State University, who analyzed the data and prepared the charts in the Appendix. We also appreciate the help of Lisa Holmes, Ph.D. candidate in political science at the University of Georgia, who created the initial database from which the analysis was performed, and of Professor Sheldon Goldman of the University of Massachusetts at Amherst, who provided additional data and assisted us in understanding the process of judicial selection.

31. *Youngstown Sheet and Tube Co. v. Sawyer,* 343 U.S. 579, 635 (1952)(Jackson, J., concurring).

APPENDIX:

DESCRIPTION OF
METHODOLOGY AND FINDINGS

The following tables and figures provide data on the nomination and confirmation process for federal judges from 1977 through 1998. They cover the entire Carter, Reagan, and Bush presidencies, and six years of Clinton's two terms. They include the judgeships of all the U.S. District Courts and U.S. Courts of Appeals, except for the district courts of the Virgin Islands, Guam, and the Northern Mariana Islands, which are not Article III courts. (Article III courts are those established under Article III of the U.S. Constitution.)

METHODOLOGY

These tables and figures were generated from a database that was created by Wendy L. Martinek, Ph.D. candidate and senior research assistant, under the supervision of Dr. Harold Spaeth of the Program for Law and Judicial Politics at Michigan State University.* The database will be made available to the public on the website of the Program for Law and Judicial Politics, as well as that of Citizens

---

* Lisa Holmes, Ph.D. candidate at the University of Georgia, also provided substantial assistance in the creation of the database.

for Independent Courts. The database will be continually updated by the Program for Law and Judicial Politics as data become available.

The data included in the database were collected by the staff of Citizens for Independent Courts from various sources, since no one source had all the desired information in a publicly available form. The primary source was the Congressional Research Service, which provided, via a senator's office, vacancy dates, nomination dates, and confirmation dates for all vacancies on the federal courts described above arising between 1977 and 1998. Data on the ethnicity, gender, and party affiliation of nominees were provided by Professor Sheldon Goldman of the University of Massachusetts-Amherst. Additional data and verification were provided by the Senate Judiciary Committee librarian and minority staff, the Federal Judicial Center, and the American Bar Association.

One of the major reasons for creating the database was to determine the average amount of time taken to nominate and confirm federal judges, and to determine whether that average amount of time has changed over the past twenty-two years. Specifically, we sought to determine the average amount of time between vacancy and the president's nomination of a candidate, and between nomination and either the Senate's confirmation or the failure of a candidate. Unfortunately, hearing dates were not available for all nominees; thus, we were unable to determine the average amount of time between nomination and hearing, and between hearing and confirmation or rejection.

There were several different ways in which we could have measured these time periods, including exclusion of congressional recesses. However, more important than what was included or excluded was ensuring that our methodology was consistent. Thus, we decided to count every calendar day, with the exceptions noted below. This method was consistent with our attempt to view the process from the vantage point of the "consumers" of the courts—those of us who require access to the courts, want timely resolution of our cases, and who do not care what the reason is that federal vacancies are not being filled.

MEASURING THE TIME BETWEEN VACANCY AND NOMINATION

To determine the amount of time between vacancy and the president's nomination of a candidate, we counted the number of days between each "nomination opportunity" that arose between 1977 and 1998 and the date a nomination was made for that opportunity (or the last day of the last congressional term during that president's service if no nomination was made). A president is faced with a nomination opportunity when a new vacancy occurs, when a prior nomination is withdrawn or fails to secure Senate approval, or when a vacancy is inherited from a previous president. This methodology ensured that presidents were not "charged" for the time period in which their predecessor failed to nominate someone; thus, the time shown for each president to nominate a candidate includes only time when he could have nominated a candidate.

At the end of each president's term of office, we excluded the days between the adjournment of Congress (*sine die*) and the inauguration of the next president, since it would not be realistic for a president about to leave office to make a nomination after Congress has already adjourned.

Although nominations that have not been acted upon terminate at the end of a Congress, numerous vacancies currently remain unfilled. We decided to "stop the clock" for all vacancies that had not yet been filled on October 21, 1998, the last day of the 105th Congress.

Measuring the Time between Nomination and Confirmation or Failure

To determine the amount of time between nomination and either confirmation or failure of a nominee, we counted the number of days between each nomination made for a nomination opportunity that arose between 1977 and 1998 and the date of one of the following: the Senate's confirmation of a nominee, the Senate's rejection of a nominee, the president's withdrawal of a nominee, or the termination of a nomination by the ending of the Congress in which the nomination was made. Because pending nominations die at the end of a Congress (*sine die* adjournment), the days between Congresses were never included.

We analyzed the amount of time to fill vacancies for district courts as compared with circuit courts, as well as the amount of time to fill vacancies under divided government (when the president is of one party and the Senate is of the other party) as compared with unified government. In addition, we analyzed the time for confirmation or rejection of female nominees as compared with male nominees. We also analyzed the time for confirmation or rejection of racial minority nominees as compared with white nominees for the 105th Congress only. The 105th Congress was the only Congress for which data on the race of nominees were available for both successful and unsuccessful nominees.

Once nominations are made, there is an opportunity to analyze them by various factors. Thus, we were able to conduct more analyses on the time between nomination and either confirmation or failure than on the time between vacancy and nomination.

CAVEAT

It is important to note that our method of counting days does not necessarily account for the total amount of time a single vacancy may have remained open. For example, if a vacancy was created in one Congress but not filled until another Congress, more than one nomination would be required to fill it (and those successive nominations might be of the same person). For such a case, our data would include the time it took for the president to make each nomination and for the Senate to confirm each nomination (or to reject it or let it die), but would not indicate that a particular vacancy remained open over several Congresses.

For greater accuracy and ease of understanding, the data in the tables and figures are presented by presidential term for action by presidents and by congressional term for action by the Senate.

FINDINGS

The tables and figures show a general trend of an increasing amount of time taken to fill vacancies on the federal bench.

Table 1 - Summary provides a summary of the amount of time taken to nominate and confirm federal judges from 1977 through 1998. For each president starting with President Carter, the table gives the number of nomination opportunities, number of actual nominations, and average number of days for the president to act on a nomination opportunity. For each congressional term, the summary shows the number of confirmations, number of nominations returned to the president, and average number of days for the Senate to act on a nomination (or, where the Senate did not act, for the nomination to expire at the end of a congressional term). The chart also includes the average number of days for Senate action during each president's administration since 1977.

Table 2 - Presidential Action and the accompanying figures show the number of nomination opportunities each president had and the number of nominations he made. Figure 2b reflects a sharp increase in nominations in 1978, 1984, and 1990, years when new federal judgeships were created by Congress.

Table 3 - Presidential Action and the accompanying figure show the average number of days between nomination opportunity and nomination, broken down by president. As can be seen, the mean has steadily increased. For example, President Clinton's average is seventy-five days higher than President Carter's.

Table 4 - Senate Action and the accompanying figure show the average number of days between nomination and final action on that nomination for both successful and unsuccessful nominees. Final action is a confirmation, a withdrawal of the nomination by the president, or a return of the nomination to the president by the Senate (because the nomination expired without Senate action at the end of a congressional term; none were rejected during this time period). The data show a steady increase in the number of days between nomination and final action, especially for unsuccessful nominees in recent years. In general, unsuccessful nominations tended to take longer for final action. This may reflect the fact that unsuccessful nominations frequently receive no action by the Senate and simply expire at the end of the congressional term, as much as two years after they are made.

There appears to be a pattern of additional delay in Senate action in each two-year period preceding a presidential election, with the exception of 1983–84. This occurred even in 1979–80, when the same party (the Democrats) had control of both the White House and the Senate.

Table 5 - Senate Action, Table 6 - Senate Action, and the accompanying figures provide the average number of days between nomination and final action on that nomination for district court and circuit court nominees, respectively. The average number of days for final action on nominations has increased for nominees to both types of court.

Table 7 - Senate Action and the accompanying figure show the average amount of time between nomination and final action, broken down by the thirteen federal circuit courts.

Table 8 - Senate Action shows the average amount of time between nomination and final action for each circuit, broken down by congressional term. In the 105th Congress, there were seven circuits with an average of two hundred or more days between nomination and final action, as compared with four circuits in the 102nd and 104th Congresses.

Table 9 - Senate Action and the accompanying figure show the average number of days between nomination and final action, broken down by president, for successful, unsuccessful, and all nominees. Again, the data show a steady increase in the amount of time. President Carter's nominees received final action in an average of 78 days, while President Clinton's nominees took an average of 144 days.

Table 10 - Senate Action and the accompanying figure provide the average number of days between nomination and final action, broken down by president and type of court (district or circuit). The data show an increase in this average from the Carter administration to the Clinton administration, with President Clinton's circuit court nominees taking the longest amount of time for final action.

Table 11 - Senate Action and the accompanying figure show the average number of days between nomination and final action during times of divided government and unified government. During times when one party had control of the Senate and the other party of the White House, the average number of days between nomination and final action was significantly higher. This difference existed for both successful and unsuccessful nominees, but the average time for unsuccessful nominees was much longer.

Table 12 - Senate Action and the accompanying figure show the average amount of time for final action for male and female nominees, broken down by president. President Clinton's female nominees have taken the longest time for final action, and President Reagan's female nominees took the shortest amount of time.

Table 13 - Senate Action and the accompanying figure show the average amount of time between nomination and final action for men and women, broken down by congressional term. The amount of time for final action on female nominees has been roughly the same as for males from the 95th through the 104th Congresses (except for the 100th Congress). The greatest disparity occurred during the 105th Congress, when it took women an average of sixty-five days longer than men for final action. It should be noted that the proportion of female nominees was much higher in the 105th Congress—they constituted over one-third of the nominees—than in the 95th Congress, when women comprised about 12 percent of the nominees.

Table 14 - Senate Action and the accompanying figure show the average amount of time between nomination and final action for male and female nominees, both successful and unsuccessful. Overall, female nominees waited an average of twenty-seven more days than men for final action over the twenty-two-year period we analyzed.

Table 15 - Senate Action and the accompanying figure show the average number of days between nomination and final action, broken down by race and success of nominee for the 105th Congress, the only Congress for which data were available on unsuccessful as well as successful nominees. The data show that nominations of nonwhites took an average of sixty days longer than those of white nominees to receive final action.

Note: The data on race were not available for unsuccessful nominees other than those nominated during the 105th Congress. Thus, it was not possible to perform an analysis on race of nominees for any Congress other than the 105th.

Table 16 - Senate Action and the accompanying figure compare the average number of days between nomination and final action in the 105th Congress for white men to the average number for white women and minorities. Overall, the nominations of white male candidates received final action an average of seventy-six days sooner than did the nominations of racial minorities and white women. Unsuccessful white male nominees received final action, on average, in 242 days, and unsuccessful white female and nonwhite nominees received final action, on average, in 386 days. Again, we were unable to provide a similar analysis for Congresses other than the 105th due to the lack of data on the race of unsuccessful nominees.

Table 17 and the accompanying figure show the number of nominations that were made per vacancy, broken down by president. Where the initial nomination for a particular vacancy failed, at least one and as many as three additional nominations were made before the Senate finally confirmed a candidate for that vacancy. The number of nominations per vacancy has increased over time. For vacancies that were filled during the Carter administration, only 1.9 percent required more than one nomination. For vacancies that were filled during President Clinton's first six years in office, 26.9 percent required more than one nomination. The accompanying figure shows, by president, the percentages of total successful nominations that were first nominations.

Table 18 and the accompanying figure show the number of nominations needed in order to fill a vacancy, broken down by congressional term. For vacancies that were filled during the 95th Congress (1977-78), 96.7 percent were filled by the first nomination, whereas for vacancies filled during the 105th Congress (1997-98), only 75.8 percent were filled by the first nomination. The accompanying figure shows, by congressional term, the percentages of total scucessful nominations that were first nominations.

SUMMARY

Between 1977 and 1998, there has been an increase in the amount of time required to fill a vacancy on the federal bench. Through 1998, President Clinton took an average of 75 more days to nominate a candidate for the federal bench than did President Carter during his time in office. In the 105th Congress, the Senate took an average of 163 more days to act on a nomination (or to let it expire) than did the

Senate in the 95th Congress. Whatever the reasons, these findings have serious implications for those Americans who require access to the federal courts and want timely resolution of their cases.

TABLE 1. SUMMARY: PRESIDENTIAL AND SENATE ACTION, 1977–98

Pres-ident	Cong. Term	Years	Party in Control of the Senate	Nominations		Avg. No. of Days for Pres. Action[c]	Confirm-ations	Nomin-ations Returned to the Pres.	Avg. No. of Days for Senate Action	
				Opp. for[a]	Made[b]				by Cong.[d]	by Pres.[d]
Carter		1977–80		296	280	240	258	19		78
	95th	1977–78	Dem.				214	10	38	
	96th	1979–80	Dem.				44	9	90	
Reagan		1981–88		432	423	254	372	42		65
	97th	1981–82	Repub.				110	5	32	
	98th	1983–84	Repub.				147	19	38	
	99th	1985–86	Repub.				75	7	45	
	100th	1987–88	Dem.				40	11	144	
Bush		1989–92		302	248	296	191	57		120
	101st	1989–90	Dem.				156	31	78	
	102nd	1991–92	Dem.				35	26	138	
Clinton		1993–98		402	368	315	297	61		144
	103rd	1993–94	Dem.				173	27	83	
	104th	1995–96	Repub.				89	26	159	
	105th	1997–98	Repub.				35	8	201	

Table 1. Summary: Presidential and Senate Action, 1977–98

Pres-ident	Cong. Term	Years	Party in Control of the Senate	Nominations		Avg. No. of Days for Pres. Action[c]	Confirm-ations	Nomin-ations Returned to the Pres.	Avg. No. of Days for Senate Action	
				Opp. for[a]	Made[b]				by Cong.[d]	by Pres.[d]
Carter through Clinton	95th through 105th	1977–98	—	1432	1319	277	1118	179	100	100

[a] A nomination opportunity arises when a new vacancy occurs, a prior nomination is withdrawn or fails to secure Senate approval, or a vacancy is inherited from a previous president.
[b] A nomination returned to the president that is resubmitted by the president counts as two separate nominations.
[c] The average number of days for presidential action is the average number of days between nomination opportunity and nomination (or last day of last congressional term of presidential service if nomination not made).
[d] The average number of days for Senate action is the average number of days between nomination and one of the following: confirmation, return of the nomination, or withdrawal.

Source: Prepared by the Program for Law and Judicial Politics at Michigan State University.

Table 2. Presidential Action: Nomination Opportunities[a] and Nominations Made, by President, 1977–98

President	Nomination Opportunities	Nominations Made
Carter (1977–80)	296	280
Reagan (1981–88)	432	423
Bush (1989–92)	302	248
Clinton (1993–98)	402	368
Carter through Clinton (1977–98)	1432	1319

[a] A nomination opportunity arises when a new vacancy occurs, a prior nomination is withdrawn or fails to secure congressional approval, or a vacancy is inherited from a previous president.

Source: Prepared by the Program for Law and Judicial Politics at Michigan State University.

FIGURE 2A. PRESIDENTIAL ACTION: NOMINATION OPPORTUNITIES[a] AND NOMINATIONS MADE, BY PRESIDENT, 1977–98

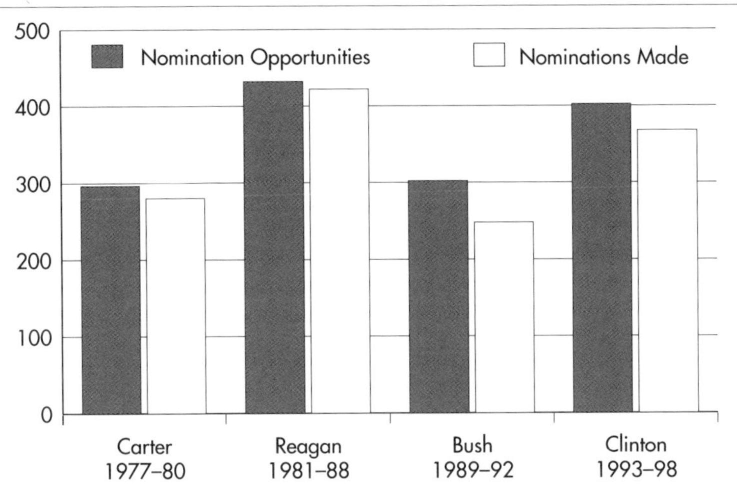

[a] A nomination opportunity arises when a new vacancy occurs, a prior nomination is withdrawn or fails to secure congressional approval, or a vacancy is inherited from a previous president.

Source: Prepared by the Program for Law and Judicial Politics at Michigan State University.

FIGURE 2B. PRESIDENTIAL ACTION: NOMINATIONS MADE, 1977–98

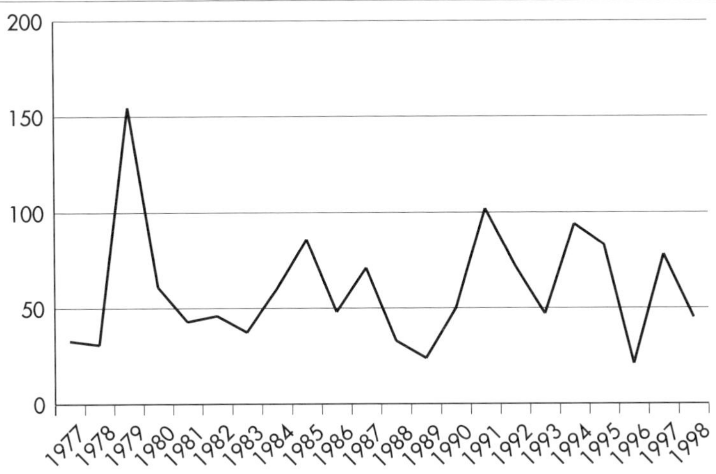

Source: Prepared by the Program for Law and Judicial Politics at Michigan State University.

TABLE 3. Presidential Action: Average Number of Days between Nomination Opportunity[a] and Nomination, by President, 1977–98

President	District Courts	Circuit Courts	District and Circuit Courts
Carter (1977–80)	244 (234)	224 (62)	240 (296)
Reagan (1981–88)	262 (332)	230 (100)	254 (432)
Bush (1989–92)	297 (240)	292 (62)	296 (302)
Clinton (1993–98)	311 (321)	329 (81)	315 (402)
Carter through Clinton (1977–98)	279 (1127)	268 (305)	277 (1432)

Note: Numbers in parentheses indicate the number of nomination opportunities.

[a] A nomination opportunity arises when a new vacancy occurs, a prior nomination is withdrawn or fails to secure congressional approval, or a vacancy is inherited from a previous president.

Source: Prepared by the Program for Law and Judicial Politics at Michigan State University.

FIGURE 3. PRESIDENTIAL ACTION: AVERAGE NUMBER OF DAYS BETWEEN NOMINATION OPPORTUNITY[a] AND NOMINATION, BY PRESIDENT, 1977–98

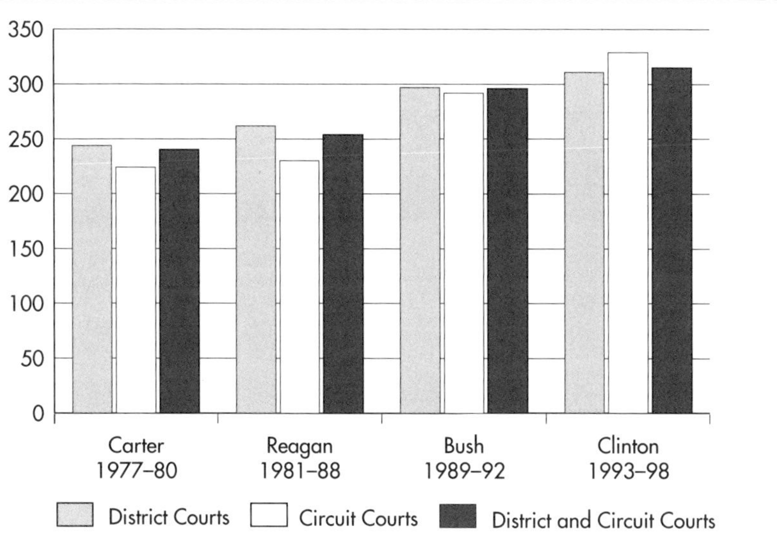

Note: Numbers in parentheses indicate the number of nomination opportunities.

[a] A nomination opportunity arises when a new vacancy occurs, a prior nomination is withdrawn or fails to secure congressional approval, or a vacancy is inherited from a previous president.

Source: Prepared by the Program for Law and Judicial Politics at Michigan State University.

TABLE 4. SENATE ACTION: AVERAGE NUMBER OF DAYS BETWEEN NOMINATION AND FINAL ACTION,[a] ALL DISTRICT AND CIRCUIT COURT NOMINEES, BY CONGRESSIONAL TERM, 1977–98

Congressional Term	Successful Nominees	Unsuccessful Nominees[b]	All Nominees
95th (1977–78)	38 (60)	35 (4)	38 (64)
96th (1979–80)	80 (198)	205 (18)	90 (216)
97th (1981–82)	33 (86)	10 (3)	32 (89)
98th (1983–84)	35 (75)	51 (21)	38 (96)
99th (1985–86)	44 (128)	71 (6)	45 (134)
100th (1987–88)	120 (83)	241 (21)	144 (104)
101st (1989–90)	77 (70)	91 (4)	78 (74)
102nd (1991–92)	111 (120)	197 (54)	138 (174)
103rd (1993–94)	81 (127)	102 (14)	83 (141)
104th (1995–96)	114 (72)	259 (32)	159 (104)
105th (1997–98)	171 (99)	326 (24)	201 (123)
95th through 105th (1977–98)	83 (1118)	194 (201)	100 (1319)

Note: Numbers in parentheses indicate the number of nominations.

[a] Final action is the confirmation, return to the president, or withdrawal of a nomination.

[b] An unsuccessful nomination is one that is either returned to the president or withdrawn by the president.

Source: Prepared by the Program for Law and Judicial Politics at Michigan State University.

Figure 4. Senate Action: Average Number of Days between Nomination and Final Action,[a] All District and Circuit Court Nominees, by Congressional Term, 1977–98

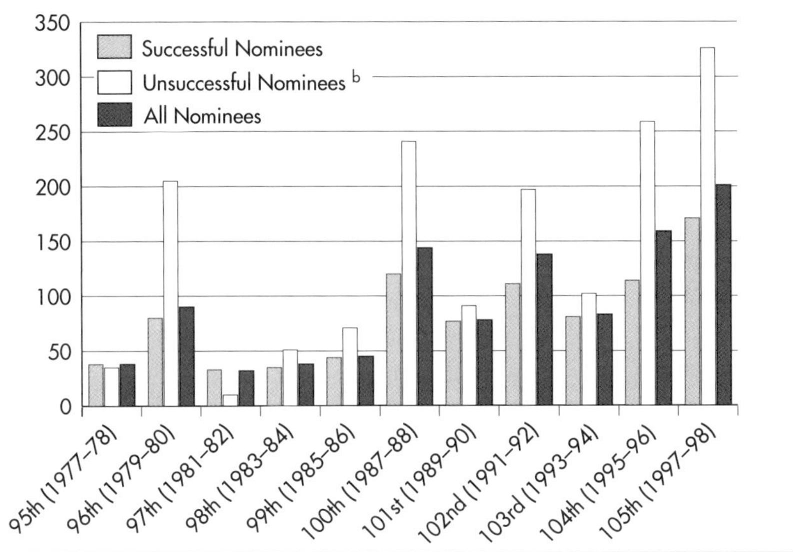

[a] Final action is the confirmation, return to the president, or withdrawal of a nomination.

[b] An unsuccessful nomination is one that is either returned to the president or withdrawn by the president.

Source: Prepared by the Program for Law and Judicial Politics at Michigan State University.

TABLE 5. SENATE ACTION: AVERAGE NUMBER OF DAYS BETWEEN NOMINATION AND FINAL ACTION,[a] ALL DISTRICT COURT NOMINEES, BY CONGRESSIONAL TERM, 1977–98

Congressional Term	Successful Nominees	Unsuccessful Nominees[b]	All Nominees
95th (1977–78)	40 (47)	35 (4)	40 (51)
96th (1979–80)	79 (154)	208 (14)	90 (168)
97th (1981–82)	33 (67)	9 (2)	32 (69)
98th (1983–84)	31 (61)	48 (15)	35 (76)
99th (1985–86)	42 (95)	71 (6)	44 (101)
100th (1987–88)	120 (66)	217 (12)	135 (78)
101st (1989–90)	77 (48)	69 (3)	76 (51)
102nd (1991–92)	112 (100)	172 (43)	130 (143)
103rd (1993–94)	76 (107)	104 (11)	79 (118)
104th (1995–96)	113 (61)	250 (23)	150 (84)
105th (1997–98)	162 (79)	300 (14)	183 (93)
95th through 105th (1977–98)	82 (885)	174 (147)	95 (1032)

Note: Numbers in parentheses indicate the number of nominations.

[a] Final action is the confirmation, return to the president, or withdrawal of a nomination.
[b] An unsuccessful nomination is one that is either returned to the president or withdrawn by the president.

Source: Prepared by the Program for Law and Judicial Politics at Michigan State University.

Figure 5. Senate Action: Average Number of Days between Nomination and Final Action,[a] All District Court Nominees, by Congressional Term, 1977–98

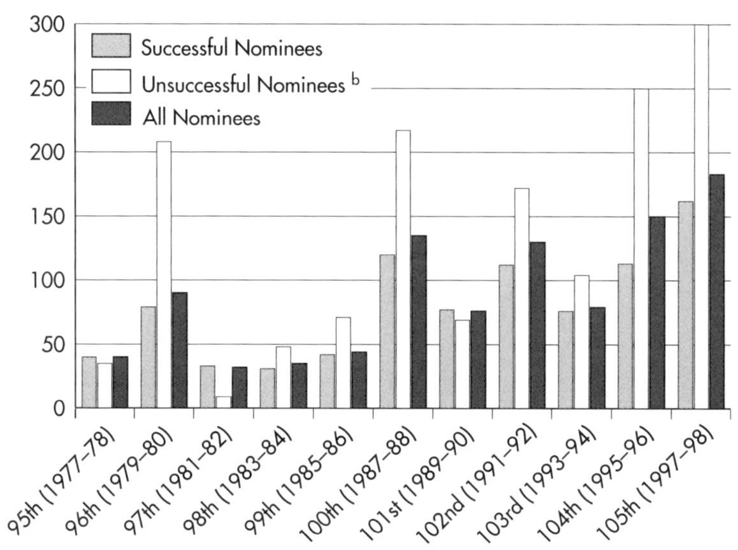

[a] Final action is the confirmation, return to the president, or withdrawal of a nomination.

[b] An unsuccessful nomination is one that is either returned to the president or withdrawn by the president.

Source: Prepared by the Program for Law and Judicial Politics at Michigan State University.

TABLE 6. SENATE ACTION: AVERAGE NUMBER OF DAYS BETWEEN NOMINATION AND FINAL ACTION,[a] ALL CIRCUIT COURT NOMINEES, BY CONGRESSIONAL TERM, 1977–98

Congressional Term	Successful Nominees	Unsuccessful Nominees[b]	All Nominees
95th (1977–78)	32 (13)	—	32 (13)
96th (1979–80)	81 (44)	195 (4)	91 (48)
97th (1981–82)	34 (19)	12 (1)	33 (20)
98th (1983–84)	51 (14)	56 (6)	52 (20)
99th (1985–86)	50 (33)	—	50 (33)
100th (1987–88)	119 (17)	273 (9)	172 (26)
101st (1989–90)	79 (22)	155 (1)	82 (23)
102nd (1991–92)	108 (20)	296 (11)	174 (31)
103rd (1993–94)	105 (20)	94 (3)	103 (23)
104th (1995–96)	124 (11)	280 (9)	194 (20)
105th (1997–98)	206 (20)	362 (10)	258 (30)
95th through 105th (1977–98)	88 (233)	248 (54)	118 (287)

Note: Numbers in parentheses indicate the number of nominations.

[a] Final action is the confirmation, return to the president, or withdrawal of a nomination.
[b] An unsuccessful nomination is one that is either returned to the president or withdrawn by the president.

Source: Prepared by the Program for Law and Judicial Politics at Michigan State University.

FIGURE 6. SENATE ACTION: AVERAGE NUMBER OF DAYS BETWEEN NOMINATION AND FINAL ACTION,[a] ALL CIRCUIT COURT NOMINEES, BY CONGRESSIONAL TERM, 1977–98

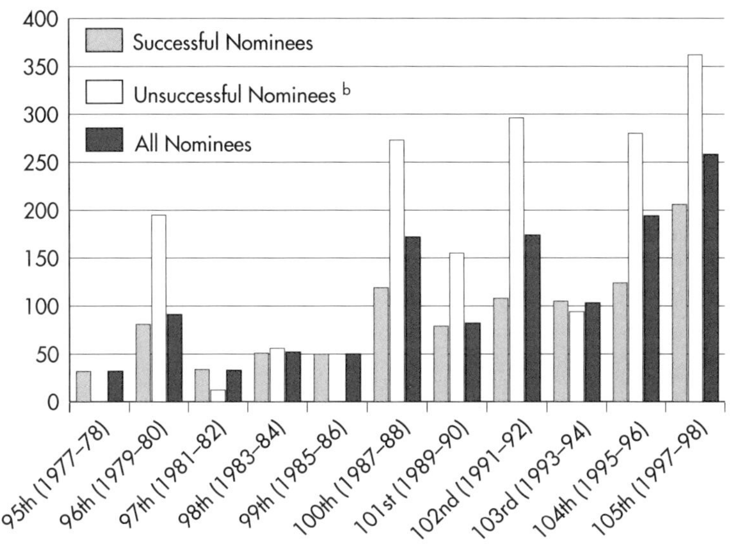

[a] Final action is the confirmation, return to the president, or withdrawal of a nomination.

[b] An unsuccessful nomination is one that is either returned to the president or withdrawn by the president.

Source: Prepared by the Program for Law and Judicial Politics at Michigan State University.

TABLE 7. SENATE ACTION: AVERAGE NUMBER OF DAYS
BETWEEN NOMINATION AND FINAL ACTION[a] FOR CIRCUIT
COURT NOMINEES, BY CIRCUIT, 1977–98

Circuit	Successful Nominees	Unsuccessful Nominees[b]	All Nominees
1st	66 (10)	61 (1)	66 (11)
2nd	105 (20)	253 (2)	119 (22)
3rd	70 (16)	324 (3)	110 (19)
4th	77 (17)	386 (5)	147 (22)
5th	78 (31)	249 (7)	109 (38)
6th	79 (23)	276 (5)	114 (28)
7th	64 (12)	88 (2)	68 (14)
8th	76 (13)	139 (1)	81 (14)
9th	121 (37)	260 (13)	157 (50)
10th	74 (15)	329 (1)	90 (16)
11th	130 (9)	193 (4)	149 (13)
DC	83 (18)	219 (4)	108 (22)
Federal	87 (12)	190 (6)	121 (18)
All Circuits	88 (233)	248 (54)	118 (287)

Note: Numbers in parentheses indicate the number of nominations.

[a] Final action is the confirmation, return to the president, or withdrawal of a nomination.
[b] An unsuccessful nomination is one that is either returned to the president or withdrawn by the president.

Source: Prepared by the Program for Law and Judicial Politics at Michigan State University.

FIGURE 7. SENATE ACTION: AVERAGE NUMBER OF DAYS BETWEEN NOMINATION AND FINAL ACTION,[a] ALL CIRCUIT COURT NOMINEES, BY CIRCUIT, 1977–98

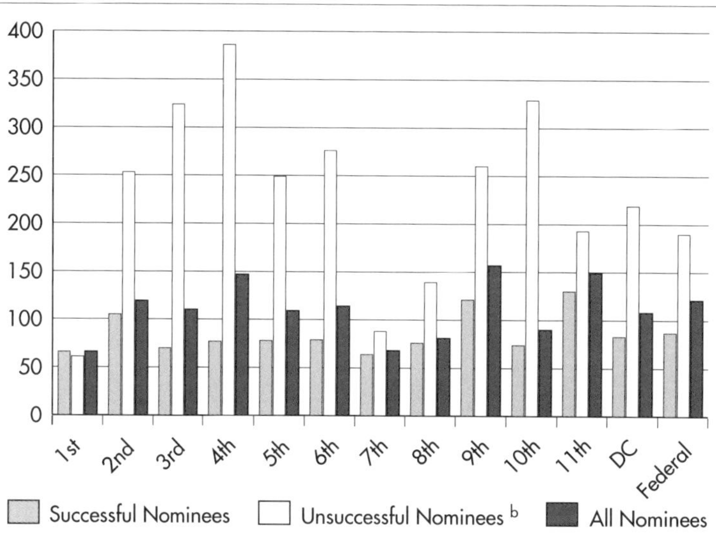

[a] Final action is the confirmation, return to the president, or withdrawal of a nomination.

[b] An unsuccessful nomination is one that is either returned to the president or withdrawn by the president.

Source: Prepared by the Program for Law and Judicial Politics at Michigan State University.

TABLE 8. SENATE ACTION: AVERAGE NUMBER OF DAYS BETWEEN NOMINATION AND FINAL ACTION[a] FOR CIRCUIT COURT NOMINEES, BY CIRCUIT AND CONGRESSIONAL TERM, 1977–98

Cong. Term	Circuit													All Federal Circuits
	1st	2nd	3rd	4th	5th	6th	7th	8th	9th	10th	11th	DC	Federal	
95th	18 (1)	—	18 (1)	22 (1)	36 (2)	44 (2)	—	50 (1)	28 (2)	30 (3)	—	—	—	32 (13)
96th	26 (1)	69 (3)	77 (1)	63 (3)	94 (14)	128 (4)	112 (2)	101 (2)	91 (13)	64 (1)	—	86 (4)	—	91 (48)
97th	—	43 (4)	17 (1)	62 (1)	29 (3)	32 (3)	29 (3)	20 (2)	—	—	—	42 (2)	12 (1)	33 (20)
98th	63 (1)	—	—	128 (2)	20 (3)	27 (1)	49 (2)	55 (1)	41 (4)	—	—	53 (2)	56 (4)	52 (20)
99th	12 (1)	46 (3)	17 (2)	10 (1)	35 (1)	47 (5)	65 (3)	33 (2)	73 (5)	57 (4)	34 (1)	59 (4)	61 (1)	50 (33)
100th	—	395 (1)	70 (5)	—	180 (4)	—	106 (1)	128 (1)	193 (6)	158 (2)	118 (1)	205 (2)	260 (3)	172 (26)
101st	87 (2)	78 (2)	66 (1)	84 (1)	112 (2)	70 (1)	—	32 (1)	81 (3)	—	106 (3)	81 (3)	68 (4)	82 (23)
102nd	70 (2)	193 (1)	224 (4)	174 (5)	150 (3)	178 (4)	41 (1)	153 (2)	112 (1)	235 (2)	200 (4)	255 (1)	162 (1)	174 (31)

TABLE 8. SENATE ACTION: AVERAGE NUMBER OF DAYS BETWEEN NOMINATION AND FINAL ACTION FOR CIRCUIT COURT NOMINEES, BY CIRCUIT AND CONGRESSIONAL TERM, 1977–98 (CONT.)

Congress		1st	2nd	3rd	4th	5th	6th	Circuit 7th	8th	9th	10th	11th	DC	Federal	All Circuits
103rd		61 (1)	88 (4)	115 (2)	111 (3)	124 (4)	84 (2)	—	71 (1)	63 (1)	86 (1)	202 (1)	111 (2)	98 (1)	103 (23)
104th		65 (1)	—	—	287 (2)	240 (1)	149 (3)	100 (2)	—	282 (5)	63 (3)	199 (1)	395 (1)	169 (1)	194 (20)
105th		164 (1)	251 (4)	200 (2)	279 (3)	454 (1)	283 (3)	—	185 (1)	310 (10)	—	136 (2)	71 (1)	204 (2)	258 (30)
95th through 105th		66 (11)	119 (22)	110 (19)	147 (22)	109 (38)	114 (28)	68 (14)	81 (14)	157 (50)	90 (16)	149 (13)	108 (22)	121 (18)	118 (287)

Note: Numbers in parentheses indicate the number of nominations for each category.

[a] Final action is the confirmation, return to the president, or withdrawal of a nomination.

Source: Prepared by the Program for Law and Judicial Politics at Michigan State University.

TABLE 9. SENATE ACTION: AVERAGE NUMBER OF DAYS
BETWEEN NOMINATION AND FINAL ACTION,[a] BY
PRESIDENT AND SUCCESS OF NOMINEE, 1977–98

President	Successful Nominees	Unsuccessful Nominees[a]	All Nominees
Carter (1977–80)	70 (258)	174 (22)	78 (280)
Reagan (1981–88)	57 (372)	129 (51)	65 (423)
Bush (1989–92)	99 (190)	190 (58)	120 (248)
Clinton (1993–98)	119 (298)	250 (70)	144 (368)
Carter through Clinton (1977–98)	83 (1118)	194 (201)	100 (1319)

Note: Numbers in parentheses indicate the number of nominations.

[a] Final action is the confirmation, return to the president, or withdrawal of a nomination.
[b] An unsuccessful nomination is one that is either returned to the president or withdrawn by the president.

Source: Prepared by the Program for Law and Judicial Politics at Michigan State University.

Figure 9. Senate Action: Average Number of Days between Nomination and Final Action,[a] by President and Success of Nominee, 1977–98

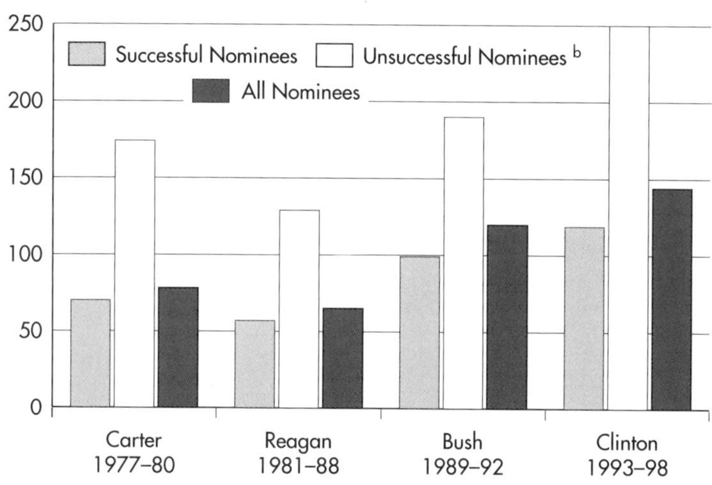

[a] Final action is the confirmation, return to the president, or withdrawal of a nomination.

[b] An unsuccessful nomination is one that is either returned to the president or withdrawn by the president.

Source: Prepared by the Program for Law and Judicial Politics at Michigan State University.

Table 10. Senate Action: Average Number of Days between Nomination and Final Action,[a] by President and Type of Court, 1977–98

President	District Court Nominees	Circuit Court Nominees	District and Circuit Court Nominees
Carter (1977–80)	78 (219)	78 (61)	78 (280)
Reagan (1981–88)	61 (324)	79 (99)	65 (423)
Bush (1989–92)	116 (194)	135 (54)	120 (248)
Clinton (1993–98)	132 (295)	192 (73)	144 (368)
Carter through Clinton (1977–98)	95 (1032)	118 (287)	100 (1319)

Note: Numbers in parentheses indicate the number of nominations.

[a] Final action is the confirmation, return to the president, or withdrawal of a nomination.

Source: Prepared by the Program for Law and Judicial Politics at Michigan State University.

Figure 10. Senate Action: Average Number of Days between Nomination and Final Action,[a] by President and Type of Court, 1977–98

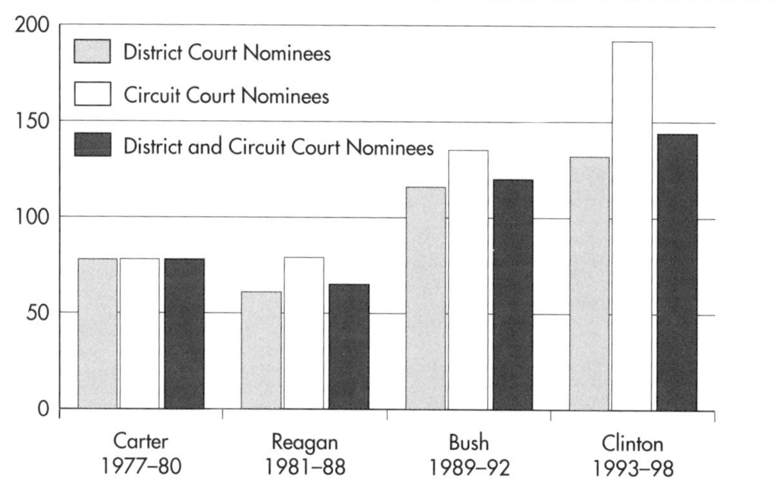

[a] Final action is the confirmation, return to the president, or withdrawal of a nomination.

Source: Prepared by the Program for Law and Judicial Politics at Michigan State University.

TABLE 11. SENATE ACTION: AVERAGE NUMBER OF DAYS BETWEEN NOMINATION AND FINAL ACTION,[a] BY DIVIDED VERSUS UNIFIED GOVERNMENT,[b] 1977–98

	Divided Government	Unified Government
District Courts		
Days between nomination and confirmation for successful candidates	120 (354)	57 (531)
Days between nomination and final Senate action for unsuccessful candidates[c]	212 (95)	103 (52)
Circuit Courts		
Days between nomination and confirmation for successful candidates	127 (90)	64 (143)
Days between nomination and final Senate action for unsuccessful candidates	300 (40)	101 (14)
District and Circuit Courts		
Days between nomination and confirmation for successful candidates	121 (444)	59 (674)
Days between nomination and final Senate action for unsuccessful candidates	238 (135)	103 (66)

Note: Numbers in parentheses indicate the number of nominations.

[a] Final action is the confirmation, return to the president, or withdrawal of a nomination.
[b] Divided government exists when one party controls the White House and the other party controls the Senate.
[c] An unsuccessful nomination is one that is either returned to the president or withdrawn by the president.

Source: Prepared by the Program for Law and Judicial Politics at Michigan State University.

FIGURE 11. SENATE ACTION: AVERAGE NUMBER OF DAYS BETWEEN NOMINATION AND FINAL ACTION,[a] BY DIVIDED VERSUS UNIFIED GOVERNMENT[b] AND SUCCESS OF NOMINEE, 1977–98

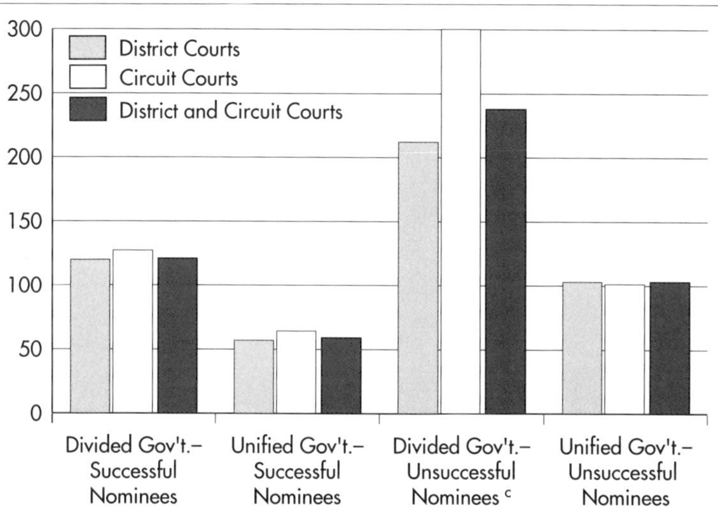

[a] Final action is the confirmation, return to the president, or withdrawal of a nomination.

[b] Divided government exists when one party controls the White House and the other party controls the Senate.

[c] An unsuccessful nomination is one that is either returned to the president or withdrawn by the president.

Source: Prepared by the Program for Law and Judicial Politics at Michigan State University.

TABLE 12. SENATE ACTION: AVERAGE NUMBER OF DAYS BETWEEN NOMINATION AND FINAL ACTION,[a] BY PRESIDENT AND GENDER OF NOMINEE, 1977–98

President	Men	Women	Men and Women
Carter (1977–80)	79 (238)	74 (42)	78 (280)
Reagan (1981–88)	65 (388)	68 (35)	65 (423)
Bush (1989–92)	119 (208)	123 (40)	120 (248)
Clinton (1993–98)	137 (260)	160 (108)	144 (368)
Carter through Clinton (1977–98)	96 (1094)	123 (225)	100 (1319)

Note: Numbers in parentheses indicate the number of nominations.

[a] Final action is the confirmation, return to the president, or withdrawal of a nomination.

Source: Prepared by the Program for Law and Judicial Politics at Michigan State University.

FIGURE 12. SENATE ACTION: AVERAGE NUMBER OF DAYS BETWEEN NOMINATION AND FINAL ACTION,[a] BY PRESIDENT AND GENDER OF NOMINEE, 1977–98

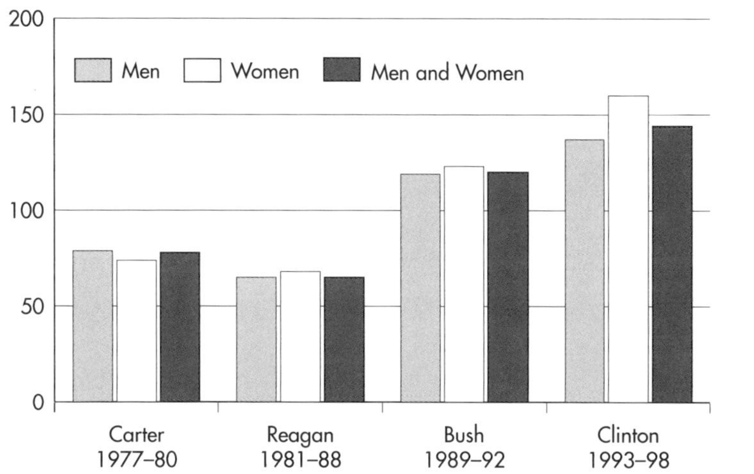

[a] Final action is the confirmation, return to the president, or withdrawal of a nomination.

Source: Prepared by the Program for Law and Judicial Politics at Michigan State University.

TABLE 13. SENATE ACTION: AVERAGE NUMBER OF
DAYS BETWEEN NOMINATION AND FINAL ACTION,[a] BY
CONGRESSIONAL TERM AND GENDER OF NOMINEE, 1977–98

Congressional Term	Men	Women	Men and Women
95th (1977–78)	38 (57)	40 (7)	38 (64)
96th (1979–80)	92 (181)	80 (35)	90 (216)
97th (1981–82)	32 (86)	32 (3)	32 (89)
98th (1983–84)	40 (83)	31 (13)	38 (96)
99th 1985–86)	47 (122)	30 (12)	45 (134)
100th (1987–88)	139 (97)	216 (7)	144 (104)
101st (1989–90)	78 (67)	77 (7)	78 (74)
102nd (1991–92)	139 (141)	133 (33)	138 (174)
103rd (1993–94)	85 (97)	78 (44)	83 (141)
104th (1995–96)	149 (72)	182 (32)	159 (104)
105th (1997–98)	184 (91)	249 (32)	201 (123)
95th through 105th (1977–98)	96 (1094)	123 (225)	100 (1319)

Note: Numbers in parentheses indicate the number of nominations.

[a] Final action is the confirmation, return to the president, or withdrawal of a nomination.

Source: Prepared by the Program for Law and Judicial Politics at Michigan State University.

Figure 13. Senate Action: Average Number of Days between Nomination and Final Action,[a] by Congressional Term and Gender of Nominee, 1977–98

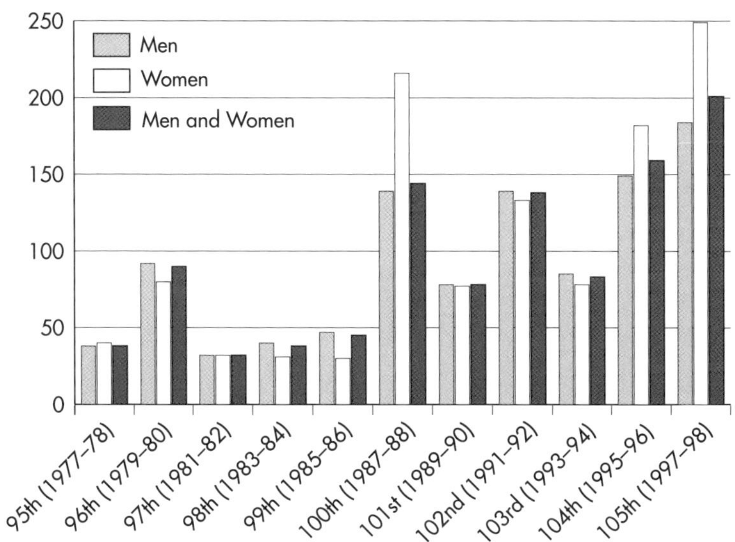

[a] Final action is the confirmation, return to the president, or withdrawal of a nomination.

Source: Prepared by the Program for Law and Judicial Politics at Michigan State University.

Table 14. Senate Action: Average Number of Days between Nomination and Final Action,[a] by Gender and Success of Nominee, 1977–98

	Men	Women	Men and Women
Successful Nominees	79 (927)	104 (191)	83 (1118)
Unsuccessful Nominees[b]	187 (167)	228 (34)	194 (201)
All Nominees	96 (1094)	123 (225)	100 (1319)

Note: Numbers in parentheses indicate the number of nominations.

[a] Final action is the confirmation, return to the president, or withdrawal of a nomination.
[b] An unsuccessful nomination is one that is either returned to the president or withdrawn by the president.

Source: Prepared by the Program for Law and Judicial Politics at Michigan State University.

FIGURE 14. SENATE ACTION: AVERAGE NUMBER OF DAYS BETWEEN NOMINATION AND FINAL ACTION,[a] BY GENDER AND SUCCESS OF NOMINEE, 1977–98

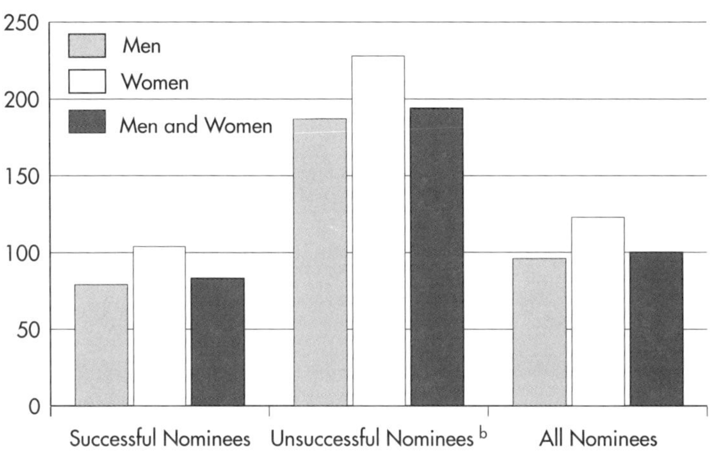

[a] Final action is the confirmation, return to the president, or withdrawal of a nomination.

[b] An unsuccessful nomination is one that is either returned to the president or withdrawn by the president.

Source: Prepared by the Program for Law and Judicial Politics at Michigan State University.

TABLE 15. SENATE ACTION: AVERAGE NUMBER OF DAYS BETWEEN NOMINATION AND FINAL ACTION,[a] BY RACE AND SUCCESS OF NOMINEE, FOR THE 105TH CONGRESS

Race	Successful Nominees	Unsuccessful Nominees[b]	All Nominees
Whites	170 (79)	285 (13)	186 (92)
Minorities	175 (20)	374 (11)	246 (31)
Whites and Minorities	171 (99)	326 (24)	201 (123)

Note: Numbers in parentheses indicate the number of nominations; the analysis is limited to the 105th Congress due to unavailability of complete race data for other than the 105th Congress.

[a] Final action is the confirmation, return to the president, or withdrawal of a nomination.
[b] An unsuccessful nomination is one that is either returned to the president or withdrawn by the president.

Source: Prepared by the Program for Law and Judicial Politics at Michigan State University.

FIGURE 15. SENATE ACTION: AVERAGE NUMBER OF DAYS BETWEEN NOMINATION AND FINAL ACTION,[a] BY RACE AND SUCCESS OF NOMINEE, FOR THE 105TH CONGRESS

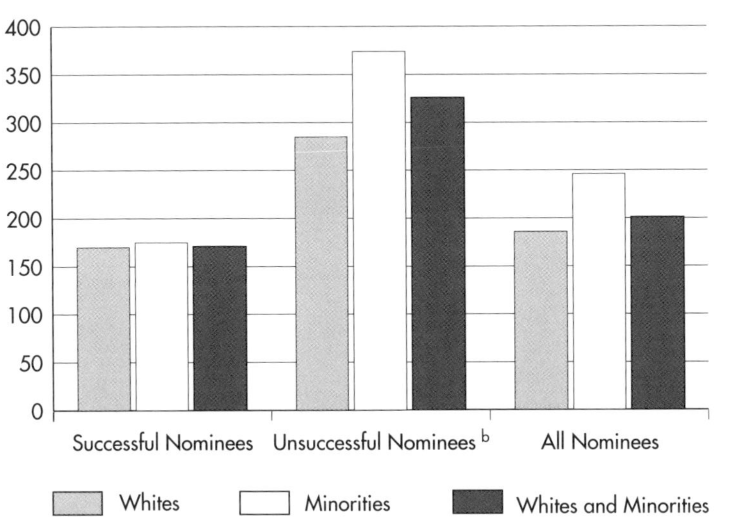

Note: The analysis is limited to the 105th Congress due to unavailability of complete race data for other than the 105th Congress.

[a] Final action is the confirmation, return to the president, or withdrawal of a nomination.
[b] An unsuccessful nomination is one that is either returned to the president or withdrawn by the president.

Source: Prepared by the Program for Law and Judicial Politics at Michigan State University.

TABLE 16. SENATE ACTION: AVERAGE NUMBER OF DAYS BETWEEN NOMINATION AND FINAL ACTION,[a] WHITE MEN VERSUS WOMEN AND MINORITIES, FOR THE 105TH CONGRESS

	Successful Nominees	Unsuccessful Nominees[b]	All Nominees
White Men	154 (58)	242 (10)	167 (68)
Women and Minorities	194 (41)	386 (14)	243 (55)
White Men, Women and Minorities	171 (99)	326 (24)	201 (123)

Note: Numbers in parentheses indicate the number of nominations; the analysis is limited to the 105th Congress due to unavailability of complete race data for other than the 105th Congress.

[a] Final action is the confirmation, return to the president, or withdrawal of a nomination.
[b] An unsuccessful nomination is one that is either returned to the president or withdrawn by the president.

Source: Prepared by the Program for Law and Judicial Politics at Michigan State University.

Figure 16. Senate Action: Average Number of Days between Nomination and Final Action,[a] White Men versus Women and Minorities, for the 105th Congress

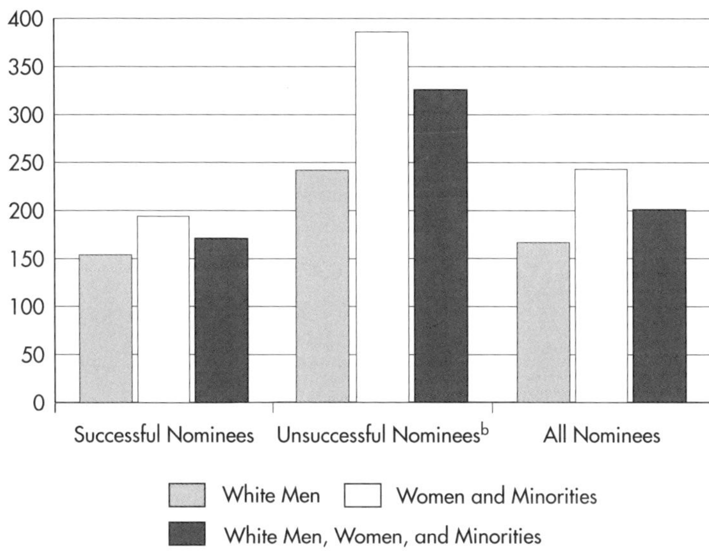

Note: The analysis is limited to the 105th Congress due to unavailability of complete race data for other than the 105th Congress.

[a] Final action is the confirmation, return to the president, or withdrawal of a nomination.

[b] An unsuccessful nomination is one that is either returned to the president or withdrawn by the president.

Source: Prepared by the Program for Law and Judicial Politics at Michigan State University.

TABLE 17. NOMINATIONS REQUIRED TO FILL A VACANCY, DISTRICT AND CIRCUIT COURTS, BY PRESIDENT MAKING SUCCESSFUL NOMINATION, 1977–98

President	Number of Nominations			
	1	2	3	4
Carter (1977–80)	253 (98.1%)	5 (1.9%)	0 (0.0%)	0 (0.0%)
Reagan (1981–88)	330 (88.7%)	36 (9.7%)	5 (1.3%)	1 (0.3%)
Bush (1989–92)	171 (90.0%)	16 (8.4%)	2 (1.1%)	1 (0.5%)
Clinton (1993–98)	217 (73.1%)	71 (23.9%)	5 (1.7%)	4 (1.3%)
Carter through Clinton (1977–98)	971 (86.9%)	128 (11.4%)	12 (1.1%)	6 (0.5%)

Note: Numbers in parentheses indicate percentages of total unsuccessful nominations.

Source: Prepared by the Program for Law and Judicial Politics at Michigan State University.

FIGURE 17. SUCCESSFUL FIRST NOMINATIONS AS PERCENTAGE OF TOTAL SUCCESSFUL NOMINATIONS, DISTRICT AND CIRCUIT COURTS, BY PRESIDENT MAKING SUCCESSFUL NOMINATION, 1977–98

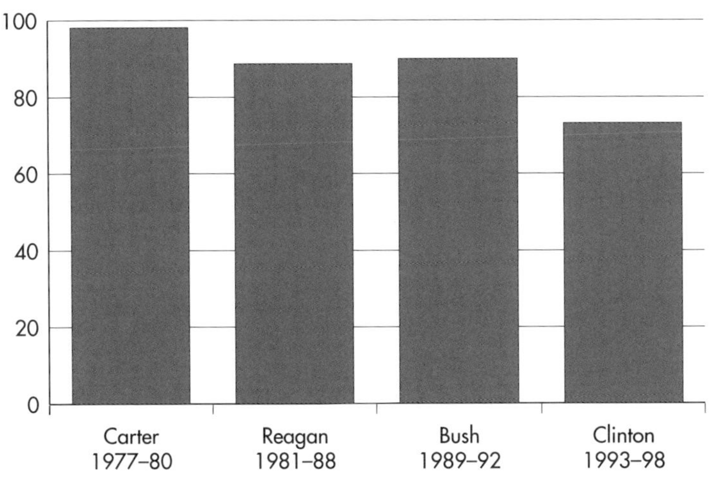

Source: Prepared by the Program for Law and Judicial Politics at Michigan State University.

Table 18. Nominations Required to Fill a Vacancy,
District and Circuit Courts, by Congressional Term
During Which Successful Nomination Was Made, 1977–98

Congressional Term	Number of Nominations			
	1	2	3	4
95th (1977–78)	58 (96.7%)	2 (3.3%)	0 (0.0%)	0 (0.0%)
96th (1979–80)	195 (98.5%)	3 (1.5%)	0 (0.0%)	0 (0.0%)
97th (1981–82)	70 (81.4%)	14 (16.3%)	2 (2.3%)	0 (0.0%)
98th (1983–84)	72 (96.0%)	1 (1.3%)	1 (1.3%)	1 (1.3%)
99th (1985–86)	109 (85.2%)	18 (14.1%)	1 (0.8%)	0 (0.0%)
100th (1987–88)	79 (95.2%)	3 (3.6%)	1 (1.2%)	0 (0.0%)
101st (1989–90)	54 (77.1%)	13 (18.6%)	2 (2.9%)	1 (1.4%)
102nd (1991–92)	117 (97.5%)	3 (2.5%)	0 (0.0%)	0 (0.0%)
103rd (1993–94)	84 (66.7%)	40 (31.7%)	0 (0.0%)	2 (1.6%)
104th (1995–96)	58 (80.6%)	10 (13.9%)	3 (4.2%)	1 (1.4%)
105th (1997–98)	75 (75.8%)	21 (21.2%)	2 (2.0%)	1 (1.0%)
95th through 105th (1977–98)	971 (86.9%)	128 (11.5%)	12 (1.1%)	6 (0.5%)

Source: Prepared by the Program for Law and Judicial Politics at Michigan State University.

FIGURE 18. SUCCESSFUL FIRST NOMINATIONS AS PERCENTAGE OF TOTAL SUCCESSFUL NOMINATIONS, DISTRICT AND CIRCUIT COURTS, BY CONGRESSIONAL TERM DURING WHICH SUCCESSFUL NOMINATION WAS MADE, 1977–98

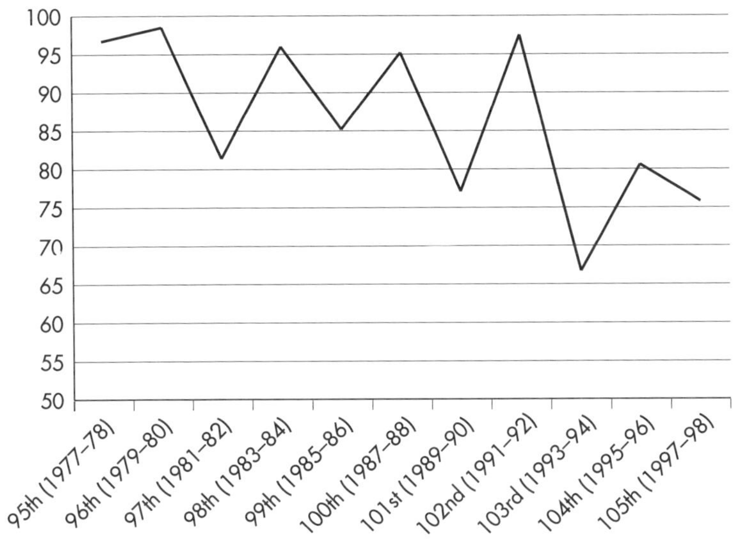

Source: Prepared by the Program for Law and Judicial Politics at Michigan State University.

CHOOSING JUSTICE
REFORMING THE SELECTION OF STATE JUDGES

THE REPORT OF THE CITIZENS FOR INDEPENDENT COURTS TASK FORCE ON SELECTING STATE COURT JUDGES

MEMBERS OF THE TASK FORCE[*]

REPORTERS

Paul D. Carrington, Chadwick Professor of Law, Duke University School of Law

Barbara E. Reed, Esq., Associate Executive Director, The Fund for Modern Courts, Inc.

MEMBERS

Seth Andersen, Director, Hunter Center for Judicial Selection, American Judicature Society[**]

Luke Bierman, Esq., Ph.D., Adjunct Faculty, Northwestern University School of Law; Presidential Assistant, American Bar Association; former Director, Judicial Division, American Bar Association

Anthony Champagne, Professor of Government and Politics, The University of Texas at Dallas, School of Social Sciences

---

[*] Affiliations of members listed for purposes of identification only. The views expressed in this report do not necessarily reflect the views of the institutions with which the members are affiliated.

[**] Member of the drafting committee.

Barry A. Currier, Dean, Samford University, Cumberland School of Law

Adrian W. DeWind, Of Counsel (Partner 1948–1983), Paul, Weiss, Rifkind, Wharton & Garrison; Tax Legislative Counsel, Department of the Treasury (1947–1948); Chief Counsel, Subcommittee on Administration of the Internal Revenue Laws, Committee on Ways and Means, House of Representatives (1951–1953); President, Association of the Bar of the City of New York (1976–1978)

Evan S. Dobelle, President, Trinity College

Victor E. Ferrall, Jr., President, Beloit College

George S. Frazza, Esq., Of Counsel, Patterson, Belknap, Webb & Tyler, L.L.P. (New York, N.Y.)

Eileen Gallagher, Esq., Project Manager, Standing Committee on Judicial Independence, American Bar Association

The Honorable Stuart M. Gerson, Assistant Attorney General, Bush administration; former Acting Attorney General, Clinton administration

Ellen Mattleman Kaplan, former Associate Director, Pennsylvanians for Modern Courts**

William Kirwan, Ph.D., President, Ohio State University

Mark Frederick Kozlowski, Esq., Staff Attorney, Brennan Center for Justice

The Honorable Thomas W. Luce III, Of Counsel, Hughes & Luce, L.L.P.; former Chief Justice Pro Tempore of Texas

Edward W. Madeira, Jr., Esq., Partner, Pepper Hamilton, L.L.P.; Chair, Commission on Separation of Powers and Judicial Independence, American Bar Association; Member, Standing Committee on Judicial Independence, American Bar Association; Permanent Member, Third Circuit Judicial Conference; Fellow, American College of Trial Lawyers

Lynn A. Marks, Executive Director, Pennsylvanians for Modern Courts

John W. Martin, Jr., Esq., former Vice President and General Counsel, Ford Motor Company**

Alan B. Morrison, Esq., Director, Public Citizen Litigation Group**

Denis J. Murphy, Director, Civil Justice, Inc.

Lawrence S. Okinaga, Esq., Immediate Past President, American Judicature Society

John A. Payton, Esq., former Corporation Counsel, District of Columbia

John H. Pickering, Esq., Senior Counsel, Wilmer, Cutler & Pickering

Traciel V. Reid, Ph.D., Associate Professor, Department of Political Science and Public Administration, North Carolina State University

The Honorable Charles B. Renfrew, former Judge, U.S. District Court for the Northern District of California; Deputy Attorney General, Carter administration

Roy A. Schotland, Professor of Law, Georgetown University Law Center**‡

Michael E. Solimine, Professor of Law, University of Cincinnati College of Law

Joseph P. Tomain, Dean and Nippert Professor of Law, University of Cincinnati College of Law**

Barry R. Vickrey, Dean, University of South Dakota School of Law

Frances Kahn Zemans, Ph.D., Justice System Consultant**

---

‡ Roy A. Schotland concurs in Recommendation 5, but abstains from the report on it.

Task Force Recommendations

1. Whether states use elective or appointive methods of judicial selection, they should provide for judicial terms of office of adequate length. For all trial judges in courts of general jurisdiction and all appellate judges, the Task Force recommends a minimum term length of eight years, and urges consideration of longer terms.

2. States in which judges face elections should adopt a nominating commission system for making *interim* appointments to the bench. The appointing authority's choice should be limited to those candidates selected by the nominating commission, which should include members from outside the legal profession.

3. In states where judges are chosen in judicial elections, stringent campaign rules should be enforced to increase public confidence in judicial neutrality. First, full disclosure of sources of all funds expended on judicial campaigns should be required. Second, the information disclosed should be made available to the public in an efficient, easily accessible manner. Third, contribution limits should be set and rigorous recusal rules should be enforced.

4. States that provide for successive terms of judicial office by means of noncompetitive retention elections should conduct systematic, objective, broadly based judicial performance evaluations, and

should disseminate the results to voters at public expense. States with competitive elective systems should provide information regarding judicial candidates to the voters at public expense.

5. In states where judges face elections, private (nongovernmental) groups should adopt methods of oversight of judicial campaigns, including campaign speech standards that make clear the requirements of the jurisdiction's canon of judicial ethics. Voters should have access to information regarding inappropriate campaign conduct by the candidates *prior* to the election.

MISSION STATEMENT OF THE TASK FORCE

The Task Force on Selecting State Court Judges was asked to study judicial selection in the states. Its recommendations, if adopted, can provide guidance to all states—whether they use elective or appointive judicial selection systems—in their efforts to improve their judiciaries. Recommendations concerning disqualification of judges from specific cases, interim vacancy merit plans, improved voter information, and judicial campaign oversight will be of special interest to states with elective systems, while almost all states will find the recommendations regarding judicial performance evaluations and judicial terms of office especially useful. Because most state judges are elected, we have paid particular attention to the influence of money in judicial campaigns, including the impact of the need to seek contributions, and the post-election impact of those contributions on the judiciary generally. We believe that the following recommendations will reduce the problems associated with judicial fundraising in states that continue to elect judges, and will help to promote the independence and integrity of all state judiciaries.

Respectfully submitted,

The Citizens for Independent Courts
Task Force on Selecting State Court Judges

REPORT OF THE
TASK FORCE ON SELECTING
STATE COURT JUDGES

INTRODUCTION

The Task Force finds that there is increasing public concern regarding the independence of many state court judges who are subject to elections.

The tradition of electing judges is uniquely American, and was widely adopted by the states in the nineteenth century for the purpose of making the judiciary independent of the executive and legislative branches of government. However, such independence has been adversely affected by a growing dependence of judicial candidates on other sources of potential influence—the individuals and special interests that finance their election campaigns.

Judicial elections have always been problematic. At a minimum, the solicitation of campaign funds creates an appearance of obligation. Indeed, a 1999 survey conducted on behalf of the Texas Supreme Court and the Texas State Bar found that 48 percent of all Texas judges believe that campaign contributions significantly influence courtroom decisions.[1] Those figures rose to 69 percent for court staff and 79 percent for lawyers.[2]

Further, voter awareness of candidates' qualifications has been limited, typically resulting in low voter turnout. Winning elections often turns on factors irrelevant to candidates' credentials, such as an easily recognizable name, a populous county of residence, strong political connections, or a good ballot position. The tenor of campaign advertising may make judicial races indistinguishable from political contests for legislative and executive offices. Moreover, the competition for campaign funds, especially for expensive televised advertisements, has placed pressure on candidates to raise money, sometimes running to several million dollars for statewide judicial offices.[3]

Election, of course, is a highly democratic method of choosing public officials. Judicial offices, however, are significantly different from positions in the legislative and executive branches, and therefore judicial elections must be assessed and treated accordingly. First, judges are not democratic representatives, as are legislators and governors. They represent the rule of law, not the will of the majority. Second, to ensure that judicial decisions will be based on the facts and law of each case, rules of judicial conduct generally forbid judicial candidates from making campaign promises regarding their future conduct on the bench. In addition, although rules in some jurisdictions forbid candidates from sponsoring certain types of advertisements attacking their opponents, some candidates still use negative advertising that may contravene their jurisdictions' rules of judicial ethics. Moreover, the candidates themselves may become the object of attacks by "issue groups" that oppose them. Indeed, because judicial candidates are constrained both in what they are permitted to say and in how they may solicit funds, they are particularly vulnerable to misleading advertising and attacks on judicial independence by opposing groups.

These problems of the electoral system present strong arguments in favor of "merit selection." Merit selection is an appointive system of judicial selection in which a nonpartisan, broad-based nominating commission recruits and evaluates judicial candidates to determine which are best qualified, and submits the names of the most qualified applicants to an appointing authority (for example, a state's governor), who may choose only from those names submitted. Most of the states that use merit selection systems also provide for "retention elections" for judges who are appointed to the bench. In general, such systems provide that, after completing a short initial term of office, a judge must stand, unopposed, for retention; the voters then decide whether to retain him or her for a full term.

Presently, twenty-four states and the District of Columbia use a nominating commission-based appointive plan for the initial selection of some or all levels of the judiciary, and an additional ten states use a similar plan only to fill midterm vacancies. Nevertheless, elective systems remain commonplace; 77 percent of all judges on courts of general jurisdiction and 53 percent of all appellate court judges in the states face contestable elections.[4]

Appointive systems do not necessarily guarantee the selection of the most capable and independent judiciary. Indeed, the Task Force recognizes the high quality and professionalism of many of the elected judges now serving on state courts. However, judges who are appointed rather than elected are relieved of the need to raise campaign funds, thereby freeing them from some vulnerability to outside influences. That there may be a link, or, perhaps more importantly, the perception of a link, between campaign contributions and judicial decision-making significantly jeopardizes public confidence in the judicial process.

A majority of the Task Force strongly endorses the merit selection process, and it is important to note that use of an appointive system of judicial selection obviates the need for the second, third, and fifth recommendations. This report and its recommendations are in no way intended to detract from the struggles of the many national and state organizations that continue to work for merit selection, nor to suggest that merit selection is unachievable. However, the political reality is that, at least for the present, in thirty-nine states, some judges face elections. Thus, particularly with regard to recommendations directed toward judicial elections, the Task Force has turned its attention to measures that it believes will substantially improve the current system.

To improve the process of judicial selection, and to enhance the independence and integrity of the judiciary, the Task Force proposes the foregoing five recommendations, which are analyzed in the next section of this report. (At the end of the analysis, Appendix 1 provides historical background on judicial selection in the states, Appendix 2 provides information on judicial term lengths in the states, and Appendix 3 provides information on interim nominating commissions.) The Task Force has chosen not to include a recommendation regarding public funding of judicial campaigns, believing that the topic raises issues that take it beyond the scope of this report.

The Task Force recognizes that there is no national prescription for reforming judicial selection completely. Rather, the history and political traditions unique to each state necessarily will dictate which reforms are likely to improve the process. Moreover, the ways in which reforms must be enacted—through revisions to a state constitution, statute, executive order, state Supreme Court rule, or a code of judicial conduct—also are not uniform among states.

It is with an understanding of these constraints that the Task Force offers for consideration the following analysis of its recommendations.

ANALYSIS

1. Whether states use elective or appointive methods of judicial selection, they should provide for judicial terms of office of adequate length. For all trial judges in courts of general jurisdiction and all appellate judges, the Task Force recommends a minimum term length of eight years, and urges consideration of longer terms.

Unlike their federal counterparts who are appointed with life tenure, most state judges are appointed or elected for a term of years. The length of the judicial term has significant consequences for reappointment or reelection, and requires maintenance of a delicate balance between judicial independence and judicial accountability. Unduly short terms increase the frequency with which judges are subjected to political pressures from the electorate or the appointing authority; on the other hand, longer terms, in the views of some, may leave judges isolated from the communities they serve.

The Task Force recommends longer tenure than many states have for two reasons. First, longer terms strike the more appropriate balance between independence and accountability.[5] Second, by reducing the frequency of campaigns, longer tenure helps to lessen the influence of money on judicial elections. Task Force members agree that a minimum term of eight years would meet these objectives.[6]

As noted in the Introduction, throughout the country, 77 percent of all judges of trial courts of general jurisdiction, and 53 percent of all appellate judges, face contestable elections. Of these trial judges, 30 percent have initial terms of four years or less (this total increases to as many as 44 percent when trial judges appointed to fill interim vacancies are included). Twenty-eight percent of elected appellate judges have initial terms of two years or less (the total increases to as many as 69 percent when appellate judges appointed to fill interim vacancies are included). Another 4 percent of elected appellate judges sit for initial terms of only three or four years.[7]

The length of subsequent terms is slightly greater: of all elected trial judges, 81 percent have subsequent terms greater than four years, and 99 percent of elected appellate judges have subsequent terms longer than four years. However, for 62 percent of elected trial judges and 45 percent of elected appellate judges, these subsequent terms are only six years in length.

Short terms are most problematic in elective systems. States with shorter terms necessarily have more elections; thus, they encounter more instances in which the necessary campaign fundraising can raise the appearance of obligations to contributors. Most importantly, the need to campaign frequently discourages qualified potential candidates, and discourages many of the ablest judges from remaining on the bench. Even where positions are almost never contested, short-term positions are inherently less attractive because of the lack of job security. Short terms also tend to result in "bedsheet ballots"—ballots that are so long and filled with so many candidates that they discourage voter participation—since, while there may be fewer candidates per race, there will be more races in an election cycle. Finally, short terms mean that candidates must raise campaign funds more frequently.

Short terms also present problems for appointed judges. Of appointed judges of trial courts of general jurisdiction, 7 percent have terms of just three to four years, and another 8 percent have terms of only five to six years. Of appointed appellate judges, 8 percent have initial terms of five to six years; 11 percent have subsequent terms of only five to six years. Thus, job security and competition for a limited number of positions on the bench remain issues for many appointed judges.

Longer terms promote judicial independence: instead of being forced to attend to the demands of reelection (and its concomitant need for fundraising) or reappointment, judges can focus on applying the law, regardless of popular sentiment. Longer terms may also in fact promote judicial accountability: the public has a greater opportunity to evaluate a judge's record and professional behavior.

Every state has a system of judicial discipline that sanctions judicial misconduct and, where the misconduct is especially egregious, removes judges from the bench. The longer the term, the greater the need for an effective disciplinary system. As a corollary to enhancing judicial accountability by increasing term lengths, the Task Force recommends that states also consider the adequacy of their judicial discipline systems.

2. States in which judges face elections should adopt a nominating commission system for making interim appointments to the bench. The appointing authority's choice should be limited to those candidates selected by the nominating commission, which should include members from outside the legal profession.

Observers of state judicial selection methods have noted that elective systems tend to be, in fact, "one-person judicial selection" where interim (or midterm) vacancies are concerned. In nearly all of the twenty-one states that elect judges directly at all court levels, the governor has the power to appoint judges to fill such vacancies.[8] In most states, more than half of all judges initially reach the bench through gubernatorial appointment to fill an interim vacancy; in some states, such as California, nearly 90 percent of judges are appointed initially, and contested elections are the exception, rather than the rule.

This system of "one-person judicial selection" presents serious problems for the independence of the judiciary. Executives who have sole authority to appoint judges are free to create their own criteria for judicial selection, which may have little or no bearing on the qualifications necessary to perform effectively and impartially as a judge. The most frequent abuse of executive power in this area is the practice of appointing only one's own political party allies to the bench. In one state, a governor appointed nearly 190 judges during his eight years in office, all of whom were members of his political party. Frequently, governors rely most heavily on recommendations from local party officials in making appointments, thereby turning judgeships into political patronage rewards.

However, a method exists to improve the appointment process for interim vacancies. For states that elect judges, adoption of merit-based nominating commissions for interim appointments helps to safeguard the traditional ideals of the elective system, by ensuring greater public involvement in and a less politicized process for choosing a significant number of judges. Currently, eleven states employ a nominating commission system only to assist the executive in making certain interim appointments.[9] (New Mexico fills all vacancies through its nominating commission. It then holds contested partisan elections for the first full term after appointment and retention elections for additional terms.) In these states, nominating commissions are not used to fill vacancies for initial terms of office.

Nominating commission systems typically contain several basic elements. First, they are broadly based, consisting of lawyer and non-lawyer members, with judges sitting ex officio on some commissions; several of these states also provide that a majority of the members must be nonlawyers. Second, to avoid domination of the process by one political party, appointment authority for selection or election of commission members is often spread among several sources, including the state bar, the supreme court, the legislature, and the governor. In seven of the eleven states described above, the executive is required to appoint only from the list of nominees provided by the nominating commission. Third, and perhaps most important, these nominating commissions are charged with recruiting, investigating, interviewing, and recommending only the most highly qualified lawyers to fill judicial vacancies.

A 1991 American Judicature Society (AJS) survey of governors using executive order merit plans shows that governors view the nom-inating commission process very favorably, because the focus is on the merits of the candidates themselves. At the time of the survey, the consensus among governors was that this kind of merit plan mini-mizes partisan political influence, provides the highest quality nomi-nees, and broadens the pool of applicants, resulting in a more diverse group of nominees in terms of race, ethnicity, gender, and practice background. One governor observed that "this system is a lot better than either popular election or unfettered gubernatorial choice," while another declared, "I believe the effectiveness of a merit plan depends a great deal on how the process is treated by the executive. I treat the process very seriously."[10] AJS has also found that citizens are sup-portive of midterm vacancy merit plans because they inject a degree of community involvement into a system that would otherwise be "one-person judicial selection."

AJS's studies show that while citizens and governors themselves support midterm vacancy plans, opposition tends to come from local- and state-level political party officials, who stand to lose the power they can wield over judicial selection when their party controls the statehouse. For this reason, it can sometimes be difficult to pass either a statute or a constitutional amendment providing for a midterm vacan-cy merit plan. Adoption of an executive order is accomplished more eas-ily, but it is vulnerable to extinction when a new governor is elected.

The Task Force thus urges states to adopt, by statute or constitutional amendment, a nonpartisan (or bipartisan) nominating commission system for interim vacancies.[11] The Task Force also recommends that any plan for a nominating commission system require that the executive must appoint *only* from the list of nominees provided by the commission; without such a provision, nominating commissions are merely advisory bodies. Further, to increase the legitimacy of the commission in the eyes of the general public, it should include members from outside the legal community.

3. In states where judges are chosen in judicial elections, stringent campaign rules should be enforced to increase public confidence in judicial neutrality. First, full disclosure of sources of all funds expended on judicial campaigns should be required. Second, the information disclosed should be made available to the public in an efficient, easily accessible manner. Third, contribution limits should be set and rigorous recusal rules should be enforced.

Money used to finance judicial elections should neither influence nor give the appearance of influencing judicial decisions. One way to ameliorate the negative influence of money on judicial campaigns is through a recusal (disqualification) rule.

DISCLOSURE

Any system of recusal requires full and effective disclosure of all campaign contributions. Disclosure should apply whenever a lawyer contributes to a judicial campaign or to a party or political action committee (PAC) that contributes to or otherwise supports judicial candidates. Such disclosure should include the lawyer's employment or professional affiliation(s) (for example, the law firm or other organization for which the lawyer works). States may also wish to require disclosure of the employers or professional affiliations of *all* contributors, including nonlawyers.

Ideally, all contributions originating from the law firm or organization should be publicly disclosed as a unit, to provide a complete picture of the contributors to a specific campaign. Contributions must be disclosed promptly, and the disclosure statements must be made readily available to the public. At a minimum, states should provide the resources to make disclosure statements publicly accessible at the courthouse where the judge regularly presides; preferably, they would be made available at *all* courthouses where the judge sits. In addition, states should make disclosure statements available in on-line format via the Internet.

RECUSAL

The U.S. Supreme Court has recognized that, to prevent the appearance of corruption, the state has a legitimate interest in limiting the amount of money that a candidate may receive from one person, even if there is no actual *quid pro quo* for a particular contribution.[12] The concern is greatest in situations where the recipient has the power to make, or to exercise great influence over, decisions that affect the interests of the contributor. Thus, a contribution of $1,000 to a judicial candidate is more troublesome than a $1,000 contribution in a legislative race, where the recipient may be one of one hundred or five hundred members.

The notion of judicial recusal, or disqualification, is well established. While recusal is generally not employed by legislators, judges are required to recuse themselves in many situations—for example, in cases in which they own stock in a company appearing before them, even where their interest is very small and it is highly unlikely that their own economic interests will be materially affected by the case. Federal law requires recusal for holding "a financial interest in the subject matter," which has been construed to mean "any" such interest.[13] Ultimately, not only must judges decide cases based on the facts of each case and the applicable law, they also must *appear* to do so, without regard for outside interests.

Mandatory Recusal. The Task Force's principal recommendation is that states in which judges face elections should require recusal of any judge who has received an excessive contribution (one that exceeds the applicable limit) from a lawyer, law firm, client, or other interested person or entity. It recommends a "bright-line rule" that would require recusal whenever a campaign contribution exceeds the limit set by the relevant jurisdiction.[14] Rules that are adopted should provide policy guidance and should contain examples of the situations in which recusal is and is not required. The following analysis discusses some of the factors and issues that jurisdictions should take into account in crafting their own bright-line rules.[15]

The Task Force recommends that a recusal rule be mandatory: a judge must recuse him- or herself in any case in which a lawyer or a client made a contribution to the judge's campaign that, at the time it was made, exceeded the prescribed legal limit. States must determine the appropriate legal limit for their jurisdictions, and how and to whom they will apply.[16]

The rule should apply throughout the length of the term during which (or in anticipation of which) the contribution was made. The Task Force recognizes that judges in some states are elected to longer terms of office (for example, ten to fifteen years); such states may deem it appropriate to shorten the period during which recusal is required. However, the Task Force urges that a mandatory rule apply, at a minimum, for the first five years after the contribution is made.

An important question involves the mechanics of recusal: Who can request that a judge recuse him- or herself? If either party is permitted to move for recusal, a lawyer (or client) in a given case who wants to avoid a particular judge need only make a contribution over the allowable limit. Such a situation encourages "judge shopping," and will not enhance public confidence in the judiciary. Thus, the Task Force recommends adoption of a rule specifying that recusal may occur only on motion of the adverse party—that is, the party to whose interests the contribution could be presumed detrimental. For purposes of determining whether the legal contribution limit has been exceeded, the Task Force does not endorse aggregation of contributions from lawyers, clients, and/or other parties on a particular side of a case.

Discretionary Recusal. In addition to establishing a bright-line rule, there is support among some members of the Task Force for urging states to formalize a judge's discretionary option to withdraw from a case, either on motion or *sua sponte,* when he or she believes that some relationship or connection with a party or counsel (for example, campaign contributions, membership on a campaign committee, hosting of a campaign fundraising event, and so on) reasonably may be perceived to affect his or her fair and impartial adjudication of the matter. Discretionary withdrawal may be appropriate when a reasonable person would conclude that, in light of the circumstances surrounding contributions or other assistance made to the campaign of the judge before whom the case is pending, the judge's objectivity may appear to be compromised in favor of the opposing side.

However, contributions that comply with the applicable limit, standing alone, are not sufficient grounds for such withdrawal. Four factors relevant to the determination of whether withdrawal may be appropriate are:

1. the aggregate amount of contributions by lawyers, parties, and other supporters of a particular side in a case (for example, trade associations, labor unions, political action committees, and so on, where there is any basis to believe that the contributions of such supporters were the result of concerted activity intended to influence the judge, or where such groups have demonstrated an intent to file *amicus curiae* briefs or to petition to intervene in support of one side);

2. the ratio of the contributions made by those listed in (1), above, to the total contributions made to the judge's campaign;

3. the timing of the contributions (how long ago they were made, and whether they were made after the identity of the judge handling the case was known to the contributors);

4. the competing concerns of preventing delay in the case in question and preventing inefficiency in managing other matters on the judge's docket, particularly in those jurisdictions where replacing a judge is a difficult matter.

A rule providing for motions for discretionary recusal must require that any such motion be *timely*. Denial of such a motion to recuse should be reviewable only on grounds of abuse of discretion.

SUMMARY

In summary, the Task Force finds, first, that disclosure requirements are necessary; second, that monetary limits must be set; and third, that states must define, for purposes of the rule, what constitutes an "adverse party." The ABA Task Force on Lawyers' Political Contributions provides guidance on these three basic issues.[17] While the Task Force recognizes that many factors must be taken into account in fashioning a rule, it endorses the creation of a bright-line rule that mandates recusal whenever a campaign contribution exceeds the jurisdiction's legal limit.

4. States that provide for successive terms of judicial office by means of noncompetitive retention elections should conduct systematic, objective, broadly based judicial performance evaluations, and should disseminate the results to voters at public expense. States with competitive elective systems should provide information regarding judicial candidates to the voters at public expense.

The Task Force finds that voters in judicial elections need more and better information about the candidates. In both competitive elections and noncompetitive retention elections, voters traditionally have very little information on which to base their decisions. While most bar associations publish evaluations of judges standing for retention, the voting public does not seem to use voter guides produced exclusively by the organized bar. This may be because such guides are not always widely distributed; some evidence indicates that voters do use guides when they receive them. However, there is anecdotal evidence that the public has greater confidence in guides produced by a committee with a broader membership than simply the organized bar.

States can help to provide better information for voters by collecting and distributing appropriate information at public expense. The type of information distributed will vary depending on the type of elective system used by the state.

JUDICIAL PERFORMANCE EVALUATIONS IN RETENTION ELECTIONS

Retention elections are designed to ensure that appointed judges are appropriately accountable to the citizens they serve.[18] Therefore, when voters go to the polls, they should be given systematic information on the overall performance of judges standing for retention. To remedy the lack of information for voters in retention elections, several states have instituted performance evaluation commissions. These commissions, composed of both lawyers and nonlawyers, conduct surveys of many different groups of people who come into contact with a judge, which may include lawyers, police and probation officers, social service personnel, jurors, litigants, witnesses, and court staff. The commissions are funded by the state, but operate as independent evaluators of judicial performance. The results of their surveys can provide systematic, relevant information to voters in retention elections. The criteria used by evaluation programs typically include such factors as the judge's judicial temperament, how expeditiously the judge resolves cases, whether the judge spends sufficient time on cases, and whether the judge treats litigants and attorneys with respect. The programs do not consider the content of the judge's decisions or his or her political ideology.

The involvement of political action committees and single-issue interest groups in several recent retention elections has served as an additional impetus for conducting performance evaluations. The most high-profile examples are those of former justice Penny White of the Tennessee Supreme Court and former justice David Lanphier of the Nebraska Supreme Court, both of whom were defeated in their retention bids in 1996 due to last-minute "Vote No" campaigns waged by groups in favor of the death penalty and term limits, respectively. Nebraska has no performance evaluation mechanism that could have countered the one-sided information disseminated by Justice Lanphier's opponents, and Tennessee's performance evaluation program did not begin until the 1998 elections. Many observers contend that performance evaluation results, if disseminated widely and effectively, can help voters make a more informed choice based on a judge's entire record, rather than on a decision in one controversial case that may be distorted by political opponents. This contention is supported by results of an American Judicature Society survey of voters in the four states that, as of 1996, had established performance evaluation programs for judges seeking retention.[19]

Currently, five states have official performance evaluation mechanisms for judicial retention elections: Alaska, Arizona, Colorado, Tennessee, and Utah.[20] New Mexico has begun limited performance evaluations of some judges, with plans to expand its program to all state judges in upcoming election cycles. Hawaii and the District of Columbia provide for additional terms through evaluation and reappointment by a commission. Performance evaluations do not necessarily require legislation or constitutional change; in 1998, the Oklahoma Supreme Court created a judicial evaluation commission to conduct a survey of attorneys who had appeared before the appellate judges up for retention that year.

These programs require modest but not insignificant funding in order to operate successfully. First, they must have adequate resources to conduct and interpret the results of broad-based surveys of those who come in contact with judges standing for retention. Second, and most important, they must have adequate funding for dissemination of results—preferably through a voter guide that is sent directly to all registered voters in a state or jurisdiction. Placement of evaluation results in newspapers and on websites is an additional means of getting information directly to the voters. States without enough funding to disseminate their evaluation results widely have been disappointed with the effectiveness of their programs. Finally, in addition to ensuring adequate funding for dissemination, states should release their evaluation results during the final few weeks leading up to the election to maximize the benefit to prospective voters.

NONPARTISAN VOTERS' GUIDES IN COMPETITIVE ELECTIONS

State-sponsored judicial performance evaluations are less feasible in contested elections, where one candidate may be an incumbent judge and the other an attorney with no judicial experience. However, states can publish and distribute nonpartisan voters' guides in state and local competitive elections. As a simple, cost-effective method to educate the public about its judiciary, such guides may reduce the influence of money and politics in judicial elections by providing candidates with a guaranteed method of reaching voters.

State-produced voters' guides are currently used in at least four states and in New York City, and exit polls and other studies have shown that these guides are voters' best sources of information about judicial candidates.[21] Voters' guides could contain biographical information, photographs, and personal statements. The guides could also include the results of bar polls or other candidate evaluations. Some states provide standardized biographical information on each candidate, while others permit the candidates themselves to supply the content.

The greatest costs associated with the guides are distribution costs; currently, the U.S. Postal Service's franking privilege (waiver of postage costs) does not apply to voters' guides. However, the total cost incurred by extending the franking privilege to the guides is small when compared to the benefits of a better-informed electorate, increased voter participation, and a reduction in negative perceptions of government. Thus, the Task Force endorses legislation to provide federal financial support in the form of postage for state and local initiatives that produce nonpartisan voters' guides for judicial elections.

5. In states where judges face elections, private (nongovernmental) groups should adopt methods of oversight of judicial campaigns, including campaign speech standards that make clear the requirements of the jurisdiction's canon of judicial ethics. Voters should have access to information regarding inappropriate campaign conduct by the candidates prior to the election.

Judicial elections are unique in terms of the restrictions placed upon candidates' speech. Canon 5 of the Model Code of Judicial Conduct exemplifies these heavy regulations.[22] Judicial campaign speech presents two difficult issues: first, as a matter of policy, whether a restriction on campaign speech is desirable; and second, whether such restrictions are constitutional. Such restrictions are intended to ensure that judicial candidates (and judges) appear neutral and unaffected by the political pressures of popular opinion. However, while courts agree on the need to construe narrowly any limits on speech, courts have not agreed on the constitutionality of several states' versions of Canon 5.[23]

On the one hand, candidates for judicial office must be able to inform the public about their credentials for office. On the other hand, candidates should not make promises regarding their future judicial decision-making. Such campaigning compromises impartiality and objectivity, thus threatening judicial independence and undermining public confidence in the judiciary.

Other examples of impermissible campaign conduct include candidates who advertise themselves as "Judge ___," even though they have never been judges, and candidates who attack decisions by their incumbent opponents in ways that distort those decisions. In 1998, for example, a Georgia Supreme Court justice was attacked by her opponent for having said in an opinion that "traditional moral standards" were "pathetic and disgraceful," whereas the justice had applied those adjectives to the majority opinion's analysis.

Public confidence in judicial neutrality is further jeopardized by campaign advertisements like the following:

"Maximum Marion" Bloss—"You do the crime, you do the time." (Texas, 1998)

"Dedicated and Experience [sic] Preserving the Rights and Needs of Victims. I'll Bring Balance to our Judicial Process." (Florida, 1998)

"Mike Burns is a tough, no-nonsense Prosecutor who believes in law and order. If elected, Mike understands his duty to uphold the law regardless of his personal views." (Florida, 1998)

This is not a new phenomenon, as demonstrated by the following advertisements from California campaigns in the 1980s:

"Sent more criminals—rapists, murderers, felons—to prison than any other judge in Contra Costa County history."

"Over 90% Convicted Criminals Sentenced. . . . Prison Commitment Rate is More Than Twice the State Average."

In Nevada, in 1997, a Supreme Court justice campaigned for reelection with advertisements that he had a "record of fighting crime," which included voting to uphold the death penalty seventy-six times. As one of his colleagues wrote after that election, dissenting from the Court's refusal to require that justice to withdraw from a capital case, "Judges are supposed to be *judging* crime, not fighting it."[24]

It is important to emphasize that the Task Force does not endorse restrictions on campaign speech that would punish a judicial candidate for personal opinions or political beliefs. Rather, it endorses those limited standards that balance judicial independence and judicial accountability by preserving the requirement that judges remain objective in the performance of their duties. As discussed earlier in this report, voters tend to have very little information regarding judicial candidates generally; and when a candidate's campaign speech or conduct violates the jurisdiction's canon of judicial ethics, fewer still are likely to recognize that there has been a violation. Campaign oversight committees are able to disseminate that information to voters when the conduct occurs, thus providing voters with additional data to use in making informed decisions in choosing judges.

There are effective and constitutional ways to encourage judicial candidates to campaign in a manner that enhances public confidence in judicial neutrality and independence. For example, for several decades, private "citizen committees" in jurisdictions around the nation have conducted active oversight of judicial campaigns. Most such groups, while usually launched by local bar associations, consist of a diverse cross section of community leaders, and their "authority" derives from the respect their members enjoy in the community. At the beginning of the election year, some groups advise candidates of the committee's criteria for evaluating judicial campaigns; some candidates actively seek the committee's opinions before running their advertisements. Occasionally, oversight committees publicly declare a candidate's conduct inappropriate for judicial office.

In addition, judicial campaign oversight committees may monitor campaign finance issues, publicizing the links between the sources of funds and the issues advanced by those sources. They may also alert the public to any violation of campaign finance laws. Such publicity can help mitigate the harm of any improper conduct before the election, and cause it to halt before it is repeated.[25]

Recent steps in Alabama and Ohio are noteworthy. For the 1998 elections, the Alabama Supreme Court appointed the nation's first Judicial Campaign Oversight Committee, composed of thirteen judges, lawyers, and lay members. The Committee was established as a result of widespread dissatisfaction with the conduct of the 1994 and 1996 judicial campaigns, which were also the most expensive in Alabama history.[26] The Committee was responsible for ensuring compliance with the relevant Canons of Judicial Conduct and the lawyers' Code of Professional Responsibility. In Ohio, the Board of Commissioners on Grievances and Discipline worked with two counties' monitoring committees to establish expedited enforcement procedures. The Board of Commissioners on Grievances and Discipline is now able to hear grievances and issue at least a preliminary ruling before the election occurs.

Two problems with official oversight should be noted. First, an official body, particularly if it is part of the judicial branch, may not be perceived to be neutral in its treatment of incumbents and challengers. Second, an official body is limited by requirements of due process and free speech, and ensuing lawsuits may be used as a campaign tool. In contrast, unofficial bodies act merely as members of the community; as a result, they are subject to fewer restrictions, and do not represent a threat to candidates' First Amendment rights. They also are likely to be able to act quickly enough to disseminate information before the election, providing voters with additional information to use in deciding which candidates are best qualified for a seat on the bench.

The Task Force thus recommends the establishment of private, nongovernmental judicial campaign oversight committees. Membership should be broad-based and diverse, including lawyers and non-lawyers; members should be representative of the community, and should have personal reputations for integrity and neutrality. Such committees should establish written procedures and standards, and should communicate with candidates at the beginning of each election year.

CONCLUSION

To help ensure that state courts remain as independent as possible, the Task Force urges state and local jurisdictions to seriously consider implementing some or all of these recommendations. The Task Force recognizes that the recommendations can only reduce, not eliminate, the influence of both politics and money on judicial selection and retention and the resulting harmful effects on judicial independence. Since elected judges will remain subject to some financial pressures, whether real or perceived, the Task Force recommends, alternatively, that states with elective systems give serious consideration to some form of merit selection system.

NOTES

1. *See* Supreme Court of Texas, State Bar of Texas, and Texas Office of Court Administration, *The Courts and the Legal Profession in Texas—The Insider's Perspective: A Survey of Judges, Court Personnel, and Attorneys,* Austin, Texas, May 1999, p. 5.

2. Ibid.

3. For extensive documentation on the problem of increased campaign spending, *see* "Report and Recommendations of the Task Force on Lawyers' Political Contributions, Part Two, Regarding Contributions to Judges and

Judicial Candidates," American Bar Association, July 1998, Appendix III, (hereafter "ABA Report and Recommendations").

4. *See* "ABA Report and Recommendations," Appendix II.

5. Some have also noted that the overall quality and productivity of the judiciary may suffer from high turnover.

6. Many Task Force members suggest that term lengths be increased to twelve years; indeed, this report recognizes that some states have had success with even longer terms. In New York, for example, justices of the Supreme Court, New York's trial court of general jurisdiction, are elected to four-teen-year terms.

7. *See* Appendix 2.

8. In Illinois, the Supreme Court makes appointments to fill vacancies, and in a few other states the governor's appointments must be confirmed by the legislature.

9. *See* Appendix 3 for a summary of these nominating commission systems.

10. American Judicature Society, Survey of Governors on Executive Order Merit Plans, 1991 (unpublished).

11. It is important to note that in some states, such as Louisiana and Arkansas, persons appointed to fill an interim vacancy are not eligible to run for a full term of office in the next general election. Therefore, adoption of a nominating commission system for interim vacancies in such states may not be a practical goal.

12. *Buckley* v. *Valeo*, 424 U.S. 1 (1976).

13. *See* 28 U.S.C. § 455(b)(4).

14. *See, e.g.*, American Bar Association, Ad Hoc Committee on Judicial Campaign Finance, Report and Recommendation, American Bar Association, May 1999.

15. Ibid., p. 4 (January 1999 Discussion Draft).

16. The report of the ABA Task Force on Lawyers' Political Contributions provides substantial guidance on this issue. *See* "ABA Report and Recommendations," p. 23.

17. *See* "ABA Report and Recommendations," pp. 19–39.

18. Only two states—Illinois and Pennsylvania—pair competitive (parti-san) elections for initial vacancies with retention elections for successive terms of judicial office. In all other states using retention elections, judges are initially appointed to their positions. In Montana, which has competitive reelections, unopposed judges run on a retention ballot. In California, unop-posed incumbent trial court judges do not appear on the ballot at all.

19. Readers seeking more information on judicial performance evalua-tion programs should contact the American Judicature Society (telephone

number 312-558-6900, extension 147) to receive a copy of the report, *Judicial Performance Evaluation Programs in Four States.*

20. These five states also conduct confidential midterm performance evaluations solely for judicial self-improvement purposes. These evaluations, which are not made public, allow judges to focus on areas of performance needing improvement.

21. Roy A. Schotland, *Elective Judges' Campaign Financing: Are State Judges' Robes the Emperor's Clothes of American Democracy?* 2 J.L. & Pol. 57, 127–28, 163–66 (1985); "ABA Report and Recommendations," pp. 54–56; Charles H. Sheldon and Linda Maule, *Choosing Justice: The Recruitment of State and Federal Judges* (Pullman: Washington State University Press, 1997), p. 62.

22. Canon 5A(3) of the Model Code of Judicial Conduct provides that "All Judges and Candidates . . . (d) shall not: (i) make pledges or promises of conduct in office other than the faithful and impartial performance of the duties of the office; (ii) make statements that commit or appear to commit the candidate with respect to cases, controversies or issues that are likely to come before the court."

23. *See, e.g.,* Randall T. Shepard (Chief Justice of Indiana), *Campaign Speech: Restraint and Liberty in Judicial Ethics*, 9 Geo. J. Legal Ethics 1059 (1996).

24. *Nevius v. Warden,* 944 P.2d 858, 860 (Nev. 1997) (Springer, J., dissenting), *cert. denied sub nom. Nevius v. McDaniel,* 119 S. Ct. 878 (1999).

25. In 1998, when the Federal Election Commission imposed its second largest fine ever against a U.S. House challenger for violations in 1994 and 1996, the former congressional staffer who had lost the 1994 nomination (after having won it in 1992), said "I knew then that he was receiving money in violation of federal law, and I screamed, yelled, asked for immediate investigation, and found there's no mechanism to remedy what would be irreparable harm. There's no temporary restraining order, no injunction, the election goes on. . . . He used illegal money and denied the [voters] the race that should have been. . . ." ("FEC Levies $280K Fine Against Ackerman Foe," *The Hill* [May 27, 1998], p. 3).

26. *See* "ABA Report and Recommendations," Table 1, Appendix III.

Appendix 1:

A Brief History of Judicial Selection in State Courts

Introduction

In 1837, Francis Lieber observed that while the ancients could not create an independent judiciary, Americans were unable adequately to appreciate the one they had.[1] Today, however, those who appreciate judicial independence also recognize the need for a measure of accountability for judges, as well as insulation from political concerns.

Because judicial authority includes the power to review legislation, judges historically have been accused of exceeding that authority and usurping the role of the legislative branch. Such criticism dates to the earliest days of the American judicial system.[2] Unlike most state courts, the federal courts are staffed by judges who enjoy tenure for life. While criticism of life tenure dates to Thomas Jefferson, the framers of the Constitution concluded that life tenure was the most effective means of shielding judges from political and financial pressures. The states, on the other hand, reached a different conclusion.

A Historical Perspective on Judicial Elections

The rationale for judicial elections was simple: because elected judges were chosen by the people themselves, they would inspire greater public trust, and their decisions, in turn, would command greater respect. Moreover, elections would provide judges with a background appropriate to the responsibilities inherent in the political role of judicial review. In theory, legislatures thus would be less likely to intrude upon judicial decisions, and if bad judges were elected, recourse would be available at the ballot box.

By the end of the nineteenth century, the weaknesses of judicial elections had become increasingly evident.[3] In rural counties, elections intensified fears of hometown prejudice against nonresident parties. Elsewhere, judicial elections were often marked by a very low level of knowledge and interest among the electorate. There were also at least three more serious weaknesses that the advocates of judicial elections had not anticipated: the role of political parties; the need for and sources of campaign funds; and the substantive content of the campaigns themselves.[4]

STATE EFFORTS TO IMPROVE JUDICIAL SELECTION

Some states included provisions in their constitutions for the recall of elected officials,[5] and seven extended these provisions to include judges. Colorado's constitution provided for public referenda to review judicial decisions. In 1911, outraged by a New York Court of Appeals decision invalidating the state's mandatory worker's compensation law,[6] former president Theodore Roosevelt proposed that New York follow Colorado's example, granting the people a referendum on the constitutionality of legislation.[7] Ohio, North Dakota, and Nebraska also amended their constitutions to require supermajority votes of their highest courts to invalidate legislation.[8] Such efforts to subject judicial decisions to popular referendum eroded the judiciary's independence, particularly under elective systems.

In the late nineteenth century, the public grew increasingly suspicious of urban political machines and feared that judges could not be trusted to decide cases independently of their party sponsors. Political parties played a significant role in judicial elections, awarding nominations and support to party regulars and contributors.[9] However, because the parties' interests extended beyond the outcome of a particular election, they did sometimes eliminate underqualified candidates who might otherwise have won election.[10]

The need for and sources of campaign funds presented a second concern.[11] Judicial candidates received contributions from lawyers and litigants who appeared in their courts, and even when such amounts were relatively small, the contributions raised at least an appearance of impropriety. This problem was exacerbated when a candidate retained surplus campaign funds or held postelection fundraisers to pay campaign debts.[12]

The substantive content of judicial campaigns presented a third difficulty (one that still exists). Political candidates had to appeal to their future constituents for votes, and they often did so by making promises regarding future policy decisions. However, judicial candidates who made such promises regarding their decisions in future cases (in which, by definition, the parties had not yet been heard) sacrificed the neutrality and objectivity they were expected to bring to the position. While professional ethical standards may have proscribed such campaign promises,[13] candidates sometimes failed to practice appropriate restraint.[14] Some also argued that free speech protection should outweigh concerns regarding judicial objectivity and its implications for due process.[15]

After 1912, the direct democracy movement faded.[16] As lengthened ballots diminished the likelihood that voters were exercising knowing choices and increased the election prospects of candidates with familiar names but few qualifications, political parties found it increasingly difficult to prevent the election of underqualified judges.[17] In this environment, a movement arose among the organized bar to improve methods of judicial selection and retention. Some states had fashioned "nonpartisan" elections by removing judicial candidates from partisan tickets. However, this weakened the parties' influence and simply made judges more vulnerable to other financial influences.[18]

This situation led to growing support among the bar for "merit selection." Under this method of judicial selection, candidates were nominated by a committee that examined their experience and credentials; those chosen were then subjected to retention elections (that is, elections in which the judge is unopposed, and voters simply decide whether the judge should remain in office). The merit selection method was first suggested by Albert Kales, vice president of the American Judicature Society, which was founded in 1913 by members of the bench and bar to improve judicial administration. In 1937, the American Bar Association adopted a merit selection policy, and in 1940, Missouri became the first state to establish a merit-selection method of choosing judges, which came to be known as "the Missouri plan." Eight more states adopted a merit selection plan for at least some judicial vacancies over the next thirty years. In the 1970s, fifteen additional states adopted a form of appointive selection for at least some levels of their judiciaries. As a result of the variety among the plans that were adopted, almost no two states now have identical systems of judicial selection, and most have different systems for different types of courts.[19] However, the trend since 1950 has been toward merit selection.

Retention elections were a device to satisfy the voters' desire for self-governance without risk of improper political influences on judges. As originally envisioned, a judge running unopposed in a retention election would be retained, in the absence of scandalous misconduct,[20] and for decades, retention elections worked as expected: no judge standing for retention failed to achieve it.

RECENT DEVELOPMENTS

About 1980, political parties and interest groups began to take an even greater interest in judicial elections. In some states, tort and insurance law moved to the top of the political agenda as campaign issues in judicial elections. By 1980, local groups of personal injury lawyers organized to work for the election of judges they believed would rule favorably for their clients. For a time, some observers felt that they controlled elections to the Supreme Court of Texas,[21] and their success evoked a response from insurance companies and others whose financial interests were threatened by what they perceived to be a "plaintiffs' court." Now, nearly two decades since, many observers believe that the pendulum has swung in the opposite direction and now characterize the court as a "defendants' court." A similar series of events has occurred in Alabama,[22] and, less visibly, in other states.[23]

During this period, television advertising also entered judicial elections. Political advertisements on commercial television have affected judicial elections in two ways. First, the cost of advertising, especially on television, has increased the need for campaign funds. Second, expert consultants and focus groups have been used to tailor such advertising, which sometimes directs negative sentiments toward political adversaries. Such attacks can be effectively countered, if at all, only by a televised response, thus further raising the cost of judicial campaigns.

Conclusion

In recent years, polls have shown that the public overwhelmingly believes that judicial decisions are influenced by campaign contributions. In some states, recent headlines have called attention to large favorable judgments and fee-paying appointments (such as receiverships) granted to lawyers or parties who previously had made large campaign contributions to the judge(s) involved.[24] These concerns weaken public confidence in the independence of the judiciary.[25] These problems show no sign of abating, making the need for the reforms discussed in the accompanying report all the more urgent.

Notes

1. Francis Lieber, *Manual of Political Ethics,* 2d ed., Theodore Woolsey, ed. (Philadelphia: J. B. Lippincott and Co., 1875), p. 363.

2. For example, in the early days of the republic, the New York State Legislature protested certain decisions made by Chancellor James Kent by forcing him into retirement. In Connecticut, a grand jury indicted its own presiding judge, Federalist Tapping Reeve, as a result of comments he made about Jefferson from the bench. Likewise, for ideological reasons, Pennsylvania Federalists deprived Jefferson's friend Thomas Cooper of his judgeship, and in 1813, a Federalist New Hampshire legislature expelled all Democratic judges from the state's courts. In 1824, as punishment for decisions adverse to tenants and debtors, Kentucky's Democratic legislature fired all Whig members of its highest court. By the 1830s, Jacksonian Democrats advocated the election of judges, and by the middle of the nineteenth century, judges were elected in all but a few states.

3. Steven P. Croley, *The Majoritarian Difficulty: Elective Judiciaries and The Rule of Law,* 62 U. Chi. L. Rev. 689, 713–29 (1995).

4. *See, e.g.,* John v. Orth, *Tuesday, February 11, 1868: The Day North Carolina Chose Direct Election of Judges: A Transcript of the Debates from the 1868 Constitutional Convention,* 70 N.C. L. Rev. 1825 (1992).

5. Recall was first adopted in Oregon in 1908, and little consideration was given to the possible exclusion of judges from that provision. Allen H. Eaton, *The Oregon System: The Story of Direct Legislation in Oregon* (Chicago: A. C. McClurg and Co., 1912).

6. J. Patrick White, *Progressivism and the Judiciary: A Study of the Movement for Judicial Reform 1901–1917* (Ph.D. dissertation, University of Michigan, 1957), p. 349.

7. Speech at Carnegie Hall, New York, October 20, 1911, *The Works of Theodore Roosevelt,* Herman Hagedorn, ed. (New York: C. Scribner's Sons, 1925). An account of this remarkable event is provided by Edward Hartnett, *Why Is the Supreme Court of the United States Protecting State Judges from Popular Democracy?* 75 Tex. L. Rev. 907, 933–49 (1997).

8. White, *Progressivism and the Judiciary,* p. 420.

9. This remains a feature of partisan judicial elections in numerous states. Roy A. Schotland, *Elective Judges' Campaign Financing: Are State Judges' Robes the Emperor's Clothes of American Democracy?* 2 J. L. & Pol. 57, 65–66 (1985).

10. Absent party control, the election is often decided by name recognition. Schotland, *Elective Judges' Campaign Financing,* pp. 86–89, gives numerous examples.

11. Ibid., pp. 59–63.

12. *See, e.g.,* the event described in David Fraser, "Letter Asks Help to Cut Judge's Debt," *Arkansas Democrat-Gazette,* July 16, 1994, p. 1A.

13. Randall T. Shepard, *Campaign Speech: Restraint and Liberty in Judicial Ethics,* 9 Geo. J. Legal Ethics 1059, 1059–68 (1996).

14. *See, e.g.,* Schotland, *Elective Judges' Campaign Financing,* pp. 66, 79–80.

15. *ACLU v. Florida Bar,* 744 F. Supp. 1094 (N.D. Fla. 1990); *J.C.J.D. v. R.J.C.R.,* 803 S.W.2d 953 (Ky. 1991); *Stretton v. Disciplinary Bd.,* 944 F.2d 137 (3d Cir. 1991); *Buckley v. Illinois Judicial Inquiry Board,* 997 F. 2d 224 (7th Cir. 1993).

16. *See generally* Patrick L. Baude, *A Comment on The Evolution of Direct Democracy in Western State Constitutions,* 28 N.M. L. Rev. 313 (1998).

17. William Howard Taft, *The Selection and Tenure of Judges,* 38 A.B.A. Rep. 418, 422–23 (1913).

18. *See* David Adamany and Philip DuBois, *Electing State Judges,* 1976 Wis. L. Rev. 731 (1976); Ray M. Harding, *The Case for Partisan Election of Judges,* 55 A. B. A. J. 1162 (1969); Philip Dubois, *Voting Cues in Nonpartisan Trial Court Elections,* 18 L. & Soc. Rev. 395 (1984).

19. A summary of the variations is provided in Polly Price, "Selection of State Court Judges," in Roger Clegg and James D. Miller, eds., *State Judiciaries and Impartiality: Judging the Judges* (Washington, D.C.: National Legal Center for the Public Interest, 1996), pp. 16–19.

20. Larry T. Aspin and William K. Hall, *Political Trust and Judicial Retention Elections,* 9 Law & Pol'y Q. 451 (1987).

21. Anthony Champagne, *The Selection and Retention of Judges in Texas*, 40 SW. L.J. 53, 90 (1986). *And see* American Tort Reform Association, *"America's Third Party": A Study of Political Contributions by The Plaintiff's Lawyer Industry*, Washington, D.C., 1994; Orrin W. Johnson and Laura Johnson Uris, *Judicial Selection in Texas: A Gathering Storm?* 23 Tex. Tech L. Rev. 525 (1992); Anthony Champagne, *Campaign Contributions in Texas Supreme Court Races*, 17 Crime, L. & Soc. J. 91 (1992); Anthony Champagne, *Judicial Reform in Texas*, 72 Judicature 146 (1988).

22. For an account of recent events in Alabama, *see* Glenn C. Noe, *Alabama Judicial Election Reform: A Skunk in Tort Hell*, 28 Cumb. L. Rev. 215 (1998).

23. For the Wisconsin experience, for example, *see* Nathan S. Heffernan, Speech, *Judicial Responsibility, Judicial Independence and the Election of Judges*, 80 Marq. L. Rev. 1031 (1997); Shirley S. Abrahamson, *Remarks Before the American Bar Association Commission on Separation of Powers and Judicial Independence*, 12 St. John's J. Legal Comment. 69 (1996). For the Michigan experience, *see* Kurt M. Brauer, *The Role of Campaign Fundraising in Michigan's Supreme Court Elections: Should We Throw the Baby Out with the Bathwater?* 44 Wayne L. Rev. 367 (1998).

24. For a recent example, the Supreme Court of Alabama upheld an enormous punitive damage award after every member of the court had received sizable contributions from counsel for the plaintiff. *ABC World News Tonight*, October 9, 1995 (transcript #5201); *Nightline*, October 24, 1995 (transcript #3762). Pennzoil lawyers contributed $315,000 to members of the Texas court deciding its enormous claim against Texaco; and four of the judges receiving contributions were not facing reelection campaigns. Madison B. McClellan, Note, *Merit Appointment Versus Popular Election: A Reformer's Guide to Judicial Selection Methods in Florida*, 43 Fla. L. Rev. 529, 555 (1991). Alabama and Texas have since modified their rules of judicial conduct to prohibit this practice.

25. *See, e.g.*, Stephen B. Bright, *Can Judicial Independence Be Attained in the South? Overcoming History, Elections, and Misperceptions about the Role of the Judiciary*, 14 Ga. St. U. L. Rev. 817, 845 (1998) (discussing "rapidly growing role of special interest groups").

APPENDIX 2:

SUMMARY OF TERM LENGTHS FOR STATE JUDGES

TABLE 1. SUMMARY OF ELECTORAL STATUS OF STATE JUDGES

Judges	Appellate Courts	Trial Courts
Stand for some form of election	1,084 (87%)	7,380 (87%)
Do not stand for some form of election	159 (13%)	1,111 (13%)
Total	1,243 (100%)	8,491 (100%)

Reprinted with permission. Excerpted from Roy A. Schotland, *Comment*, 61 Law and Contemporary Problems 149, 154–55 (1998).

Sources: ABA Task Force on Lawyers' Political Contributions, Part II, 69 (July 1998) (corrected for recategorization of one state); American Judicature Society, *Judicial Selection in the States* (1998); National Center for State Courts, *State Court Caseload Statistics* (1996).

TABLE 2. TERM LENGTH FOR ALL STATE APPELLATE JUDGES

Length of Term	Appellate Courts[a]	
	Initial Term	Subsequent Terms
2 years or fewer	305 (25.9%)	—
3–4 years	38 (3.2%)	10 (0.8%)
6 years	346 (29.4%)	510 (44.5%)
7–8 years	151 (12.8%)	194 (16.9%)
10 years	168 (14.3%)	226 (19.7%)
11–15 years	138 (11.7%)	177 (15.4%)
15 years or more	31 (2.6%)	39 (3.4%)

[a] Not included are New York's intermediate appellate judges, who are appointed from judges who had been elected to the trial courts.

TABLE 3. TERM LENGTH FOR ELECTED APPELLATE JUDGES

Length of Term[a]	Appellate Courts	
	Initial Term	Subsequent Terms
2 years or fewer	305 (28.2%)	—
3–4 years	38 (3.5%)	10 (0.9%)
6 years	332 (30.6%)	486 (44.8%)
7–8 years	89 (8.2%)	171 (15.8%)
10 years	154 (14.2%)	212 (19.6%)
11–15 years	166 (15.3%)	205 (18.9%)

[a] Of all elected appellate judges, 40.4% (438) are appointed for initial terms of four years or fewer and then face only retention elections. In all elective systems, a majority of judges initially reach the bench by appointment to vacancies.

Table 4. Term Length for All State Trial Court (General Jurisdiction) Judges

Length of Term	Trial Court of General Jurisdiction	
	Initial Term	Subsequent Terms
2 years or fewer	868 (10.2%)	—
3–4 years	1,450 (17.1%)	1,506 (18.0%)
6 years	3,966 (46.7%)	4,646 (55.5%)
7–8 years	1,134 (13.4%)	618 (7.4%)
10 years	408 (4.8%)	408 (4.9%)
11–15 years	538 (6.3%)	814 (9.7%)
15 years or more	127 (1.5%)	372 (4.5%)

Table 5. Term Length for Elected Trial Court (General Jurisdiction) Judges

Length of Term[a]	Trial Court of General Jurisdiction	
	Initial Term	Subsequent Terms
2 years or fewer	868 (11.76%)	—
3–4 years	1,377 (18.66%)	1,433 (19.41%)
6 years	3,884 (52.63%)	4,564 (61.84%)
7–8 years	428 (5.80%)	428 (5.80%)
10 years	366 (4.95%)	366 (4.95%)
11–15 years	457 (6.20%)	589 (8.00%)

[a] Of all elected trial judges, 13.8% (1,019) are appointed for initial terms of four years or fewer and then face only retention elections. In all elective systems, a majority of judges initially reach the bench by appointment to vacancies.

Appendix 3:

Summary of Midterm Vacancy Merit Plans[a]

State	Year Established	Level of Court	Legal Basis of Plan
Alabama			
Jefferson County	1951	Circuit	Constitutional
Madison County	1974	Circuit	Constitutional
Mobile County	1982	Circuit, District	Constitutional
Tuscaloosa County	1990	Circuit, District	Constitutional
Georgia	1975, 1983; revised 1984, 1991	Appellate Court Superior Court State Court	Executive Order
Idaho	1967; amended 1985	Supreme Court Court of Appeals District Court	Statutory

[a] In addition to the eleven states listed in this table, five states or localities use nominating commissions to fill initial and interim vacancies at the appellate and supreme court level while also providing for nominating commissions to help fill only interim vacancies on lower courts: Florida, New York City, Oklahoma, South Dakota, and Tennessee. These jurisdictions are not included in the above table because they use merit selection plans for initial and interim vacancies on their higher courts, and not simply as interim vacancy merit plans.

Summary of Midterm Vacancy Merit Plans (cont.)

State	Year Established	Level of Court	Legal Basis of Plan
Kentucky	1975	Supreme Court Court of Appeals Circuit Court District Court	Constitutional
Minnesota	1983; revised 1987, 1989, 1992	District Court	Statutory
Montana	1972	Supreme Court District Court	Constitutional
Nevada	1976	Supreme Court District Court	Constitutional
New Mexico	1988	Supreme Court Court of Appeals District Court Metropolitan Court	Constitutional
North Dakota	1981 1983	Supreme Court District Court County Court	Constitutional Statutory Statutory
West Virginia	1981, 1989	All levels	Executive Order
Wisconsin	1983; revised 1987	Supreme Court Court of Appeals Circuit Court	Executive Order

DEFENDING JUSTICE
THE COURTS, CRITICISM, AND INTIMIDATION

THE REPORT OF THE CITIZENS FOR INDEPENDENT COURTS
TASK FORCE ON THE DISTINCTION BETWEEN INTIMIDATION
AND LEGITIMATE CRITICISM OF JUDGES

MEMBERS OF THE TASK FORCE*

REPORTER

Charles Gardner Geyh, Professor of Law, Indiana University School of Law-Bloomington; Director, Center for Judicial Independence, American Judicature Society; Visiting Associate Professor of Law, Cleveland State University (1998–1999)**

MEMBERS

Robert M. Ackerman, Professor of Law, Pennsylvania State University, Dickinson School of Law; former Dean, Willamette University College of Law

Luke Bierman, Esq., Ph.D., Adjunct Faculty, Northwestern University School of Law; Presidential Assistant, American Bar Association; former Director, Judicial Division, American Bar Association

George M. Dennison, President, The University of Montana

John DiBiaggio, President, Tufts University

---

* Affiliations of members listed for purposes of identification only. The views expressed in this report do not necessarily reflect the views of the institutions with which the members are affiliated.

** Christopher R. George, Cleveland State University, served as assistant to the reporter.

The Reverend Dr. James M. Dunn, Executive Director, Baptist Joint Committee

John R. Dunne, Assistant Attorney General, Bush administration; former State Senator, Sixth District of New York

Eileen Gallagher, Esq., Project Manager, Standing Committee on Judicial Independence, American Bar Association

Harlan D. Hockenberg, Esq., Member, Board of Directors, National Jewish Coalition; Co-Chair, Senator Charles E. Grassley Re-election Committee

Mark Frederick Kozlowski, Esq., Staff Attorney, Brennan Center for Justice

Edward W. Madeira, Jr., Esq., Partner, Pepper Hamilton, L.L.P.; Chair, Commission on Separation of Powers and Judicial Independence, American Bar Association; Member, Standing Committee on Judicial Independence, American Bar Association; Permanent Member, Third Circuit Judicial Conference; Fellow, American College of Trial Lawyers

Paul Marcus, Haynes Professor of Law, College of William and Mary, Marshall-Wythe School of Law

Burke Marshall, Professor Emeritus of Law, Yale Law School

John J. McMackin, Jr., Esq., Williams & Jensen, P.C.

The Honorable William A. Norris, former Judge, U.S. Court of Appeals for the Ninth Circuit

LeRoy Pernell, Dean, Northern Illinois University College of Law

Burnele V. Powell, Dean, University of Missouri-Kansas City School of Law

Richard L. Rubenstein, President, University of Bridgeport

Patricia C. Shakow, Esq., former Member, Editorial Board, *The Washington Post*

Thomas H. Sponsler, Dean, Albany Law School

Paul B. Terpak, Esq., Blankingship & Keith

Daniel E. Troy, Esq., Partner, Wiley, Rein & Fielding; Associate Scholar, American Enterprise Institute

Task Force
Recommendations

1. The Task Force recommends against the adoption of any proposal that seeks to censor or sanction excessive but otherwise lawful criticism of judges.

2. Because bar-generated responses to attacks on judges may be perceived as self-serving, the Task Force recommends that legal educators, civic organizations, community leaders, and other concerned citizens be involved in response efforts.

3. The Task Force recommends that national, state, and local bar organizations develop plans for responding to unjust criticism of judges, such as those developed by the American Bar Association. Such plans should provide for a prompt response to misleading or potentially intimidating criticism, without seeking to defend judges for the sake of defending them when they are subjected to nonintimidating, nonmisleading criticism, and should involve nonlawyers as participants whenever possible.

4. The Task Force recommends the development and continuation of programs designed to better inform school children and adults on the importance of courts in protecting legal rights and responsibilities, so as to ensure public receptivity to an impartial, independent judiciary.

REPORT OF THE TASK FORCE ON THE CRITICISM OF JUDGES

I. INTRODUCTION

Our task force was assigned to address this issue: when does legitimate criticism of judges deteriorate into illegitimate, independence-threatening intimidation?

The issue of judicial criticism has received considerable attention in the past five years. It has been discussed at length in books, law review symposia, commission reports, and newspaper and magazine articles. It has been the subject of conferences hosted by the bench, the bar, and academic institutions; and it has been of central concern to Citizens for Independent Courts, which commissioned this report.

With so much having already been said and written, the question naturally arises as to what this report can hope to accomplish. The contribution of this report is ultimately twofold. First, the report reflects a consensus reached among the members of an avowedly bipartisan task force. The report thus underscores the extent to which an independent judiciary—one that is insulated from political intimidation—is valued across the political spectrum. Second, while many (though not all) members of the Task Force have law degrees, this report is written not by and for lawyers and judges, but by and for citizens who are concerned about their government and the role of courts in American society. The report thus looks beyond the bench, the bar, and the academy that have more or less monopolized the judicial independence discussion to date, in an effort to reach a broader audience.

Given its purposes and target audience, this report does not address its subject in the exhaustive detail or with the subtlety of nuance that some might say it deserves. Concededly, generalizing about judicial independence and intimidation can be perilous business. After all, mechanisms for judicial selection, tenure, and removal—to say nothing of legal culture—differ dramatically between state and federal judiciaries; among the various state judiciaries; and among trial, appellate, and supreme court judges within any given state. The kinds of criticism that could well intimidate a state trial judge who is in the midst of a bruising reelection campaign may have no impact on a justice of the United States Supreme Court, who enjoys life tenure and receives a salary that may not be diminished. In the end, the Task Force has attempted to strike a balance with a concise report that speaks in general terms accessible to all citizens, without overgeneralizing to the point of being simplistic or inaccurate.

II. THE CRITICISM OF JUDGES IN HISTORICAL CONTEXT

Judicial criticism and intimidation are not recent phenomena. In England, the 1700 Act of Settlement, which rendered English courts independent of the Crown, was a response to repeated overreaching and intimidation by the monarch.[1] Although the Act of Settlement served to protect the English courts, it did not apply in the American colonies, where the colonial courts were dependent on the King for their tenure and compensation.[2] Repeated confrontations between the colonists and the Crown over the latter's attempts to manipulate colonial judges ultimately led to a grievance in the Declaration of Independence, that King George III had "made Judges dependent on his Will alone, for the Tenure of their Offices, and the Amount and payment of their Salaries."[3]

As the new states began to frame their constitutions in the wake of independence, the generally accepted antidote to judicial dependence on the monarch or executive branch was not judicial independence, but judicial dependence on the legislative branch or the people.[4] Although the state judiciaries were appointed, judges were subject to reappointment in some jurisdictions; in other jurisdictions that provided for tenure during good behavior, they were subject to removal upon impeachment for "maladministration," or a simple address from the legislature—a process by which the Governor is authorized to remove a judge upon the request of a bare majority of the general assembly.[5] Over the course of the succeeding decade, legislatures in several states threatened judges with removal in response to courts exercising the power of judicial review to strike down legislation.[6] These and like episodes gave rise to fear of legislative tyranny, and generated significant support for judicial independence that may have reached its high point on the eve of the federal constitutional convention.

Although the phrase "judicial independence" appears nowhere in the United States Constitution, it is implicit in three provisions of Article III: the "judicial power" clause, which delegates to the judicial branch alone the judicial power to decide individual cases (and which, by implication, guarantees the judiciary sufficient independence from the political branches to protect the "judicial power" against usurpation); the "good behaviour" clause, which guarantees federal judges tenure during good behavior—which is to say for life, subject only to removal following impeachment for "treason, bribery, and other high crimes and misdemeanors"; and the "compensation" clause, which guarantees federal judges a compensation that may not be diminished during their tenure in office. It is clear from James Madison's notes of the constitutional convention, and Alexander Hamilton's defense of Article III in *The Federalist,* that these provisions were designed to provide for an independent judicial branch comprised of independent judges.[7]

As vital as the founders thought judicial independence was to the success of the fledgling government, at no time did they or their successors equate independence with immunity from harsh criticism. To the contrary, state and federal judges have weathered cycles of intense criticism that have peaked and troughed throughout our nation's history.[8] There is a tendency in the historical literature (and in the brief synopsis of that literature, which follows) to define these periods of judicial criticism with reference to attacks upon the Supreme Court of the United States. It is important to understand, however, that each state judiciary has a unique history, with periods of criticism unique to itself, that limitations of space and time prevent the Task Force from exploring in this report.

THE JEFFERSONIAN REPUBLICANS' CONFRONTATION WITH THE FEDERAL COURTS

The election of Thomas Jefferson ushered in the first sustained wave of national anger directed at federal judges. Although reform of the judicial system had been sought for several years, it was lame duck President John Adams, with the aid of a lame duck Federalist Congress, who established new courts and packed them with Federalist partisans. That, in turn, catalyzed a drive by the incoming Jeffersonian Republicans to disestablish the courts the Federalists had created, and impeach the Federalist judges whose offices had not been abolished. "[T]he only check upon the Judiciary system as it is now organized and filled," wrote Republican Congressman William Giles to Thomas Jefferson, "is the removal of all its executive officers indiscriminately."[9]

The Jeffersonian Republicans succeeded in repealing the judgeships the outgoing federalists had created, but with the exception of the inebriated and insane Judge Thomas Pickering, failed in their efforts to remove federalist judges by means of the impeachment process. The Republicans' inability to secure the conviction of Justice Samuel Chase in his 1805 impeachment trial effectively ended this initial assault on the federal courts.

JACKSONIAN DEMOCRATS' ATTACKS ON STATE AND FEDERAL COURTS

With the ascendancy of Jacksonian Democracy at the close of the 1820s came a new wave of antagonism directed at the state and federal courts. President Andrew Jackson's unique brand of majoritarian democracy was very much in tension with an appointed judiciary (on the federal or state level) that imposed limits on the will of the majority. Legislation was introduced in Congress to strip the United States Supreme Court of jurisdiction to hear appeals from the decisions of state courts; the president himself openly confronted the authority of the Supreme Court;[10] and several states did the same.[11] A groundswell of support for elective judiciaries directly challenged the notion of an independent judiciary. Jacksonian Democrat Frederick Robinson made the point bluntly:

> [J]udges should be made responsible to the people by periodical elections. The boast of an independent judiciary is always made to deceive you. We want no part of our government independent of the people.[12]

John Marshall's death in 1835 and the end of Jackson's presidency in 1837 effectively ended, for the time being, the confrontation between the White House and the Supreme Court. In the states, Jackson's continued influence is credited with the rise of elected judiciaries. Beginning with Mississippi in 1832 and resuming in earnest after 1845, every new state entering the Union provided for elected judiciaries. The persistence of the movement toward elected state judiciaries, however, is attributable less to a Jacksonian-era suspicion of judicial independence than to the increasingly prevalent view that elected judges approved by the people were stronger and more independent than were judges beholden to the governors or legislatures who appointed them.[13]

The *Dred Scott* Decision and Its Aftermath

The issue of slavery became increasingly heated in the decades preceding the Supreme Court's 1857 decision in *Dred Scott* v. *Sanford*. The Missouri Compromise of 1820, the Compromise of 1850, and the Kansas-Nebraska Act of 1854 were all testament to the contentiousness of the sectional divide over the direction of the nation on the slavery issue.[14]

In *Dred Scott*, the Supreme Court held, first, that freed black slaves could not invoke the jurisdiction of the federal courts because they were not citizens of the United States, and second, that because the Constitution acknowledged and protected the right to own slaves as property, Congress lacked the power to prohibit slavery in the territories.[15] In so holding, the Court simultaneously appeared to manifest a proslavery bias and crippled congressional moderates in their efforts to preserve any semblance of detente between pro- and anti-slavery forces.

Reaction to *Dred Scott* was swift and severe. The "five slave-holders and two or three doughfaces on the bench" who decided the case were accused of "rush[ing] into politics voluntarily and without other purpose other than to subserve the cause of slavery."[16] It was a decision "entitled to just so much moral weight as would be the judgment of a majority of those congregated in any Washington barroom,"[17] wrote one critic. "If epithets and denunciation could sink a judicial body, the Supreme Court of the United States would never be heard of again."[18]

The *Dred Scott* decision is widely identified as a contributing cause of the Civil War. It was not until after the end of the war, adoption of the Thirteenth through Fifteenth Amendments to the United States Constitution, and the painful period of Reconstruction (which included its own round of attacks on the federal courts) that some semblance of equilibrium was restored.

PROGRESSIVE-POPULIST AND NEW DEAL CRITICISM OF THE LOCHNER ERA COURT

The Populist period at the end of the nineteenth century, and the progressive era in the early twentieth century, ushered in another wave of resentment directed at the courts. As progressive reformers sought to address social ills through legislation, they came into conflict with state courts and a national Supreme Court that read the due process clauses of the Fifth and Fourteenth Amendments to the United States Constitution as imposing distinct limits on the power of state and federal legislatures to regulate business and industry. Senator George Norris declared that federal judges on the trial and appellate levels were "not responsive to the pulsations of humanity [because] the security of a life position and a life salary makes them forget too often the toiling masses who are struggling for an existence."[19] Accordingly, as one scholar observed:

> [T]he Populist-Progressives during the early decades of the century sought to infuse federal judicial institutions with elements of popular democracy, to alter the substance of judicial decisions, to change the selection of federal judges, and to circumscribe their power and the jurisdiction of their courts.[20]

On the state level, progressive reformers grew disenchanted with the partisan nature of judicial elections. Earlier in the nineteenth century, appointed judges had been perceived as weak-kneed shills for the governor or the general assembly. This perception helped give rise to elective judiciaries. Now, however, judges selected in partisan elections were increasingly criticized as too beholden to the political parties. To address the problem, some states adopted nonpartisan judicial election systems. In 1913, the American Judicature Society was formed, and soon thereafter began to advocate "merit-selection" systems. Several states adopted these systems, in which judges would be appointed with the assistance of a merit-selection commission, and later stand for "retention elections." In such elections, the judges would run unopposed and remain in office if a majority of the electorate voted to retain them.

On the federal level, Chief Justice William Howard Taft and the United States Congress responded to widespread criticisms with groundbreaking reforms in federal judicial administration, which served to allay some of the public criticism targeting defective administration of justice.[21] Attacks on the Supreme Court (sometimes called the "Lochner Court" because of its interpretation of the due process clause exemplified by its decision in the case of *Lochner* v. *New York*) accelerated, however, after Franklin Roosevelt took office, when the Court continued to strike down New Deal legislation. Roosevelt brought the issue to a head with his so-called Court-packing plan, which would have increased the size of the Supreme Court, under the guise of lessening the workload of the aging Supreme Court justices. His avowed purpose was to add enough New Deal justices to tip the balance of power on the Court in Roosevelt's favor. The confrontation was finally defused when a member of the Supreme Court, who had previously ruled against New Deal legislation, changed his voting behavior before Congress had acted on the Court-packing proposal—the so-called "switch in time that saved nine."

ATTACKS ON THE WARREN COURT

Under Chief Justice Earl Warren's leadership in the 1950s and 1960s, the Supreme Court of the United States interpreted the Constitution to protect a greatly expanded array of civil and criminal rights. Supreme Court decisions invalidating racial segregation of public institutions, disallowing prayer in public schools, and affording criminal defendants a range of previously unrecognized procedural protections provoked sharp criticism in some quarters.

The John Birch Society accused Warren of voting "92 percent in favor of Communists," and "sanction[ing] treason."[22] Congress received a torrent of letters calling for Warren's impeachment, a sentiment echoed on billboards across the country.[23] Warren was not the only target. Then-congressman Gerald Ford called for the impeachment of Justice William O. Douglas, because of Douglas's allegedly leftward leanings.

Although the calls for impeachment were never acted upon, the perceived excesses of the Warren Court were among the campaign issues that helped win the presidency for Richard Nixon in 1968.[24] The retirement of Earl Warren in 1969, and the resignation of Justice Abe Fortas that same year, enabled President Nixon to appoint Chief Justice Warren Burger and Justice Harry Blackmun, thereby closing the book on the Warren Court and the attendant period of criticism.

Opinions have differed as to who is to "blame" for these periods of criticism—the judges, for inviting attacks when they allegedly exceeded their proper roles; or overly vituperative critics, for seeming to lack the necessary appreciation for an independent judiciary. As a consequence, periods of intense criticism have often been greeted by a counterresponse from those who charge the critics with threatening to compromise judicial independence.[25]

One consequence of these recurrent altercations between critics and defenders of the courts may have been to preserve a semblance of interbranch equilibrium over time:

- The Jeffersonian Republicans may have succeeded in their efforts to disestablish federal courts, but their critics succeeded in convincing future Congresses that such a tack was inappropriate and not to be repeated.[26]

- The Jeffersonian Republicans, in turn, by failing in their effort to remove Justice Chase, thus set a precedent against Congress's impeaching a judge on account of his or her judicial decisions. At the same time, however, others have noted that for its part, the judiciary ceased to provide so many targets as obvious as Justice Chase.[27]

- Progressive-era defenders of the courts staved off extreme assaults on judicial independence, such as proposals to end good behavior tenure for federal judges, but the widespread dissatisfaction with the courts, as highlighted by court critics, led to major structural reforms in the state and federal courts systems.

- During the New Deal, President Roosevelt's Court-packing plan was never adopted, which set a precedent against such transparent efforts to manipulate Court decision-making in the future. At the same time, Roosevelt's threat to implement the plan may have led to a one-vote shift on the Supreme Court that tipped the balance of power in favor of upholding the constitutionality of New Deal programs.

- While calls to impeach Chief Justice Earl Warren and Justice William Douglas were successfully resisted, critics of the Warren Court ultimately had their concerns addressed with the election of Richard Nixon and his appointment of more conservative justices to replace the outgoing members of the Warren Court.

As the Task Force and others seek to address the current period of judicial criticism, described below, it is important to understand it in a broader historical context—to keep in mind the push and pull of court critics and defenders, and the interplay of confrontation and compromise, that have typified such periods in the past and helped bring debates over the courts to peaceful resolution.

III. Recent Developments Concerning Criticism of Judges

A new wave of criticism directed at the courts is now upon us. Unlike many of the previous waves, the focus today is not so much on the Supreme Court as on state and lower federal court judges. Opinions differ as to whether such criticism represents an unprecedented assault on judicial independence, an inevitable response to unprecedented usurpations of power by the courts, or simply another high tide in the ebb and flow of judicial criticism described in the preceding section. There is, however, general agreement that judicial criticism has intensified, relative to recent years past.

For purposes of this report, we have isolated six basic categories of criticism that some have identified as troubling: (A) threats to life and safety; (B) threats of impeachment or related forms of removal from office; (C) threats amid pending cases; (D) misleading criticism; (E) judicial discipline as a form of criticism; and (F) threats of electoral defeat. What follows is a brief description of these categories of criticism, and the explanations offered for why they do or do not threaten judicial independence.

ISSUE A: THREATS TO LIFE AND SAFETY

Threats to the life or safety of judges and their families are periodically reported. They are unlawful, and subject to criminal prosecution. Moreover, there is no serious disagreement that such threats are inimical to judicial independence. Judges cannot be expected to render impartial justice in the teeth of threats to kill or injure them or their loved ones unless they decide cases in a particular way.

Judges have been occasionally attacked or killed on account of their decisions. District judge John H. Wood, Jr., was murdered in 1979; district judge Richard Daronco was shot and killed in 1988; and circuit court judge Robert Vance was killed by a bomb blast in 1989.[28] In 1996, a militia group in central Texas reportedly plotted to kidnap a federal judge,[29] and the Associated Press recently reported on a plan devised by three prison inmates to murder three federal judges.

The so-called Nuremberg Files web page has given rise to a more controversial issue concerning implied death threats directed at judges, among others. The antiabortion Internet web site solicited and published the names of abortion providers, and it differentiated between those who were "working," "wounded," or a "fatality." Physicians shot and killed were moved from the "working" category to the "fatality" category within hours of the incident. Following the list of abortion providers was a list of judges, identified as the "shysters" of the abortion providers.[30] A civil jury recently found in favor of several abortion providers who sued the authors of the website on the grounds that listing their names in this manner constituted a threat to their lives. Others have expressed the concern that holding the authors of the site liable for their speech violates their First Amendment freedom of speech.

Issue B: Threats of Impeachment or Removal

Over the course of the past three years, Speaker of the House Newt Gingrich, Senate Majority Leader Robert Dole, and House Majority Whip Tom DeLay have each threatened to bring impeachment proceedings against one or more federal judges on the basis of rulings those judges issued in specific cases.[31] And President Clinton, through his press secretary, at one point threatened to request a judge to resign if he did not reverse a ruling. Six judges who have been specifically targeted include:

- United States district judge Harold Baer, who was threatened with impeachment proceedings by several members of Congress, and with President Clinton's resignation request, after he issued a pretrial ruling excluding evidence in a drug case.[32]

- United States district judge Fred Biery, who was targeted for removal by impeachment after he preliminarily enjoined the seating of two Texas county office holders who had recently won election, pending resolution by the state courts of whether voters who cast 800 absentee ballots met state residency requirements.[33]

- United States district judge Thelton Henderson, who was identified as an impeachment target after he issued a preliminary injunction against the implementation of California Proposition 209, on the grounds that the proposition was likely to be ruled unconstitutional.[34]

- United States district judge John T. Nixon, whose investigation and possible impeachment was urged by the Tennessee state senate and the state house judiciary committee after he overturned five death penalty convictions.[35]

- United States district judge Ira DeMent, who issued several rulings prohibiting school-sponsored prayer in public schools in Alabama, which resulted in his being targeted for impeachment by religious groups.[36]

- United States district judge Stewart Dalzell, whose impeachment was sought by the family and supporters of a slain woman after

he overturned the conviction of Lisa Michelle Lambert, convicted of the woman's murder, and barred the state from retrying
Lambert.[37]

Some have characterized these threats of impeachment as a form
of independence-compromising intimidation. In response to the
threats directed at Judge Baer, three present and former chief judges
of the United States Court of Appeals for the Second Circuit issued a
joint statement, which declared in part that:

> The framers of our Constitution gave federal judges life
> tenure, after nomination by the President and confirmation
> by the Senate. They did not provide for resignation or
> impeachment whenever a judge makes a decision with which
> elected officials disagree. . . .
> When a judge is threatened with a call for resignation or
> impeachment because of disagreement with a ruling, the
> entire process of orderly resolution of legal disputes is under-
> mined.
> We have no quarrel with criticism of any decision ren-
> dered by a judge. . . .
> But there is an important line between legitimate criticism
> of a decision and illegitimate attack upon a judge. . . . Attacks
> on a judge risk inhibition of all judges as they conscientious-
> ly endeavor to discharge their constitutional responsibilities.[38]

Others have been less sympathetic, arguing either that Congress
is within its rights to define impeachable high crimes and misdemeanors to include what they regard as activist decision-making,[39]
or that judges with life tenure and a guaranteed salary have all the
insulation they need to endure essentially idle threats of removal.[40]
Senator Robert Dole responded to the above-quoted joint statement
of the Second Circuit judges calling him to task for his attacks on
Judge Baer, with a letter of his own:

> Although I share your concerns about maintaining the inde-
> pendence of the federal judiciary, I believe you were wrong to
> suggest that I overstepped my bounds in criticizing Judge
> Baer's ruling in the *Bayless* case. Simply put, judges are not the
> only ones in our constitutional system who have "important

responsibilities" relating to the proper administration of justice in the federal courts. The Legislative Branch, along with the President, has a significant role to play in ensuring that judges, no less than other officers of the United States, faithfully perform their duties under the Constitution. That is why . . . Congress is given the solemn power under the Constitution, where warranted, to remove from office judges and other officers of the United States.[41]

Other actions short of threats to impeach may also have an impact on public confidence in the courts, if not the independence of the judge in question. President Clinton's suggestion, through his press secretary, that he might ask for Judge Baer's resignation if the judge did not reverse the unpopular ruling described above, is an example.[42] Shortly thereafter, a circuit court judge announced that he was resigning in protest of widespread attacks on federal judges, including those on himself.[43]

Although threats to remove a judge by means other than electoral defeat have been directed primarily at federal judges, state judges have occasionally been targeted as well. Members of the New Hampshire legislature recently responded to a state Supreme Court decision invalidating the use of local property taxes to fund public schools with an effort to remove Chief Justice David Brock by means of legislative address.[44]

Issue C: Threats amid Pending Cases

One of the previously mentioned episodes—that concerning Judge Baer—occurred in the context of a pending case.[45] The judge subsequently reversed his ruling, and said that he did so on the basis of new information introduced at a second hearing. Some, however, assumed that he responded to political pressure and criticized the president and members of Congress who, in their view, intimidated him. Others complained that even if the reversal was solely merits-based, those who threatened the judge made it *appear* as though they had bullied him into changing his decision.[46] In either case, the fact that the threats were issued at a time when they could have influenced the decision-making process made such threats especially problematic in the minds of some.[47] Others, in contrast, thought it was all for the best that the judge responded to political pressure,[48] or blamed the judge for creating his own problems by reversing himself instead of standing firm and allowing the appellate process to run its course.

ISSUE D: MISLEADING CRITICISM

Judges have been targeted with arguably misleading criticism in a variety of contexts. In some cases, judges have been criticized by lawyers in their capacity as election opponents or as attorneys who have appeared before the judge in question, or who otherwise have an interest in the court system. Lawyers who criticize judges in unfair or misleading ways may be subject to discipline under applicable codes of professional responsibility, as discussed in Appendix A (see pages 165–71). In other cases, judges have been criticized by nonlawyers who are members of special interest groups, representatives of the media, or disgruntled litigants.

The following examples are illustrative:

- Georgia justice Leah Sears' election opponent accused her of writing a dissenting opinion in which she "referred to traditional moral standards as pathetic and disgraceful," when in fact she had referred to the analysis of the majority opinion as "pathetic and disgraceful."[49]

- United States district judge Norma Shapiro is reported to have "placed a population cap on [Philadelphia's] crowded jail system, causing people arrested on felony charges to be released."[50] As a consequence, she has been accused by *Wall Street Journal* Editorial Features writer Max Boot of being "responsible for as much crime in Philadelphia as any street gang,"[51] and more specifically, by National Rifle Association president Charlton Heston, of releasing prisoners who subsequently "committed seventy-nine murders, ninety rapes, seven hundred and one burglaries, nine hundred and fifty nine robberies, one thousand one hundred and thirteen assaults," among other offenses.[52] Heston apparently obtained these statistics from the Philadelphia district attorney's office.[53] In fact, Judge Shapiro had originally dismissed the case on the grounds that it was inappropriate for the federal courts to decide a matter that was the subject of ongoing state court proceedings. Her decision to abstain, however, was reversed by the Third Circuit Court of Appeals, which ordered her to decide the case.[54] She did not then impose a prison population cap on her own initiative; rather, she approved a consent decree agreed to by all parties—including the city of Philadelphia—which called for such a cap.[55] Finally, she took pains to ensure that no prisoner released under the consent decree had been arrested for violent crimes.[56]

- Opponents in Tennessee justice Penny White's retention election focused their attention on a single capital case, in which they asserted that "Penny White felt the crime wasn't heinous enough for the death penalty—so she struck it down."[57] In fact, Justice White wrote no opinion in that case, but merely joined in the opinion of the court which did not disallow imposition of the death penalty, but instead remanded the case for resentencing.[58]

- Ad hominem attacks may represent a special subset of misleading criticism. Shrill and unfounded attacks on a judge's character, motives, competence, or allegiance arguably misinform listeners or readers as to the basis for the decisions in question. Examples include a recent series of articles in the *New York Post*, published under headlines such as "Three Stooges Are Court Clowns";[59] a Philadelphia journalist's reference to a judge as the "Queen of Murder Lite";[60] and Alabama governor Fob James, who accused a trial judge of lacking the "personal integrity and fortitude to obey his oath of office" because, in the governor's view, the judge followed the decisions of the Supreme Court at the expense of the Constitution.[61]

Some have singled out misleading criticism of judges as especially troublesome.[62] Most public officials, they argue, are in a position to address misleading criticism by defending their decisions publicly and thereby setting the record straight. Judges, in contrast, are restricted in their authority to do so by the canons of judicial ethics.[63] Even when ethics rules are not technically violated, judges have been chastised for making extrajudicial comments about judicial decisions. Thus, for example, when the present and former chief judges of the United States Court of Appeals for the Second Circuit issued the joint statement defending Judge Baer, described above,

Senator Dole's initial response was to question the propriety of the judges speaking out on the issue:

> It has come to my attention that you have issued a joint statement criticizing me for expressing my belief that U.S. District Judge Harold Baer's decision in *United States* v. *Bayless* . . . has no basis in law. I must say I was surprised to learn that you had commented publicly on a case that may well appear before you on appeal. Judges, unlike elected officials such as Senators, perform what your statement calls their "important responsibilities in a constitutional democracy" in the courtroom, not in the court of public opinion.[64]

Others, less sympathetic to the view that publication of misleading criticism poses a particular problem, point out that counterspeech remains alive and well, as reflected in each of the illustrations recounted above, in which misleading accusations against the judges in question were ultimately exposed in counterreports.[65]

ISSUE E: THREATS OF DISCIPLINE

Judicial discipline (short of removal) was unheard of prior to the 1960s. In the last thirty years, however, judicial conduct organizations have been established in all fifty states, and Congress has created a disciplinary mechanism for the federal courts. These disciplinary bodies serve a vital role, by providing a means to detect and remedy a wide range of judicial misbehavior, such as drunkenness, abusiveness, gender and racial bias, and chronic decision-making delay.

In several states, judges have recently been subjected to disciplinary proceedings on the basis of their rulings.[66]

* In California, state court of appeals justice Anthony Kline issued a dissenting opinion in which he indicated that he would "refuse to acquiesce" in a 1992 decision of the California Supreme Court, which had authorized parties to settle their disputes posttrial by stipulating to reversal of the trial court judgment.[67] Justice Kline's stated rationale was "based on [his] deeply felt opinion that the doctrine of stipulated reversal announced in [the 1992 decision]—a doctrine employed in no other jurisdiction in this

nation and unanimously repudiated by the Supreme Court of the United States—is destructive of judicial institutions."[68] The California Commission on Judicial Ethics subsequently initiated an inquiry into Justice Kline on the grounds that his "refusal to follow the law" violated the Code of Judicial Ethics.[69] The press has subsequently reported that Justice Kline "is only the latest in a series of similar investigations by the Commission on Judicial Performance."[70]

- In New York, the New York Court of Appeals approved the removal of Brooklyn Criminal Court judge Lorin M. Duckman from office, in light of what the court characterized as "[t]he substantial record of petitioner's intentional disregard of the requirements of the law in order to achieve a personal sense of justice in particular cases before him."[71] In particular, the court concluded that Duckman had "willfully disregard[ed] the law" by dismissing sixteen misdemeanor cases after prosecutors declined to reduce the charges or offer more lenient plea arrangements.[72] The Duckman case is complicated by the fact that the judge's alleged misconduct also included a "substantial record of improper courtroom conduct and unresponsiveness to concerns flagged for him," over and above the charges that he disregarded the law in the decisions he made.[73]

- A different but related problem has arisen in the federal court system. There, the Fifth Circuit Judicial Council has sanctioned Texas U.S. district judge John McBryde for, among other things, abusive and inappropriate courtroom demeanor. Judge McBryde has challenged the sanction—which banned him from hearing new cases for one year—on the grounds that it effectively removed him from office in violation of the United States Constitution.[74]

Some have argued that the targeted judges' independence is threatened when judicial conduct organizations pursue disciplinary actions against judges on account of their decisions. Professor Stephen Barnett, of the University of California Boalt Hall School of Law, accused the California Commission on Judicial Performance of "trying to set itself up as a Super Court to punish judges who don't decide cases the way the commission thinks they should."[75] Two judges who dissented from the majority's decision to remove Judge Duckman argued that "the majority has sent a message that the State's judicial disciplinary procedures are susceptible to manipulation by public officials and that judges whose rulings displease those public officials may find themselves singled out for exceptional, and possibly ruinous, scrutiny."[76]

Others have argued, however, that a judge's refusal to follow the law is a form of misconduct that is subject to discipline. In response to the Kline episode, the director of New York's judicial discipline commission argued that the California commission's decision to bring charges against Judge Kline "was a very courageous thing to do," because "[i]f a judge disregards the law, statutory law or case law, it is judicial misconduct."[77] The point was echoed by the legal affairs correspondent to the *California Political Review,* who argued that "intermediate appellate court judges . . . are sworn to uphold the law. When they refuse to follow the law, they violate their oath." He characterized Kline's actions as a form of "judicial nullification," and "a lot more serious offense than drinking at lunch or being rude to jurors."[78]

ISSUE F: THREATS OF ELECTORAL DEFEAT

In several states, grassroots organizations have launched sometimes successful campaigns against the reelection or retention of particular judges, on the basis of the judge's decision in an isolated case or on an isolated issue. Certainly the most highly publicized recent example is Tennessee justice Penny White, who lost her retention election following a campaign to unseat her on account of her joining a majority opinion reversing the imposition of the death penalty in a murder case, and remanding the case for resentencing.[79] Mississippi justice James Robertson likewise lost his reelection bid following an effort to unseat him on account of his decision to invalidate the death penalty in a rape case.[80]

Although comparatively few judges have been turned out of office because of unpopular decisions rendered in isolated cases, many more have survived close calls—stiff challenges to reelection posed by groups or opponents upset by a single decision or set of decisions. Examples include:

- Tennessee justice Adolpho Birch, who authored the opinion that Justice Penny White joined;[81]

- California chief justice Ronald George and California justice Ming Chin, who were opposed on account of their abortion rulings;[82]

- Illinois judge Dan Locallo, whose retention was opposed on account of a sentence he imposed in a single case.[83]

- Ohio justice Paul Pfeifer, whose reelection was opposed on the basis of his decision in a school funding case.[84]

Some assert that judicial independence is threatened when judges are voted out of office, not on the basis of their records as a whole, but in light of how they ruled in particular cases. As Florida justice Ben Overton put it: "It was never contemplated that the individual who has to protect our individual rights would have to consider what decision would produce the most votes."[85]

Others argue that voters are merely exercising their franchise, and holding judges accountable for their record. In the wake of Penny White's defeat, Tennessee governor Don Sundquist observed: "Should a judge look over his shoulder [when making decisions] about whether they're going to be thrown out of office? I hope so."[86] A letter to the editor of a Tennessee newspaper added: "[I]t is disturbing to hear the public being chastised for threatening judicial independence. This kind of rhetoric threatens voter independence."[87]

V. TASK FORCE ANALYSIS

The Task Force believes that judges must be permitted to decide cases according to the law as they conceive it to be written, without fear of reprisal. This is not because judicial independence is an end in and of itself. Rather, it is because judicial independence is a critically important means to the larger end of enabling judges to render impartial justice and to enforce our individual and collective rights. Our cherished constitutional rights would not long endure if the judges sworn to uphold them could be intimidated by public officials or a fleeting majority of the electorate into disregarding or minimizing those rights in order to achieve "popular" results.

To say that judges must be independent enough to render impartial justice and resist intimidation is not to say that they must be so independent as to be unaccountable. Judges, of course, must ultimately be accountable to the people. Accountability, in turn, often begins with criticism. Judges will be criticized whenever they decide controversial cases. Moreover, criticism is inevitable when they make mistakes, and when they press the limits of their constitutional power. Such criticism provides judges with an opportunity to rethink their views and to correct their errors.

It must be remembered, moreover, that criticizing public officials, including judges, is not only instrumental to good government— it is every citizen's constitutional right. On those occasions in which legitimate criticism degenerates unjustifiably into intimidation that may threaten judicial independence, we must nevertheless err on the side of tolerating dissent by making no recommendation that could be construed as threatening court critics with punishment, censorship, or reprisal for lawful criticism.

To say that criticism must be tolerated and encouraged is not to deny that certain forms of criticism may undermine judicial independence, or at least the appearance of judicial independence in the public's mind.

In this report, the Task Force has identified and analyzed a number of significant problems that have arisen in isolated areas where the line separating criticism from intimidation has been crossed, and which together constitute a serious concern that needs to be addressed.

ANALYSIS OF ISSUE A: THREATS TO LIFE OR SAFETY

Threats to the life or safety of judges, their families, or their friends represent an obvious and extreme form of judicial intimidation. Explicit threats are subject to criminal prosecution. Implied threats, varying in their subtlety, can present difficult questions as to when concern for a judge's physical safety ends and critics' First Amendment rights begin. Regardless, however, of where that line is drawn for purposes of criminal prosecution or civil liability, court critics should be taken to task for any criticism that could be construed as threatening to a judge's life or safety.[88]

Direct threats to a judge's life or safety pose more than a theoretical problem, as evidenced by the judges discussed in Section IV of this report who have been assaulted or killed. Although such threats represent the most extreme form of judicial intimidation imaginable, the Task Force has no evidence to suggest that ongoing law enforcement efforts to protect judges are inadequate or in need of reform.

ANALYSIS OF ISSUE B: THREATS OF IMPEACHMENT

The Task Force is troubled by recent threats to impeach and remove judges for making unpopular decisions in isolated cases. The problem is twofold: first, the specter of calls for their impeachment may cause some judges to think twice about interpreting the law as they conceive it to be written, on those occasions in which the law dictates an unpopular result. Second, even if impeachment threats do not in fact compromise a judge's capacity for independent judgment, the public perception may be to the contrary, thereby undermining public confidence in the courts and the appearance of a fair and impartial justice system.

The appropriate remedy for correcting erroneous judicial decisions is not impeachment, but appeal. The point was made powerfully by Representative Robert Kastenmeier in 1986, when he explained the House Judiciary Committee's decision not to initiate impeachment proceedings against three judges who had voted to reverse a death penalty conviction:

> A judicial decision (right or wrong), standing alone, cannot rise to the level of a "high crime or misdemeanor." If this were otherwise, the impeachment remedy would become merely another avenue for judicial review: a sort of legislative referendum on the quality of judicial decision-making. To the contrary, impeachment is a constitutional last step and an extraordinary response at that.[89]

The threat posed by essentially idle calls for impeachment should not be overstated. No federal judge has ever been removed from office for rendering an unpopular decision. Federal judges thus appear to remain sufficiently insulated from such threats to ignore them—as they should. At the same time, recently renewed interest in the impeachment process in Congress in light of the Clinton impeachment counsels against dismissing impeachment threats as empty. Moreover, public confidence in an impartial judiciary can only be undermined by threats to remove judges who make unpopular rulings—regardless of whether those threats are viable, or whether the judges in question are in fact intimidated.

In the past several years, threats of judicial removal (other than by election) have targeted federal judges, for which reason our discussion here has thus far been confined to the impeachment process in the federal system. The recent efforts by members of the New Hampshire Assembly to remove a justice of the New Hampshire Supreme Court by means of legislative address—in large part because of a widely criticized ruling in a particular case—demonstrate that removal threats are no longer an issue limited to the federal system. Moreover, some state removal mechanisms, such as the legislative address, are less cumbersome to employ than impeachment[90] and so have the potential to be more viable tools for judicial intimidation. Accordingly, the Task Force is especially concerned by the possibility that efforts to remove state judges on account of their rulings could become more commonplace.

ANALYSIS OF ISSUE C: THREATS IN PENDING CASES

Threats to remove a judge or to exact retribution of other kinds are especially troublesome in the context of a pending case, when the judge is put on notice that if he or she decides the case a particular way, negative consequences may follow. Unlike the previously discussed threats to remove a judge for a decision already made—a decision that the judge is no longer in a position to reverse—threats issued while a decision is still within the judge's control can be uniquely intimidating. Even if the judge is able to remain uninfluenced by such threats, the appearance will be to the contrary whenever the judge's decision coincides with the views of those issuing the threats.

ANALYSIS OF ISSUE D: MISLEADING CRITICISM

Misleading criticism poses a problem of a different nature. Previously discussed forms of criticism raise the specter of intimidation—the possibility that judges will be deterred by threats to their lives, safety, or tenure in office, from deciding cases according to the law as they conceive it to be written. Misleading criticism, in contrast, may not be any more intimidating than accurate criticism.

This is not to say, however, that misleading criticism has no impact on judicial independence. When a judge's decisions are criticized in materially misleading ways, public confidence in the judge and the justice system are unjustifiably undermined. It is only when public confidence in the courts is at low ebb that proposals to curb or undermine the judiciary's independence gain significant public support.

Ordinarily, when a public official is criticized in unfair or misleading ways, there is an obvious and effective remedy: the official can set the record straight in a press release, at town meetings, in television or newspaper interviews, and so on. Unlike other public officials, however, judges are generally foreclosed by ethics restrictions from publicly explaining and defending their decisions. (A memorandum describing these ethics restrictions is attached as Appendix B.) As a consequence, their ability to set the record straight is compromised, and the possibility that misleading criticism will go unanswered becomes correspondingly greater. If misleading speech is to be corrected, the task must fall to concerned citizens other than the targeted judge.

ANALYSIS OF ISSUE E: JUDICIAL DISCIPLINE

Although the Task Force believes that judicial discipline should be used sparingly, if at all, to address the content of a judge's judicial opinions, the Task Force is convinced that judicial discipline, properly administered, is critically important to preserving an independent judiciary. By providing a meaningful remedy for judicial misbehavior when it arises, disciplinary mechanisms preserve public confidence in the integrity of the judicial system. Obviously enough, however, judicial discipline can serve that vital role only if the public is aware of its existence. In the *Report of the Twentieth Century Fund Task Force on Federal Judicial Responsibility*, published in 1989, that Task Force came to the following conclusion with respect to the Judicial Councils Reform and Judicial Conduct and Disability Act of 1980, which established a disciplinary structure in the federal system:

> [F]or the 1980 act to be truly effective, all of those involved—the bench, the bar, and the public—must be aware

of its existence and must have access to it. We do not believe
that public awareness of the act is widespread. *The Task
Force therefore endorses measures to educate the public
about the 1980 Act.*[91]

Ten years later, our Task Force continues to believe that public
awareness of disciplinary mechanisms in the state and federal judicial
systems is insufficient, and needs to be more adequately publicized.

Subjecting judges to disciplinary action on account of their rulings in specific cases presents a complicated issue. The problem is
not an issue in the federal system, where the disciplinary statute
directs chief circuit judges to dismiss disciplinary complaints related
to the merits of a case. Not all state judicial conduct organizations,
however, are similarly restricted.

Ordinarily, appellate review is the appropriate remedy for errant
judicial decisions. Alternatively, errors can sometimes be corrected
by remedial legislation or constitutional amendment, or circumvent-
ed by changes in executive branch enforcement. In contrast, resort to
judicial discipline as a vehicle for discouraging or correcting judicial
error can be problematic. Judges' independence could be compromised if they must decide cases in the shadow of a judicial conduct
organization poised to take action against them, should it deem one
of their decisions sufficiently erroneous or unjustified.

At the same time, judges take an oath to uphold the law. In rare
and extreme cases, deliberate disregard of that oath, as manifested in
a judicial opinion, may constitute a form of misconduct. The propriety of disciplinary action in these rare instances must necessarily turn
on the unique circumstances of the situation at hand.

ANALYSIS OF ISSUE F: JUDICIAL ELECTIONS

Nowhere is the tension between judicial independence and
accountability more obvious than in the context of judicial elections.
If judges believe that they may be voted out of office if they make
unpopular decisions in highly publicized cases shortly before they
stand for reelection, the possibility exists that they will decide such
cases differently than if the law is their only guide.

On the other hand, the point of having judges stand for reelection
is to hold them accountable to the electorate. If the electorate believes

that a judge ought to be removed because of a decision rendered in an isolated case, that is its right.

Striking an appropriate balance between independence and accountability may depend on efforts to persuade voters that if a judge's reelection is made to turn on how he or she ruled in an isolated case, it can undermine judicial independence. If voters want judges to be impartial and to uphold their constitutional rights, they must be convinced to cast their ballots in light of the judge's record as a whole.

Alternatively, voters may be persuaded to reconsider the methods by which state judges are selected. Jurisdictions with highly partisan or politicized elections may wish to consider adopting the so-called Missouri plan, long supported by the American Judicature Society and the American Bar Association, among other organizations. In Missouri-plan states, judges are initially chosen by judicial selection commissions, rather than by election. At the conclusion of their terms, they stand for retention election, in which they do not run against other candidates, but against their own record, and must receive majority voter support to remain in office.

VI. Task Force Recommendations

The preceding section details the variety of circumstances in which legitimate judicial criticism can degenerate into a form of intimidation threatening not just to judicial independence, but also to our individual rights and freedoms that only independent judges can protect. The question then becomes what to do about it.

Analysis and Recommendation 1

Although some forms of judicial intimidation—death threats, for example—are unlawful, the vast proportion of independence-threatening speech at issue in this report is protected by the First Amendment, and for good reason. We depend upon the largely unfettered expression of views to expose problems in government and to find solutions. Occasionally, such expression takes the form of unfair or intimidating criticism. Were we, however, to punish or censor such excesses, we would risk chilling the dissemination of reasoned criticism by speakers fearful that their speech might be subject to sanction. Therefore, despite the adverse impact on judicial independence, legislators cannot and should not be prevented from threatening judges with impeachment; interest groups cannot and should not be barred from campaigning against judges' reelection on account of their decisions in isolated cases; and neither press nor public can or should be silenced on the grounds that their criticism is misleading.

Recommendation: The Task Force recommends against the adoption of any proposal that seeks to censor or sanction excessive but otherwise lawful criticism of judges.

ANALYSIS AND RECOMMENDATION 2

In a constitutional democracy that depends for its success upon the freedom of speech to provide the people with the information they need to govern themselves intelligently, there is only one appropriate response to unfair, excessive, and even intimidating speech, and that is counterspeech.

Without denigrating the importance of a response from the organized bar to excessive judicial criticism, there are inherent limits on what lawyers can accomplish in their responses to unjust judicial criticism. A skeptical public may remain unpersuaded by arguments that a judge has been attacked unfairly if the only people making those arguments are lawyers who may have clients with cases to be decided by that judge. Further, responses that come primarily from lawyers may create the perception that the judicial system is protecting its own.

To the extent possible, responses to unjust criticism should not come only from practicing lawyers. Law professors, for example, are well situated to serve as a credible source of information. Concerned citizens who are not necessarily lawyers, such as those who are members of Citizens for Independent Courts and the League of Women Voters, likewise have an important role to play. Participation by such citizens can help the public to think of the judicial system as one that serves all citizens and is worth defending against attacks.

Nonlawyers may be most effective in their responses if they work with local bar associations and bear in mind the guidelines provided for responses from bar associations as outlined in Analysis and Recommendation 3.

Recommendation: Because bar-generated responses to attacks on judges may be perceived as self-serving, the Task Force recommends that legal educators, civic organizations, community leaders, and other concerned citizens be involved in response efforts.

ANALYSIS AND RECOMMENDATION 3

Given ethics restrictions on counterspeech by targeted judges, primary responsibility for the task of defending judges against unjust criticism frequently falls to officers of the court—the practicing bar. The bar is uniquely well-positioned to be aware of intimidating or otherwise unjust judicial criticism when it arises, and to respond accordingly.

The American Bar Association has developed a model plan for responding to unjust criticism, which is attached as Appendix C to this report. In the Task Force's view, the key to the success of this or any counterspeech initiative is at least fourfold.

First, the response to unjust criticism must be prompt. A delay of only a few days allows the criticism to have more impact and the response to be overlooked or ignored.

Second, those responding to criticism must be mindful not only of when a response to criticism is appropriate and necessary, but also when it is not. In Section V above, the Task Force identified the limited circumstances in which independence-threatening criticism occurs, which is where remedial counterspeech would be in order. That leaves all manner of legitimate criticism—however harsh—with respect to which a response from the bar is neither necessary nor appropriate. It is incumbent on the bar to familiarize itself sufficiently with the facts of those cases in which judges are severely criticized to enable it to make an intelligent assessment of when intervention is warranted, and when it is not.

The third point follows from the second. An effective plan for responding to unjust criticism of judges must recognize that the goal is not to protect judges, but to protect the rights of the people. If judges are intimidated, they may seek to appease their intimidators at the expense of disfavored litigants and their constitutional rights. For that reason, neutralizing judicial intimidation with counterspeech is enormously valuable. At the same time, when judges make erroneous decisions at the expense of our constitutional rights and responsibilities, they deserve criticism. To attempt to protect judges from legitimate criticism also disserves the individual rights that we seek to protect and preserve.

Fourth, if the bar is to play a credible role in responding to unjust criticism, it must not be perceived as a "shill" for the judges it defends. When the bar decides to respond in a given case, it should be because the bar has made an independent assessment that a response is necessary and appropriate—and not simply because a judge has requested that the bar intercede on his or her behalf.

Recommendation: The Task Force recommends that national, state, and local bar organizations develop plans for responding to unjust criticism of judges, such as those developed by the American Bar Association. Such plans should provide for a prompt response to misleading or potentially intimidating criticism, without seeking to defend judges for the sake of defending them when they are subjected to nonintimidating, nonmisleading criticism, and should involve nonlawyers as participants whenever possible.

ANALYSIS AND RECOMMENDATION 4

A reasoned response to intimidating criticism can have the desired effect only if it persuades the target audience. Unless the public understands and supports judicial independence in principle, it is unlikely to be troubled by judicial intimidation when called to its attention. Indeed, the public may even support efforts to intimidate judges into deciding cases as the majority would have them decided, as a means to preserve judicial accountability. The effectiveness of any short-term plans to respond to unjust criticism when it arises must therefore be coupled with a long-term plan to educate the public on the role of courts and judicial independence and accountability in American government. Such plans might also logically include efforts to better publicize existing mechanisms for judicial discipline, as discussed earlier in this report.

Citizens for Independent Courts, along with the American Judicature Society and the American Bar Association, among other organizations, have initiated a range of programs designed to reach school children and adults with general information on the role of courts and the importance of judicial independence. The Task Force supports such efforts.

Recommendation: The Task Force recommends the development and continuation of programs designed to better inform school children and adults on the importance of courts in protecting legal rights and responsibilities, so as to ensure public receptivity to an impartial, independent judiciary.

VII. CONCLUSION

In this report, the Task Force has identified and analyzed a number of significant problems that have arisen in isolated areas, where the line separating criticism from intimidation has been crossed, and which together constitute a serious concern that needs to be addressed. Specifically, the Task Force has identified problems in the following areas: (A) threats to judges' lives or safety; (B) threats of removal; (C) threats in pending cases; (D) misleading criticism; (E) judicial discipline; and (F) judicial elections. To address these problems, the Task Force recommends a counterspeech campaign that responds to unjust or intimidating criticism when it occurs, and that seeks to educate the public on the role of courts and the importance of judicial independence in American government.

NOTES

1. Peter M. Shane, *Who May Discipline or Remove Federal Judges? A Constitutional Analysis*, 142 U. Pa. L. Rev. 209, 216 (1993).

2. Joseph H. Smith, *An Independent Judiciary: The Colonial Background*, 124 U. Pa. L. Rev. 1104, 1112–13 (1976).

3. Declaration of Independence, para. 11 (U.S. 1776).

4. Gordon S. Wood, *The Creation of the American Republic, 1776–1787* (Chapel Hill: University of North Carolina Press, 1969), p. 161.

5. *Ibid.*

6. Julius Goebel, Jr., *History of the Supreme Court of the United States: Antecedents and Beginnings to 1801*, vol. 1 (New York: Macmillan, 1971), pp. 133–41.

7. Alexander Hamilton, *The Federalist* Nos. 78, 79.

8. For an excellent historical treatment of the early periods of counter-majoritarian criticism, *see* Barry Friedman, *The History of the Counterma-joritarian Difficulty, Part I: The Road to Judicial Supremacy*, 73 N.Y.U. L. Rev. 333 (1998). The discussion that follows draws to a significant extent on Professor Friedman's work.

9. William Giles to Thomas Jefferson, March 16, 1801, *reprinted in* Dice Robins Anderson, *William Baruch Giles: A Biography* (Menasha, Wisc.: George Banta Pub. Co., 1915), p. 77.

10. The most notable example is President Jackson's alleged statement that "John Marshall has made his decision, now let him enforce it." Charles Warren, *The Supreme Court in United States History,* vol. 1 (Boston: Little, Brown and Co., 1926), p. 759.

11. *Ibid.,* p. 773.

12. *Quoted in* Mary L. Volcansek and Jacqueline Lucienne Lafon, *Judicial Selection: The Cross-Evolution of French and American Practices* (New York: Greenwood Press, 1988), p. 90.

13. Kermit L. Hall, *Progressive Reform and the Decline of Democratic Accountability: The Popular Election of State Supreme Court Judges, 1850–1920,* 1984 Am. B. Found. Res. J. 345, 346–48. Although, with few exceptions, the independence of state judges is no longer preserved by life tenure, various other mechanisms have, over the course of time, been included in state constitutions to preserve some measure of state judicial independence. Illustrative mechanisms include: lengthy terms of office; merit selection systems in which judges stand for retention elections only after they are initially appointed on the basis of merit; oaths of office obligating judges to uphold the law; specific constitutional guarantees of a separate, unified, or independent judicial branch; and tri-branch governmental structures in which the judiciary keeps the political branches in check through the exercise of judicial review, which by implication requires that the judiciary remain independent of those branches.

14. Paul Finkelman, *The Dred Scott Case, Slavery and the Politics of Law*, 20 Hamline L. Rev. 1 (1996).

15. *Dred Scott v. Sanford*, 60 U.S. 393 (1857).

16. *New York Daily Tribune,* March 10, 1857, p. 5.

17. *New York Daily Tribune,* March 17, 1857, p. 4.

18. *New York Daily Tribune,* March 7, 1857, p. 5.

19. *Quoted in* Peter Graham Fish, *The Politics of Federal Judicial Administration* (Princeton: Princeton University Press, 1973), p. 18 (alteration in original).

20. *Ibid.* (citations omitted).

21. *Ibid.*, p. 19. The establishment of the Conference of Senior Circuit Judges (later renamed the Judicial Conference of the United States), and later the circuit judicial councils and the Administrative Office of the U.S. Courts, were among the improvements.

22. *Quoted in* Bernard Schwartz, *Super Chief: Earl Warren and His Supreme Court—A Judicial Biography* (New York: New York University Press, 1983), p. 280.

23. *Ibid.*, p. 281.

24. Jack Harrison Pollack, *Earl Warren: The Judge Who Changed America* (Englewood Cliffs, N.J.: Prentice Hall, 1979), p. 289 (discussing "Nixon's campaign fulminations over the need to replace 'Warrenite' justices with 'law and order' appointees").

25. Thus, for example, when the Jeffersonian Republicans disestablished the federal courts created by the Judiciary Act of 1801—which had the effect of putting the Federalist judges occupying those courts out of their jobs—the Federalists protested vociferously that the repeal undermined judicial independence as embodied in the good behavior clause. The Federalists objected again in 1805, this time to greater effect, that the Jeffersonian-Republican-led effort to impeach Justice Samuel Chase because of his inflammatory rulings and statements from the bench, was an inappropriate attempt to muzzle the courts and compromise their independence. A century later, when the courts were under sustained attack by progressive reformers, the president of the American Bar Association came to the courts' defense: "Judicial judgments are not accorded the same reception as formerly," he said, noting that "the courts . . . are frequently and fiercely attacked," which, in his view, threatened to "destroy confidence in the courts and . . . make a subservient judiciary." American Bar Association, Address of the President, 33 Report of the Thirty-First Annual Meeting of the American Bar Association 341, 359 (1908). President Franklin Roosevelt's Court-packing plan likewise prompted strenuous objections from opponents who argued that it would render the Supreme Court subservient to the president. *Reorganization of the Fed. Judiciary: Hearings on S.1392 Before the Senate Comm. on the Judiciary*, 75th Cong., pt. 3, p. 546 (1937) (statement of Raymond Moley) (characterizing the Court-packing plan as a "deliberate attempt by one branch of the Government to weaken another branch," which has "very few parallels in our history," "none of [which] is creditable").

26. Thus, for example, in 1913, when Congress abolished the Article III Commerce Court it had created three years earlier, it took special care to relocate the judges whose offices were being abolished. *See* Philip B. Kurland,

The Constitution and the Tenure of Federal Judges: Some Notes from History, 36 U. Chi. L. Rev. 665 (1969).

27. Stephen B. Burbank, *The Architecture of Judicial Independence*, 72 S. Cal. L. Rev. 315, 321–22 (1999) ("Notwithstanding the well-known frustration of President Jefferson in response to this failure, however, it did have effect, if only in curbing partisan behavior on the bench.") (footnotes omitted).

28. Deborah Tedford, "Federal Judges Warned of Abduction Plot," *Houston Chronicle*, February 21, 1996, p. 17.

29. *Ibid.*

30. David E. Rovella, *Judges Target of Abortion Foe Web Site*, Nat'l L.J., November 23, 1998, p. A6.

31. The judges at issue included Harold Baer, Fred Biery, and Thelton Henderson. *See* Ralph Z. Hallow, "Republicans Out to Impeach 'Activist' Jurists," *Washington Times*, March 12, 1997, p. A1 (reporting on the majority whip's efforts to initiate impeachment proceedings against Baer, Biery and Henderson); Don Van Natta, Jr., "Judges Defend a Colleague from Attacks," *New York Times*, March 29, 1996, p. B1 (discussing the Baer episode).

32. Van Natta, Jr., "Judges Defend a Colleague from Attacks," p. B1.

33. Ross E. Milloy, "Suit Fights Absentee Vote By Soldiers at Texas Base," *New York Times*, March 2, 1997, p. A22; Hallow, "Republicans Out to Impeach 'Activist' Jurists."

34. Hallow, "Republicans Out to Impeach 'Activist' Jurists."

35. Michael Finn, "Tenn. Senate Asks Congress to Impeach U.S. Judge Nixon," *Chattanooga Free Press*, May 20, 1997, p. B3; Karin Miller, "House Panel OKs Weakened Judge Impeachment Resolution," *Chattanooga Free Press*, May 28, 1997, p. B3.

36. Associated Press, "Effort to Impeach Federal Judge Stalls," February 9, 1999.

37. Joseph Slobodzian, *Did this Judge Free a Killer?* Nat'l L. J., November 3, 1997, p. A6.

38. Jon O. Newman, *The Judge Baer Controversy*, 80 Judicature 156, 158 (1997).

39. David Barton, *Impeachment! Restraining an Overactive Judiciary* (Aledo, Tex.: Wallbuilder Press, 1996), p. 49 ("Judges who ignore jury decisions, or who pander to criminals while ignoring the obvious harm to society, clearly fulfill the standards for impeachment . . .").

40. *Hearing of the ABA Commission on Separation of Powers and Judicial Independence,* pp. 203–04, (February 21, 1997) (testimony of John Choon Yoo) (observing that "of all the elected or appointed officials in our government, either national or state, federal judges are the only ones who are

institutionally independent and institutionally immune from political pressure," and that Judge Baer was too "sensitive to political criticism," because "[t]here was no real threat he was going to be impeached").

41. Letter from Robert Dole to Jon O. Newman, et al., April 9, 1996, *reprinted in* Newman, 80 Judicature at 161, *supra* note 38.

42. *See* Martin Kasindorf, "Judgments Raise Some Objections/Clinton Denies Pressuring Baer," *Newsday,* April 3, 1996, p. A19.

43. *See* Neil MacFarquhar, "Federal Judge to Resign, Citing Political Attacks," *New York Times,* June 5, 1996, p. B4 (discussing resignation of circuit judge Lee Sarokin). Many greeted Judge Sarokin's explanation for his resignation with skepticism. *See, e.g., Hearing of the ABA Commission on Separation of Powers and Judicial Independence,* pp. 195–96 (October 11, 1996) (testimony of Fred Graham) ("I do not believe [Sarokin] really makes a case or attempts to make a case that he or any other federal judge—that their independence was, in fact infringed upon, by . . . the kind of criticism that he cited").

44. Associated Press, "Committees Starting From Scratch Handling Unusual Bill," March 8, 1999.

45. The episode, involving United States district judge Harold Baer, is reported in Van Natta, Jr., "Judges Defend a Colleague from Attacks."

46. Stephen B. Bright, *Political Attacks on the Judiciary*, 80 Judicature 165, 172 (1997) ("Regardless of why Judge Baer eventually changed his ruling . . . there will always be the appearance that he backed down due to the barrage of criticism he received").

47. *Hearing of the ABA Commission on Separation of Powers and Judicial Independence,* pp. 139–40 (October 11, 1996) (testimony of Andrew Coats) ("[T]he pending case aspect of [the Baer incident] seems . . . to make it somewhat more difficult" because "interference in the process seems . . . to be more of a danger than just the criticism after the fact").

48. William Schneider, "Getting Out Front on the Crime Issue," *National Journal,* April 11, 1996 ("Did a federal judge respond to political pressure . . . ? Of course he did. And by doing so, he saved Clinton, the federal judiciary and himself a whole lot of grief").

49. Bill Rankin, "Campaign Flier Targeting Judge Criticized by Legal Ethics Experts," *Atlanta Constitution,* June 19, 1998, p. 6F.

50. Brad Stetson, "Author Scathingly Indicts Judiciary," *Orange County Register,* August 16, 1998, p. F37.

51. *Ibid.*

52. NBC-TV, *Today,* transcript, June 8, 1998.

53. Although Heston did not indicate his source in the interview, he was apparently relying on data generated by the Philadelphia District Attorney's office.

Transcript of speech by Judge Norma Shapiro before the American Judicature Society Task Force on Judicial Independence, October 28, 1998 ("I have tried in the last few years to verify those statistics. I can find no basis for it whatsoever. The figures are totally and exclusively in the control of the district attorney").

54. *Hearing of the ABA Commission on Separation of Powers and Judicial Independence,* pp. 191, 198 (December 13, 1996).

55. *Ibid.,* p. 199.

56. Transcript of speech by Judge Norma Shapiro ("I didn't release people fast enough to suit the class or the city so there was a new consent decree in which a special prison master would do it. However, in each one of those 7,000 decrees I personally reviewed what he did to be sure he complied with one thing: it couldn't be anyone accused of a violent offense such as rape, homicide and no one who had been accused of doing anything with a gun. And to my knowledge, those rules were never violated").

57. *Quoted in* Stephen B. Bright, *Political Attacks on the Judiciary: Can Justice Be Done Amid Efforts to Intimidate and Remove Judges from Office for Unpopular Decisions?* 72 N.Y.U. L. Rev. 308, 314 (1997).

58. *Ibid.*

59. Jack Newfield and Maggie Haberman, "Three Stooges Are Court Clowns," *New York Post,* September 29, 1998, p. 12.

60. Don Russell, "Temin's Gig Is Up," *Philadelphia Daily News,* December 3, 1998, p. 3.

61. Press Release, State of Alabama, Governor's Office, November 4, 1997.

62. Bright, *supra* note 46, at 167–70 (detailing the misleading criticism aimed at former Tennessee justice Penny White and Mississippi justice James Robertson during their reelection campaigns).

63. *Ibid.* at 172. For example, Canon 3B(9) of the ABA Model Code of Judicial Conduct provides that "a judge shall not, while a proceeding is pending or impending in any court, make any public comment that might reasonably be expected to affect its outcome or impair its fairness or make any nonpublic comment that might substantially interfere with a fair trial or hearing." The accompanying commentary adds that "the requirement that judges abstain from public comment regarding a pending or impending proceeding continues during any appellate process and until final disposition."

64. *Reprinted in* Newman, *supra* note 38, at 161.

65. In his testimony before the ABA Commission, Court Television anchor Fred Graham was unapologetic about the role of the media in its reporting of judicial criticism, noting that after Senator Dole attacked several Democratic appointees, the press responded by putting Dole's arguably

misleading accusations in context, for example, by reporting that Dole had voted to confirm the appointees he criticized President Clinton for nominating. *Hearing of the ABA Commission on Separation of Powers and Judicial Independence*, p. 194 (October 11, 1996).

66. *See, e.g.*, Harriet Chiang, "Judicial Watchdog's Probes Assailed," *San Francisco Chronicle*, July 24, 1998, p. A1 (discussing disciplinary proceedings filed by the state Commission on Judicial Performance against Justice J. Anthony Kline and other California judges, on the basis of statements made in judicial opinions); Gary Spencer, *Court of Appeals Removes Duckman; Dissents Stress Threats to Independence*, N.Y. L. J., July 8, 1998, p. 1 (reporting on removal of Judge Lorin Duckman, in part because of his rulings in misdemeanor cases).

67. *Morrow v. Hood Communications, Inc.*, 59 Cal. App. 4th 924, 927 (1997) (Kline, J., dissenting).

68. *Ibid.* (citation omitted).

69. Notice of Formal Proceedings in *Inquiry Concerning J. Anthony Kline, No. 151*, Before the State of California Commission on Judicial Performance 2 (filed June 30, 1998).

70. Chiang, *supra* note 66.

71. Spencer, *supra* note 66.

72. *Ibid.*

73. *Ibid.*

74. Laura Vozella, "Judicial Panel Affirms Rebuke of McBryde," *Fort Worth Star-Telegram*, September 20, 1998, p. 1.

75. *Quoted in* Chiang, *supra* note 66.

76. *See, e.g.*, Spencer, *supra* note 66.

77. *Quoted in* Chiang, *supra* note 66.

78. Jean Guccione, "Discipline Board: Charges Resulted From Kline's Vote," *Los Angeles Daily Journal*, July 13, 1998.

79. *See, e.g.*, Kirk Loggins, "Activists Target Tennessee Judge," *Tennessean*, July 8, 1998, p. 1A (discussing election defeat of Tennessee justice Penny White, and ongoing effort to defeat Tennessee justice Adolpho Birch, because of rulings in criminal cases).

80. "Judicial Independence Crucial, Justice Warns," *Chicago Tribune*, December 6, 1998, p. C13.

81. *Ibid.*

82. Jenifer Warren, "State's Chief Justice Says He Will Fight Back," *Los Angeles Times*, March 6, 1998, p. A3; Pete Wilson and Dianne Feinstein, "Don't Let Factions Oust Judges Over Single Decision," *Los Angeles Daily News*, October 29, 1998, p. N19.

83. R. Bruce Dold, "Judges Up For Election Walking a Delicate Tightrope," *Chicago Tribune,* October 23, 1998, p. N27.

84. Thomas Suddes, "Editorials and Forum," *Plain Dealer,* May 6, 1998, p. 11B (discussing opposition to Pfeifer's reelection based on the school funding cases and concluding: "So, by this November, Republican Justice Pfeifer just may have a race—and, possibly, some additional insights into the school-funding case").

85. *Quoted in* Stephen B. Bright, *Political Attacks on the Judiciary*, 80 Judicature 165, 166 (1997).

86. *Ibid.* (alteration in original) (footnote omitted).

87. Letters to the Editor, *Tennessean,* August 3, 1998, p.14A.

88. For a discussion of *how* such critics might be taken to task, please see the Recommendations section of this report.

89. *Quoted in An Independent Judiciary: Report of the ABA Commission on Separation of Powers and Judicial Independence,* p. 48 (1997).

90. The legislative address, for example, typically enables the general assembly to petition the governor for removal of a judge upon a simple majority vote of both houses of the legislature.

91. Thomas E. Baker, *The Good Judge: Report of the Twentieth Century Fund Task Force on Federal Judicial Responsibility* (New York: Priority Press Publications, 1989), p. 10.

Appendix A:

Memorandum on Ethical Restrictions on Lawyers Who Criticize Judges

To: Charles Geyh, Reporter to Citizens for Independent Courts Task Force on the Distiction between Intimidation and Legitimate Criticism of Judges

From: Lisa Dewey, Associate, Piper & Marbury, L.L.P., Amy Potter, Law Clerk, Piper & Marbury, L.L.P.

Date: May 28, 1999

Subject: Ethical Restrictions on Lawyers Who Criticize Judges

Introduction and Summary

Lawyers may criticize judges as long as the statements made are true and do not disrupt the functioning of the judicial system.[1] Lawyers have the same First Amendment right as non-lawyers to criticize judges, but lawyers must also abide by the ethical rules of their states. State ethical rules are based largely on the ABA Model Rules of Professional Conduct and the Model Code of Professional Responsibility.[2] These ethical rules impose sanctions on lawyers who make false statements about judges or whose criticism interferes with the fairness of judicial proceedings.[3] Lawyers are uniquely well-situated to inform the public of possible problems with the judicial system but, at the same time, must ensure that their comments do not interfere with the administration of justice.[4]

Lawyers rarely face sanctions for criticism unless they knew or should have known that the criticism was false.[5] When imposing sanctions under ethical provisions, courts must take into account the guarantee of freedom of speech found in the First Amendment. Courts will also consider when the comment took place and what effect, if any, it had on an impending trial. A lawyer retains his or her First Amendment rights to free speech, and sanctions cannot be imposed unless the statements of facts are false or the statements impede the ability of the judiciary to function.

ABA MODEL RULES AND MODEL CODE OF PROFESSIONAL CONDUCT

The ABA's ethical codes governing lawyers are useful in determining what limitations exist on lawyers' criticism of the judiciary. The Model Rules of Professional Conduct and the Model Code of Professional Responsibility[6] serve as a basis for many state codes of ethics for lawyers. The Model Rules are the most current standard adopted by the ABA, replacing the Model Code in 1983.[7] Nearly two-thirds of the states have modeled their ethical standards on the Model Rules.[8] Model Rule 8.2, "Judicial and Legal Officials," states:

> (a) A lawyer shall not make a statement that the lawyer knows to be false or with reckless disregard as to its truth or falsity concerning the qualifications or integrity of a judge, adjudicatory officer or legal officer, or of a candidate for election or appointment to judicial or legal office.

> (b) A lawyer who is a candidate for judicial office shall comply with the applicable provisions of the Code of Judicial Conduct.[9]

MR 8.2 differs slightly from the provisions in the Model Code, which refers only to "knowingly mak[ing] false statements."[10] Under MR 8.2, it is possible for a lawyer to be sanctioned for statements he or she did not know were false, but could have reasonably discovered were false. The general standard for determining if a statement can be proscribed is that (1) the statement must be false and (2) the lawyer must have known it to be false or have had reckless disregard for the truth of the statement.

The limits on speech imposed by MR 8.2(a) are consistent with the U.S. Constitution's guarantee of freedom of speech.[11] The comments to the rules recognize that honest and candid opinions by lawyers can improve the administration of justice, whereas false statements by lawyers can unfairly undermine public confidence in the administration of justice.[12] In addition, lawyers are encouraged to defend judges who are unjustly criticized by others.[13]

A LAWYER'S DUTY TO THE PUBLIC AND TO THE COURTS

Some courts have held that, because they are officers of the court and members of a profession that has developed ethical guidelines, lawyers do not have the same right as non-lawyers to criticize the judiciary.[14] Lawyers have a duty to avoid undermining public opinion of the judiciary by exhibiting disrespect for the courts.[15] Rather, lawyers are encouraged to help promote public confidence in the judicial system. Unfair or inaccurate criticism will not help to improve the judiciary.[16]

FIRST AMENDMENT ISSUES ARISING FROM LAWYERS' CRITICISM OF JUDGES

There is a tension between the ethical rules governing a lawyer's conduct when criticizing a judge and that lawyer's First Amendment guarantee of freedom of speech. Ethical rules that limit what a lawyer can or cannot say regarding a judge restrict his or her freedom of speech. Yet such restraints have been upheld in some situations because certain conduct by lawyers may undermine the ability of the judicial system to function.[17] The Supreme Court of the United States has generally held that conduct protected by the First Amendment cannot be restricted by ethical codes unless the conduct "obstruct[s] the administration of justice."[18] Thus, criticism by lawyers is protected as long as it does not interfere with judicial functioning. This standard is especially applicable during a trial, but can be used to restrict criticism made at other times.

Courts apply the standards used in libel and defamation cases to situations in which lawyers criticize the judiciary. Public figures, including judges, do not receive as much protection as ordinary citizens. Nevertheless, a defendant will be held liable for statements about public figures that are false and said with "actual malice."[19] This standard has been applied to lawyers who criticize judges and it is consistent with the standards developed in MR 8.2.

Distinctions are drawn between comments made during or prior to a trial, comments made after the litigation has been resolved, and comments made during an election campaign. These three situations carry with them different levels of obligations concerning what types of speech are allowed and protected by the First Amendment.

A. Comments Made during a Trial. Generally, criticisms made by lawyers involved in a pending or recently concluded trial are more suspect than statements made by lawyers not involved in the proceedings.[20] This is because of the fear that publicity may interfere with the parties' ability to get a fair proceeding. In addition to MR 8.2, lawyers must also abide by Model Rules 3.5 and 3.6, which pertain specifically to a lawyer's duty not to influence a judge in a specific case and to ongoing trial publicity, respectively.[21] First Amendment guarantees in many cases are superseded by the guarantees of fair trials and judicial proceedings. Thus, with certain exceptions, lawyers involved in a pending case cannot comment publicly on matters that would disrupt the proceedings. This includes criticisms of judges in and out of court.

B. Comments Made after a Trial. After a trial, there are two different situations in which a lawyer's criticism of a judge may be sanctioned. The general standards in MR 8.2 are applicable to these situations. The first situation is criticism of the lower court judge contained in documents submitted to an appellate court. Some criticism is acceptable and may even be required in pleadings in order to fulfill an obligation to a client, but those criticisms must not be false and should serve the client's interest.[22] There is no First Amendment right to accuse judges of criminal acts during a trial that have no basis in the truth.[23] Some courts have read the ethical rules to apply primarily to out-of-court statements to the public, not to papers filed with the court.[24]

The second situation is general statements made out of court. Again, the nature of the statement and whether it is false determines whether it is protected under the First Amendment.

C. Campaigns for Judicial Office. Candidates for judicial office have a constitutionally protected right to criticize the incumbent judge during the campaign. However, the libel and defamation standards and MR 8.2 apply. None of the candidates may make false statements in violation of MR 8.2.

CONCLUSION

A lawyer may not make false statements regarding a judge and has a general duty, as a member of the profession, to help maintain the public's confidence in the judicial system. The ethical rules of the states punish lawyers who exceed those limitations when criticizing the judiciary. States cannot prohibit all criticism of judges because lawyers as well as non-lawyers enjoy the First Amendment protection of freedom of speech. Sanctions are generally imposed only on lawyers who knowingly make false statements or make statements with a reckless disregard for the truth. Such statements are normally not protected by the First Amendment. However, lawyers have been disciplined for statements that fail to uphold the dignity of the judicial process, or that disrupt the administration of justice or undermine the ability of the judicial system to function. Lawyers do not abandon their constitutional rights when they join the bar, but they do face ethical guidelines that nonlawyers do not in order to help to ensure that the integrity of the judicial system is maintained.

NOTES

1. *See Model Rules of Professional Conduct*, Rule 8.2 (1998); *ABA/BNA Lawyers' Manual on Professional Conduct* §101:601 (1993).

2. *Model Code of Professional Responsibility*, reprinted in *ABA/BNA Lawyers' Manual on Professional Conduct*, §101:601.

3. *ABA/BNA Lawyers' Manual on Professional Conduct* §101:601-604.

4. 2 Geoffrey C. Hazard, Jr. and W. William Hodes, *The Law of Lawyering: A Handbook on the Model Rules of Professional Conduct*, §8.2:101(2d ed., 1998).

5. *Model Rules of Professional Conduct*, Rule 8.2. *But see In re Johnson*, 729 P2d 1175 (Kan. 1986) (lawyer may be disciplined for criticisms motivated by reasons other than a desire to improve the legal system).

6. *Model Code*, note 3, *supra*.

7. *Model Rules of Professional Conduct*, Preface, p. viii.

8. *Id*. However, some states still use the provisions established in the Model Code, so consideration of the Code is important.

9. *Model Rules of Professional Responsibility*, Rule 8.2.

10. *Model Code of Professional Responsibility*, DR 8-102, 8-103, reprinted in *ABA/BNA Lawyers' Manual on Professional Conduct*, § 101:601.

11. *See Hazard, supra*.

12. *Model Rules of Professional Conduct*, Rule 8.2, cmt. 1, 2.

13. *Model Rules, supra* at cmt. 3.

14. *See Hazard, supra*; e.g., *In re Riley*, 691 P.2d 695, 705 (Ariz. 1986) (public criticism of judge by lawyer not appropriate because private grievance could have been submitted).

15. *See Comm. v. Rubright*, 414 A.2d 106, 110 (Pa. 1980) (there is an absolute duty to uphold dignity of judicial process); *ABA/BNA Lawyers' Manual on Professional Conduct* §101:602.

16. *See generally Matter of Palmisano*, 70 F.3d 483 (7th Cir. 1995), *cert. denied*, 517 U.S. 1223 (1986) ("indiscriminate accusations of dishonesty . . . do not help cleanse the judicial system of miscreants").

17. *See, e.g., United States Dist. Court for the Eastern Dist. of Washington v. Sandlin*, 12 F.3d 861, 866 (9th Cir. 1993) ("although [lawyer] does not surrender freedom of expression, he must temper his criticism in accordance with professional standards of conduct").

18. *In re Sawyer*, 360 U.S. 622, 636 (1959). *See also, Gentile v. State Bar of Nevada*, 501 U.S. 1030 (1991) (cannot punish speech protected by First Amendment unless there is "substantial likelihood of material prejudice").

19. *See New York Times Co. v. Sullivan*, 376 U.S. 254, 279-80 (1964). *See also Garrison v. Louisiana*, 379 U.S. 64 (1964) (applying standard in *New York Times Co. v. Sullivan* to lawyer who disparaged eight judges and holding that true statements are protected by First Amendment).

20. *Hazard, supra*, §8.2:201.

21. *Model Rules of Professional Conduct*, Rules 3.5, 3.6.

22. *ABA/BNA Lawyers' Manual on Professional Conduct* §101:611.

23. *See, e.g., Ramirez v. State Bar of California*, 619 P.2d 399 (Cal. 1980).

24. *See United States v. Brown*, 72 F.3d 25 (5th Cir. 1995).

APPENDIX B:

MEMORANDUM ON ETHICAL CONSTRAINTS LIMITING A JUDGE'S FIRST AMENDMENT FREEDOM OF SPEECH

To: Edward W. Madeira, Jr., Member of Citizens for Independent Courts Task Force on Criticism of Judges
From: Daniel M. Schaffzin, Pepper Hamilton, L.L.P.
Date: June 1, 1999
Subject: Ethical constraints limiting a judge's First Amendment freedom of speech

I. SCOPE OF MEMORANDUM

This memorandum discusses the recognized canons of judicial conduct as they limit a judge's constitutional right to free speech. Pursuant to instructions, the memorandum does not engage in a survey of the pertinent codes and common law governing judicial conduct in each of the fifty states. The "Discussion" section does, however, utilize case law and judicial canons from several states to demonstrate current standards and conflicts pertaining to the issue at hand. Future users of this memorandum may use the following West's key numbers in updating its research: *Judges* 11(2), 11(4), 11(7), 11(8), 21; and *Constitutional Law* 82(11), 90.1(1.5).

Secondary sources consulted include Martin J. McMahon, Annotation, *First Amendment Protection for Judges or Government Attorneys Subjected to Discharge, Transfer, or Discipline Because of Speech*, 108 A.L.R. Fed. 117 (1992 & Supp. 1997); Jeffrey M. Shaman ET AL., *Judicial Conduct and Ethics* §§ 10.01–10.38 (2nd ed. 1995 & Supp. 1997); Robert M. O'Neil, *Assaults on the Judiciary*, TRIAL, September 1998, at 54; Judith S. Kaye, *Safeguarding a Crown Jewel: Judicial Independence and Lawyer Criticism of Courts*, 25 HOFSTRA L. REV. 703 (1997); Gregory C. O'Brien, Jr., *Speech May Be Free, and Talk Cheap, But Judges Can Pay a Heavy Price for Unguarded Expression*, 28 LOY. L.A. L. REV. 815 (1995); Erwin Chemerinsky, *Is It The Siren's Call: Judges and Free Speech While Cases Are Pending*, 28 LOY. L.A. L. REV. 831 (1995); Talbot D'Alemberte, *Searching for the Limits of Judicial Free Speech*, 61 TUL. L. REV. 611 (1987); Edmund B. Spaeth, Jr. with Peggy B. Wachs, *The Judge's Three Worlds: A Judicial Ethics Course* (1996); Steven Lubet, *Judicial Conduct: Speech and Consequences*, 4 The Long Term View 71 (1997); Erwin Chemerinsky, *In Defense of Speech: Judges and the First Amendment*, 4 The Long Term View 78 (1997); William G. Ross, *Extrajudicial Speech: Charting the Boundaries of Propriety*, 2 GEO. J. LEGAL ETHICS 589 (1989); and Clarence W. Wolfram, *Modern Legal Ethics* §17.5 (Practitioner's ed. 1986).

II. QUESTION PRESENTED

What are the nature and extent of the ethical constraints that limit a judge's First Amendment right to speak openly to members of the public, both to address matters of public importance and to defend, clarify, and explain his or her judicial rulings?

III. DISCUSSION

A judge does not forfeit his or her First Amendment rights upon ascending to the bench. William G. Ross, *Extrajudicial Speech: Charting the Boundaries of Propriety*, 2 GEO. J. LEGAL ETHICS (1989)

589, 594. Under the Model Code of Judicial Conduct (hereinafter "Model Code") and similar state canons of judicial ethics, however, a judge may face more stringent limitations on his or her free speech than an ordinary citizen. *See generally* Martin J. McMahon, Annotation, *First Amendment Protection for Judges or Government Attorneys Subjected to Discharge, Transfer, or Discipline Because of Speech*, 108 A.L.R. Fed. 117 (1992 & Supp. 1997). The Model Code expressly prohibits a judge from making any public statement that affects the outcome or impairs the fairness of a pending proceeding. *Model Code* Canon 3B(9) (1990); *see also Pennsylvania Code of Judicial Conduct* (hereinafter "Pennsylvania Code") Canon 3A(6) (1999)(prohibiting public comment about pending proceeding in any court); *New Jersey Code of Judicial Conduct* (hereinafter "New Jersey Code") Canon 3A(8) (1999)(same). In addition to this express prohibition, a judge must "act at all times in a manner that promotes public confidence in the integrity and impartiality of the judiciary," *Model Code* Canon 2A; *see also Pennsylvania Code* Canon 2A (same); *New Jersey Code* Canon (same), and may not act in a way which casts reasonable doubt upon the impartiality of the judge, demeans the judicial office, or interferes with the performance of judicial duties. *Model Code* Canon 4A; *see also Pennsylvania Code* Canon 4A (directing judge to "engage in activities to improve the law, the legal system, and the administration of justice"); *New Jersey Code* Canon (allowing quasi-judicial activities that do not cast doubt on judge's ability to decide issue impartially and for which judge receives no compensation). A judge may, however, "speak, write, teach, and participate in other extra-judicial activities concerning the law . . . subject to the requirements of this code." *Model Code* Canon 4B; *see also Pennsylvania Code* Canon 5 (avocational activities must not "detract from the dignity of his office or interfere with the performance of his judicial duties"); *New Jersey Code* Canon 4A (same as Model Code section). Abiding by the direct and implied prohibitions on speech set forth in the canons of judicial conduct, a judge speaking to the public must be wary of both the content of his speech and the possible effect on its audience. *See* Judith S. Kaye, *Safeguarding a Crown Jewel: Judicial Independence and Lawyer Criticism of Courts*, 25 HOFSTRA L. REV. 703, 712–13 (1997).

The United States Supreme Court has not yet considered what limits the First Amendment imposes on a state's authority to restrict judges from publicly commenting on pending cases or engaging in public debate. *See Broadman v. Commission on Judicial Performance*, 959 P.2d 715, 727 (Cal. 1998). Accordingly, courts have weighed ethical provisions regulating extrajudicial speech against a variety of constitutional standards. *See, e.g., In re Judicial Conduct*, 603 So.2d 494, 498 (Fla. 1992)(state must accomplish legitimate interest in restraining judicial speech through narrowly-tailored limitations not exceeding that necessary to accomplish state's interests); *In re Inquiry of Broadbelt*, 683 A.2d 543, 552 (N.J. 1996)(regulation of judicial speech permitted if furthering substantial government interests unrelated to suppression of expression and no more restrictive than necessary). Generally, courts evaluating the constitutionality of restrictions on judicial speech balance the effect of the challenged speech on "the independence and integrity of the judiciary" against the "imposition of restrictions on a judge's free speech rights." *Broadbelt*, 683 A.2d at 552; *see also In re Disciplinary Proceeding Against Sanders*, 955 P.2d 369, 376 (Wash. 1998)(balancing "government's interest in a fair and impartial judiciary" against "judge's interest in the right to express his or her views").

Courts have assessed the validity of four types of extrajudicial expression: statements concerning pending cases, statements concerning courts and case procedure, statements responding to public criticism, and statements concerning controversial legal issues. *See, e.g., Broadbelt*, 683 A.2d at 543 (assessing conduct of judge who gave television commentary on cases pending outside of jurisdiction); *Office of Disciplinary Counsel v. Souers*, 611 N.E.2d 305 (Ohio 1993)(assessing judge's media statements defending overturned sentencing order); *Sanders*, 955 P.2d at 369 (Wash. 1998)(assessing speech of state supreme court justice at anti-abortion rally); *In re Conard*, 944 S.W.2d 191 (Mo. 1997)(assessing judge's response to public attacks on ruling of his court). In addition, courts have evaluated the limits on the speech of candidates for judicial office. *See, e.g., Buckley v. Illinois Judicial Inquiry Board*, 997 F.2d 224 (7th Cir. 1993)(assessing state election rule regulating speech of judicial candidates). For the purposes of this memorandum, each form of extrajudicial expression will be considered individually:

A. Judicial Comment on Pending Cases. The issue of the appropriateness of a judge's public statements of opinion arises most frequently in situations where the commentary concerns a matter pending before the judge. Edmund B. Spaeth, Jr., with Peggy B.

Wachs, *The Judge's Three Worlds: A Judicial Ethics Course* 135 (1996). Under the 1990 Model Code, a judge may not "while a proceeding is pending or impending in *any court,* make any public comment that might reasonably be expected to affect its outcome or impair its fairness or make any nonpublic comment that might substantially interfere with a fair trial or hearing." *Model Code* Canon 3B(9) (emphasis added). In many states, including Pennsylvania and New Jersey, proscriptions against judicial speech concerning pending matters may be broader than the Model Code. *See Pennsylvania Code* Canon 3A(6)(1999)(ordering judges to "abstain from public comment about a pending proceeding in any court" without regard to the potential impact of the judge's statements); *New Jersey Code* Canon 3A(8)(same); *see also Michigan Code of Judicial Conduct* Canon 3A(6)(identical provision). Under both the Model Code and parallel state codes, the prohibition on speech concerning pending cases "continues during any appellate process and until final disposition," but does not extend to "public statements in the course of [a judge's] official duties or explan[ations] for public information purposes the procedures of the court." *Model Code* Canon 3B(9); *Model Code* Commentary to Canon 3B(9).

Acting on these express prohibitions, courts have with rare exception upheld disciplinary action taken against judges who have willfully chosen to speak publicly on the merits of pending matters. *See In re Schenck,* 870 P.2d 402, 442 (Or. 1994)(upholding suspension of judge whose newspaper editorial discussed specific case and criticized district attorney handling pending cases); *Ryan v. Commission on Judicial Performance,* 754 P.2d 724 (Cal. 1988)(upholding discipline of judge who discussed draft opinion with press before notifying parties of his ruling). *But see U.S. v. Yonkers Board of Education,* 946 F.2d 180,184 (2d. Cir. 1991)(Canon 3B(9) not violated when judicial statements about a pending case restate comments previously made by commenting judge in open court); *Goldman v. Nevada Comm'n on Judicial Discipline,* 830 P.2d 107, 136–137 (1992)(judge may comment on case no longer pending). While judges rarely offer unprompted statements on ongoing cases, a judge must use great caution when facing media requests to speak publicly on the merits of a pending case. Gregory C. O'Brien, Jr., *Speech May Be Free, and Talk Cheap, But Judges Can Pay a Heavy Price for Unguarded Expression,* 28 LOY. *L.A. L. REV.* 815, 824 (1995). Two recent cases outline the considerations made by courts evaluating the propriety of extrajudicial statements made in response to such requests. *See Broadman v. Comm'n on Judicial Performance*, 959 P.2d at 715; *In re Inquiry of Broadbelt*, 683 A.2d at 543.

In *Broadman*, a trial judge made comments to several television stations and magazines about a case pending on appeal in which he ordered the use of the Norplant contraceptive device as a condition of probation. *Id.* at 725. The Supreme Court of California held that the judge "engaged in unjudicial conduct by violating a canon of judicial conduct . . . with knowledge of its restrictions. By making public comments in an attempt to justify and defend his decisions while those decisions were pending, [the judge] adopted the role of an advocate." *Id.* at 729. The court concluded that the judge's comments subjected him to discipline where they discussed the merits of ongoing cases and were "prejudicial to public esteem for the judicial office." *Id.*

In *Broadbelt*, a trial judge who had appeared on "Court TV" and CNBC over fifty times as a commentator on high-profile cases questioned the validity of a request of an overseeing judge to refrain from further television appearances. *Id.* at 545. Although the judge made no statements about cases pending in New Jersey, the state Supreme Court found his conduct to violate New Jersey Code Canon 3A(8)'s restriction on judicial statements regarding cases pending "in any court" in any jurisdiction. *Id.* at 546 (citing *In re Hey*, 425 S.E.2d 221, 222–24 (W.Va. 1992)). Additionally, where the judge's frequent appearances caused him to be identified with the program, his conduct violated New Jersey Code Canon 2B in "lend[ing] the prestige of judicial office to advance the private interests of others." *Id.* at 550. Because the judge's television commentary "was inappropriate and had the potential to compromise the integrity of the judiciary," the court defended its broad reading of the judicial canons as a means of "avoid[ing] the possibility of undue influence on the judicial process and the threat to public confidence posed by a judge from one jurisdiction criticizing the rulings or technique of a judge from a different jurisdiction." *Id.* at 548.

Although the U.S. Supreme Court has not set forth a binding standard strictly prohibiting extrajudicial commentary on pending matters, the limitation on a judge's speech about ongoing cases "is clearly a content-based restriction." Chemerinsky, *Is It The Siren's Call: Judges and Free Speech While Cases Are Pending*, 28 Loy. L.A. L. Rev. 831, 841 (1995). Any public statement by a judge involving "the facts, applicable law, or merits" or "the parties or their attorneys" in a pending case risks violating Model Code Canon 3B(9). William G. Ross, *Extrajudicial Speech: Charting the Boundaries of Propriety*, 2 GEO. J. LEGAL ETHICS 589, 598 (1989). Judges should therefore deliberately avoid any extrajudicial statement about a pending proceeding; both discrete public remarks and those that are objectively innocuous may be interpreted to create an appearance of bias. *Id.*

B. Judicial Comment on Courts and Procedure. Appreciating the need for limited judicial response to inquiries by the public and press in particular, Canon 3B(9) expressly omits from the prohibition against extrajudicial comment on pending cases those statements clarifying court procedures or otherwise discussing the law, the legal system or the administration of justice. *Model Code* Canon 3B(9); *see also* Jeffrey M. Shaman ET AL., *Judicial Conduct and Ethics* §10.33 (2nd ed. 1995 & Supp. 1997). In *In re Sheffield*, 465 So.2d 350 (Ala. 1984), the court noted the confusion likely to emerge among judges who are "strictly prohibited from public comments on the merits of a pending case" but "encouraged to explain a pending case in abstract terms." *Id.* at 355. Recognizing the "fine line between the duties and prohibitions" of Canon 3B(9), the court explained:

> Judges should encourage representatives of the news media [to] inquire of them for background information relating to the operation of the court system. While judges may not comment on the merits of a pending case, a judge may and should explain legal terms and concepts, procedures, and the issues involved in the case so as to permit the news representatives to cover the case more intelligently . . . Often there is no one, other than the judge, who is in a position to give a detailed and impartial explanation of the case to the news media.

Sheffield, 465 So.2d at 355 (quoting National Conference of State Trial Judges Commission on News Reporting and Fair Trial, *Judicial Guidelines for Dealing With News Media Inquiries and Criticism* (5th Draft, June 5, 1984)).

Recognizing this exception to the pending proceeding restriction, some courts have held that a judge's remark explaining the reason for a decision is a comment on the court's procedure rather than a comment on the merits of a case. *See Office of Disciplinary Counsel v. Souers*, 611 N.E.2d 305 (Ohio 1993). In *Souers*, the Ohio Supreme Court refused to discipline a judge who, in a newspaper interview, defended a ruling that had been overturned by the court of appeals. *Id.* at 306. Although the judge described the ruling as "ludicrous" and chastised the appellate court for failing to get to "the merits of the case," the Court noted that Ohio Code of Judicial Conduct Canon 3A(6) permitted the judge's "defense of his sentencing order, while less than judicious, to explain his procedure in the underlying criminal case." *Id.*

In contrast, other courts using Canon 3B(9) to assess allegations of judicial misconduct have not viewed "the freedom to explain the court's procedures . . . [as] an absolute license." Jeffrey M. Shaman ET AL., *Judicial Conduct and Ethics* §10.33 (2nd ed. 1995 & Supp. 1997). In *In re Charge of Judicial Misconduct*, 47 F.3d 399 (10th Cir. 1995), a judge discussed a pending case during a press conference in chambers, interviews, and appearances on television news shows in hopes of obtaining compliance with a judicial decree. *Id.* at 400. Noting that the judge's "public comments clearly related to a matter before him and were outside the context of official proceedings," the Tenth Circuit Judicial Council held that the Tenth Circuit acted appropriately in subjecting the judge to disciplinary action. *Id. See also In re Schenck*, 870 P.2d at 201 (presence of some permissible information about court procedure in context of judicial comment "does not sanitize" other material amounting to comment about pending cases).

While a judge is encouraged to clarify court procedure to the press and the public, a judge choosing to do so must be "discrete and self-disciplined" to avoid making statements which step beyond the authorized range of comment under the canons of judicial conduct. *See* William G. Ross, *Extrajudicial Speech: Charting the Boundaries of Propriety*, 2 GEO. J. LEGAL ETHICS 589, 600 (1989). One commentator has suggested that unethical judicial commentary or potential misquotation by the press may be avoided through off-the-record judicial statements concerning a case. *Id.* This alternative would meet the public's need for basic information while precluding public perception that the judge had made remarks that suggested bias. *Id. See also* Illinois Judicial Ethics Committee, Op. 96-5 (1996)(presenting suggested responses for judge faced with reporter's inquiry about ruling in pending case). Seemingly, a judge whose comments exhibit "a genuine interest in an educated citizenry" and not a desire for "personal notoriety" is less likely to face scrutiny over public statements on court procedure and current law. Gregory C. O'Brien, Jr., *Speech May Be Free, and Talk Cheap, But Judges Can Pay a Heavy Price for Unguarded Expression*, 28 LOY. L.A. L. REV. 815, 827 (1995).

C. Judicial Response to Public Criticism. Although a trend of intensified judicial condemnation has emerged in the late 1990s, judges seeking to respond to public criticism can do so only in conformity with the canons and norms of judicial ethics. *See* Robert M. O'Neil, *Assaults on the Judiciary*, TRIAL, September 1998, at 55–56. Generally, judges cite the need to maintain impartiality as a deterrent to judicial response to verbal attacks from the press or public:

> [T]o secure an impartial forum, even for their most vocal critics, and to assure the dignity of the judicial process, judges by and large must stay out of the fray. They do not duel with public officials about the correctness of their decisions; they do not conduct press conferences about cases; and they have no call-in radio and television shows to explain their rulings. They rely on their decisions whether written or oral, to speak for themselves.

Judith S. Kaye, *Safeguarding a Crown Jewel: Judicial Independence and Lawyer Criticism of Courts*, 25 HOFSTRA L. REV. 703, 712 (1997).

Throughout history, however, judicial speech answering critics has faced various levels "of tolerance . . . depending upon the passion of the speech, the popularity of the speaker, and the power of those against whom the speech was directed." Talbot D'Alemberte, *Searching for the Limits of Judicial Free Speech*, 61 TUL. L. REV. 611, 620 (1987). In one well-documented instance, Supreme Court Justice John Marshall used a pseudonym in defending *McCulloch v. Maryland* in newspaper editorials. Ross, *supra* at 607. More recently, Justice Clark spoke publicly in defense of the Supreme Court's harshly criticized 1962 decision prohibiting state-prescribed prayer in public schools. *Id.*

In fact, recent cases seem to suggest a more sympathetic view of judges wishing to counterattack aggressive assaults on the judiciary. *See* Robert M. O'Neil, *Assaults on the Judiciary*, TRIAL, September 1998, at 57. In *In re Conard*, 944 S.W.2d 191 (Mo. 1997), a judge ruling in a domestic violence suit was attacked in the press by a police chief and the wife of the accused after the judge allowed the accused to be released from jail and filed a contempt charge against the police chief. *Id.* at 204. Following these attacks, the judge participated in several newspaper interviews to explain the reasoning and motivations underlying his rulings. *Id.* at 198–200. While the Missouri Supreme Court found that the judge's responses through the press had overstepped the scope of permissible judicial speech where he spoke on the merits of pending criminal charges, the court held that judges do possess a qualified privilege to respond to public criticism. *Id.* at 204–05. The court clarified that a judge may react to public attack so long as the reaction "is limited to a moderate and dignified response to the attack made upon the judge and [is] not of a nature in quantity or substance that creates more harm than benefit to the judicial system." *Id.* at 204. *See also In re Miera*, 426 N.W.2d 850, 856 (Minn. 1988)(judge has qualified privilege to "publicly explain his side of the affair in moderate, unmalicious, and unabusive language").

In a similar situation, Los Angeles Superior Court judge Roosevelt Dorn, presiding over the trial of the defendants accused of beating victim Reginald Denny following the Rodney King verdict, called a press conference "to set the record straight" after the prosecutor used a peremptory bench challenge to bar the judge from the case because of problems with the judge's calendar. *See* Robert M. O'Neil, *supra* at 58. The only African-American on the court, Judge Dorn labeled the prosecutor's stated reasons for seeking his recusal an "out and out lie" and asserted that a recusal would only create a notion "that the black judge was not effectively able to handle the calendar." *Id.* Later, addressing members of a church during the prosecutor's unsuccessful attempt for reelection, Judge Dorn stated that "the issue is how African Americans are being treated by elected officials in this community." *Id.*

Although Judge Dorn's comments spoke directly about an attorney in a pending case and political election, the judge was never charged with violating the judicial canons governing such conduct. *Id.* Commentators suggest three reasons behind the tolerance of the judge's borderline conduct. First, the prosecutor's stated reasons for seeking Dorn's removal from the case were arguably "false," "personally insulting," and "racially derogatory" to the point of potentially undermining citizen confidence among the African American community. *Id.* Second, Dorn's responses did not discuss the merits of the pending case in a way that tainted the fairness of the matter before another judge. *Id.*

Finally, the judge himself was the best person to answer the allegations of the prosecutor given the serious nature of those allegations and the inability of other judicial officials to adequately speak to knowledge possessed uniquely by the judge himself. *Id.*

In spite of the movement toward recognition of a broader capacity for judicial response, it is suggested that "judges ordinarily should refrain from explaining or defending their decisions even if their decisions have ignited a firestorm of hostility." William G. Ross, *Extrajudicial Speech: Charting the Boundaries of Propriety*, 2 GEO. J. LEGAL ETHICS 589, 606 (1989). *See also In re Jimenez*, 841 S.W.2d 572, 581 ("Judicial service . . . is not for the meek or the sensitive. It requires a thick skin and an ability to ignore criticism."). Still, in addition to personal attacks on individual judges, several situations may warrant judicial defense of a ruling or series of rulings subjected to public scrutiny. Where the general direction of the court has resulted in diminished confidence among a significant portion of the public, a judge may appropriately defend a court in general terms without mentioning any specific decision. Ross, *supra* at 606. Moreover, a judge may deem it necessary to justify the rulings of his or her court "if the institutional prerogatives of the court are threatened," i.e., where unpopular decisions create a threat that the legislature will curb the court's jurisdiction or overrule the court's decisions. *Id.* Finally, it may be appropriate for judges to counter inaccurate reports regarding individual judges or the internal procedures of the court. *Id.* at 612. Ultimately, a judge seeking to combat intense criticism of his or her court should do so "only if the defense is more likely to preserve judicial integrity than diminish it." *Id.*

D. *Judicial Comment on Controversial Legal Issues.* Model Code Canon 5A(1) specifies that "a judge or candidate for election or appointment to judicial office shall not: (a) act as a leader or hold office in a political organization; (b) publicly endorse or publicly oppose another candidate for public office; (c) make speeches on behalf of a political organization; (d) attend political gatherings; or (e) solicit funds for . . . or make a contribution to a political organization or candidate . . ." *Id.*; *see also Pennsylvania Code* Canon 7 (same); *New Jersey Code* Canon 7 (same). Although Canon 5A(1) expressly prohibits only partisan electoral activities, Canon 3B(9) advises against "any public comment" by a judge that "impair[s] the fairness" of any pending or impending proceeding. *Id.*; *see also* Vincent

Martin Bonventre, *Yes: Litigants Deserve a Justice With An Open Mind*, 83 A.B.A.J. 72 (1997). Moreover, Canon 4A(1) warns judicial officers to refrain from "extra-judicial activities" that might "cast reasonable doubt on the judge's capacity to act impartially." *Id.*; *see also* Bonventre, *supra* at 72. Accordingly, a judge must exercise caution where opining on a controversial legal or political issue apart from a pending case. Ross, *supra* at 638. Because, however, the canons of judicial ethics do not decisively prevent judicial statements concerning controversial legal issues, courts and commentators alike have offered a wide variety of rules attempting to define the external limits of permissible judicial opinion. *Compare* Steven Lubet, *Judicial Conduct: Speech and Consequences*, 4 The Long Term View 71 (1997) *with* Erwin Chemerinsky, *In Defense of Speech: Judges and the First Amendment*, 4 The Long Term View 78 (1997).

In *In re Sanders*, 955 P.2d 369 (Wash. 1998), Washington Supreme Court Justice Sanders told those in attendance at an anti-abortion rally that "[n]othing is more fundamental in our legal system than the preservation of innocent human life." *Id.* at 371. In response, the Washington Commission on Judicial Conduct's ruled that Justice Sanders's words transcended "the mere expression of opinion" into "align[ment]" with a particular political organization involved in pursuing a political agenda" and were thus in violation of the Code of Judicial Conduct. *Id.* Overturning the Commission's ruling, the Washington Supreme Court held that the Justice's appearance at the rally to express his beliefs and to thank his supporters did not force the conclusion that he could not rule impartially on the abortion issue as he might encounter it in his role as a judge. *Id.* at 370. In order to restrict the judge's speech in this context, the court specified, the challenging party must offer "clear and convincing evidence of speech or conduct that casts doubt on a judge's integrity, independence, or impartiality." *Id.*

Similarly, in *In re Gridley*, 417 So.2d 950 (Fla. 1982), the Supreme Court of Florida reviewed the conduct of a judge whose published letters to a newspaper announced his views on "Christian forgiveness" and against "capital punishment." *Id.* at 954. Concluding that the judge did not violate the Canons of Judicial Conduct in submitting the letters, the court noted:

> [t]here is no doubt that a judge in an appropriate forum
> may express his protest, dissent, and criticism of the present

state of the law as long as he does not appear to substitute his concept of the law for what the law actually is, and as long as he expresses himself in a manner that promotes public confidence in his integrity and impartiality as a judge.

Id. at 954–55. Because the judge's letters made clear that he would abide by his duty as a judge and accept the law as written, he avoided sanction for criticism "close to the dividing line between what is appropriate and what is not." *Id.* at 955.

While the recent cases demonstrate that judges may face diminished scrutiny when publicly offering insight into a legal issue that is not "pending or impending," a judge must take great care to avoid demonstrating a clear bias about a public matter that he or she is quite likely to face sooner or later in court. Ross, *supra* at 638. When Justice Antonin Scalia told an audience at Catholic University that it is "absolutely plain there is no constitutional right to die," many questioned his ability to consider the right to die issue as a neutral and detached magistrate:

> It is not that judges should keep their opinions to themselves; they should keep their minds open. It is not that judges should feign neutrality; they should actually remain undecided. It is not that judges should give litigants a false sense of confidence; they should truly listen to and consider the arguments. A judge—like anyone—may be predisposed; but his or her decision ought not to be preordained.

Bonventre, *supra* at 72. Opinions like those of Justice Scalia, however, are found frequently throughout history. *See* Talbot D'Alemberte, *Searching for the Limits of Judicial Free Speech*, 61 TUL. L. REV. *611, 622.* (1987). For example, Justice Mclean and Justice Story were both noted critics of slavery. *Id.* Likewise, Chief Justice Warren publicly championed changes in the criminal justice and jury systems. *Id.* at 623.

Overall, judges desiring to speak publicly and critically on a controversial legal or political issue should be able to do so "as long as neither the words nor the context suggest an unwillingness to follow the law, nor amount to impermissible political endorsement." Jeffrey M. Shaman ET AL., *Judicial Conduct and Ethics* §10.17.1 (2nd ed. 1995 & Supp. 1997). If, however, the contents of a judge's commentary demonstrate a predisposition on the factual and legal merits of a "reasonably litigated issue," the judge should not hear a case concerning the matter. Clarence W. Wolfram, *Modern Legal Ethics* §17.5 (1986). Responsible methods to be used by a judge expressing views on law reform or a legal issue include preparing dissenting opinions, petitioning the state supreme court for changes in the rules of procedure, submitting suggested changes to state bar committees, participating in Committee on Legal Education seminars, and actively taking part in the state and local conferences of judges. *See Gridley*, 417 So.2d at 954 (citing *In re Kelly*, 238 So.2d 565, 569 [Fla. 1970]).

E. Speech of Candidates for Judicial Office. Independent of sitting judges, a judicial candidate may not make any statement that "commit[s] or appear[s] to commit the candidate with respect to cases, controversies or issues that are likely to come before the court." *Model Code* Canon 5A(3)(d)(ii). In adhering to this express prohibition, however, a judicial candidate may pledge improvement to court administration, comment privately to other judges or court personnel, and "respond to personal attacks or attacks on the candidate's record as long as the response does not violate Section 5A(3)(d)." *Id.* at Commentary to Canon 5A(3)(d); *Id.* at 5A(3)(e). Where making public statements that may lend the appearance of bias, a judicial candidate should stress his or her obligation to uphold the law regardless of personal opinion. *Id.* at Commentary to 5A(3)(d). *See also Pennsylvania Code* Canon 7B (setting boundaries on permissible judicial campaign conduct); *New Jersey Code* Canon 7 (same). Courts considering the validity of state provisions regulating the speech of judicial candidates have struggled to balance the need for judicial independence with the rights reserved to judicial candidates as citizens entitled to freedom of expression. *See, e.g., Stretton v. Disciplinary Board of the Supreme Court of Pennsylvania*, 944 F.2d 137 (3d Cir. 1991); *Buckley v. Illinois Judicial Inquiry Board*, 997 F.2d 224 (7th Cir. 1997).

In *Stretton*, 944 F.2d at 137, the Court of Appeals for the Third Circuit upheld as constitutional a Pennsylvania Code of Judicial Conduct provision prohibiting a judicial candidate's announcement of "his views on disputed legal or political issues." *Id.* at 141. In reaching its conclusion, the court noted that the Pennsylvania restriction did not violate the First Amendment where the state had a "compelling interest in the integrity of its judiciary" and its restriction on political speech did not "unnecessarily curtail protected speech." *Id.* at 144. Accordingly, the court looked to the public's need for judicial impartiality as a justification for the limitation of the expression of judicial candidates:

> The public has a right to expect that a court will make an assessment of the facts based on the evidence submitted in each case, and that the law will be applied regardless of the personal views of the judge. Taking a position in advance of litigation would inhibit the judge's ability to consider the matter impartially. Even if he or she could reach the correct result in a given case, the campaign announcement would leave the impression that . . . the case was prejudged rather than adjudicated through a proper application of the law to facts impartially determined.

Id.

Alternatively, in *Buckley*, 997 F.2d at 224, the Court of Appeals for the Seventh Circuit held that Illinois could not prevent a judicial candidate, during an election, from "announc[ing] his views on disputed legal or political issues." *Id.* at 225. The court recognized that its decision created "undoubted tension" with the Third Circuit's decision in *Stretton*, and admitted that "the principle of impartial justice . . . is strong enough to entitle government to restrict the freedom of speech of participants in the judicial process." *Id.* at 231. The court concluded, nonetheless, that the Illinois proscription was invalid where it was "so sweeping that only complete silence would comply with a literal . . . interpretation of the rule." *Id.*

To date, the Supreme Court has chosen not to settle the conflict existing at the circuit court level on the issue of permissible speech by judicial candidates. Still, as both the *Stretton* and *Buckley* courts made clear, in order to maintain an open-minded and unbiased judiciary, a judicial candidate should temper any campaign statements that seem to "leave the impression that a case ha[s] been prejudged." *See Stretton*, 944 F.2d at 142; *Buckley*, 997 F.2d at 230–31. Given the unsettled nature of the law in this particular area, a judicial candidate should avoid making any statement that asserts a bias for a particular side of a political issue.

III. CONCLUSION

Subject to the canons of judicial ethics, a judge does not possess an unlimited right to free speech. Clearly, a judge risks censure when he or she speaks about the merits of a matter pending in any court. Furthermore, a judge may face disciplinary sanction for speech otherwise acceptable from other citizens where "the state has a compelling interest in protecting the good reputation of the judiciary." *In re Kaiser*, 759 P.2d 392, 399 (Wash. 1988)(judge disciplined for speech discussing political party affiliation and attorneys in pending case). These restrictions on judicial free speech, however, should not be translated as an absolute ban on all forms of extrajudicial speech.

Independent of statements on pending matters, judges maintain a reasonable degree of freedom where desiring to speak publicly. As expressly stated in the various codes of judicial conduct, a judge may speak to educate the public on court procedure or address the law, legal system, or administration of justice. Additionally, a judge may speak to remedy public misconception about a ruling or address criticism which, if not countered, could diminish public confidence in the judiciary among members of a particular community. Finally, a judge may offer his or her opinion on a controversial legal matter so long as that opinion does not indicate a bias that would affect a case likely to come before his or her court. Seemingly, public judicial speech gives rise to sanction only where it does "measurable damage to the court's dignity, available time and energy, or appearance of impartiality." Jeffrey M. Shaman ET AL., *Judicial Conduct and Ethics* §10.07 (2nd ed. 1995 & Supp. 1997).

Although an unequivocal proscription on all forms of judicial expression might allay public fears of judicial bias and self-interest in the short run, such a measure will ultimately work to the detriment of both judges and those served by the judicial system. A judge who, using discretion, participates in public debate will maintain the practical knowledge of the public necessary to hand down practical legal decisions. Likewise, a judge with a qualified right to speak publicly and responsibly may enhance public confidence in the judiciary. Judge Kaufman, a drafter of the 1972 Model Code of Judicial Conduct, believed that an appropriate code of conduct would "encourage, rather than discourage, judicial activities that exceed the four corners of cases presented for disposition." Talbot D'Alemberte, *Searching for the Limits of Judicial Free Speech*, 61 TUL. L. REV.

611, 628 (1987). In an ever-changing world marred by fluctuating faith in the judiciary, Judge Kaufman's thoughts on extrajudicial activity and speech best state the need for qualified judicial freedom of expression:

> There are times when we need men who can feel and understand what goes on in the world about them; we shall not find such men in a gray "bureaucracy" divorced from all outside activities and interests . . . [T]here are times when we need men who are not afraid to roar should the occasion demand it.

Id. Upon this premise and subject only to the per se rules found in the respective codes of judicial conduct, a judge who wishes to speak publicly is limited only by his or her own discretion and common sense. *See* William G. Ross, *Extrajudicial Speech: Charting the Boundaries of Propriety,* 2 GEO. J. LEGAL ETHICS *589, 642* (1989).

Appendix C:
Response to Criticism of Judges[*]

American Bar Association
Judicial Division Lawyers Conference and
Special Committee on Judicial Independence

The Lawyers Conference of the Judicial Division of the American Bar Association (ABA) has given the lawyers and the courts of America an exceptionally good opportunity to insure that all Americans have a better understanding of the operation of the judicial system, the courts and the judges. The Special Committee on Judicial Independence was proud to cosponsor this measure in the ABA House of Delegates when adopted as ABA policy in February 1998.

There is a strong and understandable inclination on the part of lawyers to shy away from their ethical responsibility to protect the courts from unjust and untrue criticism, particularly when the judge involved is ethically prevented from commenting.

---

[*] *Response to Criticism of Judges*, written by the American Bar Association Judicial Division Lawyers Conference and Special Committee on Judicial Independence, was originally published by the American Bar Association as a booklet in July 1998. Copyright © 1998 American Bar Association. All rights reserved. Reprinted by permission.

This concise and well thought out model plan charts a course for appropriate response beginning with a policy statement on why a plan is needed, when a response to criticism should be made by the bar and how to implement the policy and the plan. The plan will serve not only the courts and judges involved in the particular incident, but will provide a basis for community dialogue and education that can strengthen public understanding of the crucial role played by an independent judiciary in a democracy governed by law.

Judges and lawyers across the country should review the ABA plan and then move enthusiastically to put their own bar association plan into action to respond vigorously to unjust or untrue criticism. The benefits to the individual lawyers, the courts and the communities that they serve will far outweigh the efforts required to put the record straight.

William S. Sessions
Chair, ABA Special Committee on Judicial Independence

July 1998

PREFACE: RESPONDING TO CRITICISM OF JUDGES

American judges do important work that is not always clearly understood or adequately appreciated. The Bar has a special responsibility to ensure that judges, as essential leaders of the legal system, are not only treated fairly and with appropriate dignity, but that misunderstandings of the law and the role of judges are addressed and clarified. Our goal is to develop a responsible dialogue that does not end with the Bar. The legal community must work cooperatively, hand in hand, with civic groups and involved citizens to ensure that the judiciary remains a highly respected institution. Activities recommended in this publication should also be coordinated with the courts themselves, acting through their public information officers. It is only through a fully integrated informed dialogue that inevitable criticism can be transformed into a vehicle for furthering understanding of our justice system.

While many of the references to Bar Associations in this publication refer to state and local Bars, national Bars and specialized Bar Associations can also provide effective responses. We hope that this publication will be used by all associations of lawyers to foster further understanding of the role of our judges. So too, references to criticism of "judges" should include criticism of all judicial officers, whether state or federal. This publication does not limit itself to "unjust" criticism of judges, but is meant to guide appropriate responses to a variety of criticisms. There are, in fact, limited instances where it may be appropriate for the judge concerned to respond directly as well. However, these situations are limited, should occur only after careful consideration of the ethical restrictions on public comment and, therefore, are not assisted by this pamphlet.

This revision owes a tremendous debt to the original Subcommittee on Unjust Criticism of the Bench that prepared the 1986 version of this protocol. Recent events, however, convinced the Lawyers Conference that revision was warranted. We thank the many state and local Bars that responded to our survey concerning activities in this area, and the many reviewers who offered excellent suggestions that we have included wherever possible. We also thank the California Judges Association for sharing their insights into the issues presented. The Lawyers Conference especially thanks Larry Polansky for taking pen to paper and pushing this protocol to completion. Finally, Judicial Division Chair Norma L. Shapiro, who encouraged this work and entrusted the Lawyers Conference with its development, deserves a special thank you, as do the members of the Lawyers Conference subcommittee who reviewed outlines and participated in numerous meetings.

These recommendations were prepared with judges in mind. Judges inevitably will be involved in deciding difficult and unpopular cases. The ethical dilemmas that judges face were considered carefully. Our protocols outlined here are consistent with the American Bar Association's various model provisions governing the conduct of lawyers and judges. We hope that our work will promote appreciation, respect and understanding for the unique role of the judiciary in our government.

Marla N. Greenstein, Chair
ABA Judicial Division
Lawyers Conference

July, 1997

MODEL PROGRAM OUTLINE FOR STATE, LOCAL AND TERRITORIAL BAR ASSOCIATIONS: SUGGESTED PROGRAM FOR THE APPROPRIATE RESPONSE TO CRITICISM OF JUDGES AND COURTS

I. POLICY STATEMENT

A. Why a Plan Is Needed. The effectiveness of the administration of justice depends in a large measure on public confidence. The reporting of inaccurate or unjust criticism of judges, courts, or our system of justice by the news media erodes public confidence and weakens the administration of justice. It is vital that nonlitigants as well as litigants believe that the courts, their procedures and decisions are fair and impartial.

Generally, it is undesirable for a judge to answer criticism of her or his own actions by appearing in the news media. This policy has been developed to insure the dignity of the administration of justice, to prevent interference with pending litigation, and to reaffirm the commitment to an independent judiciary, a judiciary dedicated to decision-making based on facts and law as presented.

The risk is apparent that a response by a judge to criticism of her or his own actions may be perceived by the community as "self-serving" and/or as a "defensive" position which fails for lack of credibility. Also, since there invariably is more at stake than an individual judge's ego or feelings, the bar should recognize the negative reflection on the dignity of the administration of justice if a judge should make an intemperate or emotional response to such criticism.

Further, a judge's comment contains the potential of reflecting on pending litigation and may have an undesirable effect on litigants. In addition, an inappropriate response may give encouragement to those who would control the judiciary by intimidation and thus weaken the independence of the judiciary.

Finally, judges subjected to criticism may be prevented from responding by ethical restrictions relating to a judge's ability to engage in public comment, a judge's need to maintain the appearance of impartiality and the impropriety of ex parte communications. Therefore, cooperation of lawyers and bar associations is necessary to successfully meet and accurately, quickly and fairly respond to criticism of judges and courts. This model plan implements the American Bar Association Model Code of Professional Responsibility (EC 8-6) and the Model

Rules of Professional Conduct (Comment Model Rule 8.2) which entitle adjudicatory officials to the support and the early and accurate response where their official actions are criticized.

B. When Action in Response to Criticism Should Be Taken by the Bar. Implementation of this plan is selective. To avoid infringing on the freedom of the press, this plan is designed to effect a response on behalf of the judiciary and courts to criticism that is serious as well as inaccurate or unjustified. There should be no attempt to prevent criticism, but inaccurate or unjust criticism should be answered through an organized public information program. Such criticism typically results from a lack of understanding of the system—the reason for a decision, a sentence or a courtroom action.

The bar should respond publicly to attacks upon a judge only in the following two instances:

1. a public utterance that is unwarranted or an unjust attack on a judge in relation to specific cases, regardless of the source of the attack, or,

2. any "unwarranted" or "unjust" attack or series of attacks on a judge or court which may adversely affect the administration of justice.

Guidelines to determine when a response to criticism is appropriate in a particular case are provided in Section II.C. of the Bar Association Model Program below.

C. Implementation of the Policy and Plan. Because of the restraints placed on judges both by tradition and by the Code of Judicial Conduct, and the ethical obligations imposed by the ABA Model Code of Professional Responsibility and the ABA Model Rules of Professional Conduct for lawyers, it is recommended that state, local and territorial bar associations adopt a policy and program to provide appropriate and timely responses to criticism of judges and courts.

The following are suggestions for implementation of such a policy and program:

1. Adopt a policy statement that supports the position that judges should generally not respond to criticism and that the bar, state,

local and territorial, should, when appropriate, respond to criticism of judges and courts.

2. Adopt a structure and process for receiving, screening and evaluating criticisms of judges and/or courts. (See Sections II.A. and B. for suggested program.)

3. Develop guidelines to determine when the bar association should respond. (See Section II.C. for suggested guidelines.)

4. Since timing is key to responding, provide a method whereby the bar can respond quickly, accurately and with authority. (See Section II.D.)

5. Coordinate state, local and territorial bar association programs to broaden the base of the response. In some cases, it may be appropriate for the state, local and territorial bar to respond. In other cases, only one or the other should respond.

6. Coordinate the program with the appropriate federal, state, local or territorial judiciary and recommend to other local bar associations the implementation of a comparable policy and program.

7. Provide federal, state, local and territorial judges and court officials with copies of the program and encourage them to contact named bar officials to alert them to media criticism which the judge(s) and/or court believe to be deserving of an appropriate bar association response.

II. Model Program for State and Local Bar Associations

A. Purposes and Functions of Program. The primary purposes and functions of the program are:

(a) To deal with errors in reporting or inaccuracies in reporting criticism of judges, courts and/or the administration of justice, as further provided in this policy statement;

(b) To be available to the news media as a resource for obtaining information concerning judicial activities, court process or other technical or legal information about the administration of justice;

(c) To encourage broad dissemination of information to the public about noteworthy achievements and improvements within the justice system;

(d) To suggest means by which judges and lawyers can improve the public image of the legal system; and

(e) To generally seek a better understanding within the community of the legal system and the role of lawyers and judges.

B. Referral Procedure

1. Assign the task of administering the program to an appropriate designee, committee and/or contact person.

2. All referrals of criticism of judges and courts should be forwarded to the appropriate contact person at the state, local and/or territorial bar association headquarters. The referral may be oral or written, but in all cases the referring person must be available to assist in gathering background and factual information and must present written material when requested. All referrals should be undertaken with the specific permission of the judge or court criticized with the understanding that the judge or court also will assist in gathering necessary information for the bar association to evaluate.

3. The contact person assigned should immediately begin to gather all pertinent background and factual information including a copy of the text (whether in live or print media) of the criticism.

4. The contact person then should immediately notify the president of the state, local or territorial bar association and the designee or chairperson of the committee assigned the overall responsibility.

5. The designee or committee chairperson should promptly investigate the underlying facts, discussing them to the extent possible

with other committee members and the judge involved, and then promptly prepare and release the response.

Upon securing approval of the president of the state, local or territorial bar association, the designee or committee chairperson may speak in the name of the association.

C. Guidelines to Determine When the Bar Should Respond

1. The following are the kinds of cases in which responding to criticism is appropriate, except in unusual circumstances:

   (a) When the criticism is serious and will most likely have more than a passing or de minimis negative effect in the community;

   (b) When the criticism displays a lack of understanding of the legal system or the role of the judge and is based at least partially on such misunderstanding; and

   (c) When the criticism is materially inaccurate; the inaccuracy should be a substantial part of the criticism so that the response does not appear to be "nitpicking."

2. The following factors should be considered in determining whether a response should be made in a close case and considered in every case in determining the type of response:

   (a) Whether a response would serve a public information purpose and not appear "nitpicking";

   (b) Whether the criticism adequately will be met by a response from some other appropriate source;

   (c) Whether the criticism substantially and negatively affects the judiciary or other parts of the legal system, or whether continuing discussion of the controversy would serve to lower public perceptions as to the dignity of the court, the judiciary or the judicial system;

   (d) Whether the criticism is directed at a particular judge but unjustly reflects on the judiciary generally, the court, or another element of the judicial system (e.g., grand jury, lawyers, probation, bail, etc.);

(e) Whether a response provides the opportunity to inform the public about an important aspect of the administration of justice (e.g., sentencing, bail, evidence rules, due process, fundamental rights, etc.);

(f) Whether a response would appear defensive or self-serving;

(g) Whether the critic is so obviously uninformed about the judicial system that a response can be made on a factual basis;

(h) Whether the criticism or report, although generally accurate, does not contain all or enough of the facts of the event or procedure reported to be fair to the judge or matter being criticized;

(i) Whether the overall criticism is not justified or fair;

(j) Whether the criticism, while not appearing in the local press, pertains to a local judge or a local matter;

(k) Whether the timing of the response is especially important and can be best met by the committee.

3. The following are the kinds of cases in which response to criticism IS NOT appropriate, except in unusual circumstances:

(a) When the criticism is a fair comment or opinion;

(b) When the feud is between the critic and the judge on a personal level;

(c) When the criticism is vague or the product of innuendo, except when the innuendo is clear;

(d) Where criticism raises issues of judicial ethics appropriate for presentation to the Judicial Inquiry or Disciplinary body;

(e) When a lengthy investigation to develop the true facts is necessary;

(f) When the response would prejudice a matter at issue in a pending proceeding;

(g) When the controversy is insignificant;

(h) When the criticism arises during a political campaign and the bar's response may be construed as an endorsement of a particular candidate for judicial office.

D. *The Response*

1. TIMING. To be effective, the response must be prompt, but accurate. If at all possible, the response should be made within 24–48 hours of publication of the criticism or report, especially keeping in mind the deadline(s) of the news media that reported the original criticism. Ideally a response can be more immediate and occur even before publication, for example, through direct communication with a reporter or editor which may clarify the facts and serve to defuse the situation.

2. FORM OF RESPONSE. The form and manner of the response should be such that it will receive the same exposure and notoriety as the criticism. A letter to the editor is an effective form of response, because it is the most likely to be printed fully and accurately. Press releases are usually more subject to editing and are frequently viewed as less credible, and pamphlets are too elaborate. Television or radio talk shows may be effective forms of response but should be used more cautiously and sparingly. In some circumstances, press conferences provide effective means to disseminate a response. Direct communication with reporters and editors intended to clarify facts and present another position is encouraged. Whenever possible, any response should be coordinated with the court public information officer if one exists.

3. DRAFTING CONSIDERATIONS.

(a) The response should be a concise, accurate, "to the point" statement, devoid of emotional, inflammatory or subjective language;

(b) The statement should be informative and not argumentative or condescending;

(c) The statement should include a correction of the inaccuracies, citing facts and relevant authorities where appropriate;

(d) The statement should be written in lay terms suitable for inclusion in a newspaper story;

(e) Where appropriate, the statement should include the point that the judge had no control or discretion (e.g., decision required by state law);

(f) Where appropriate, the statement should include an explanation of the process involved (e.g., sentencing, bail, temporary restraining order, etc.);

(g) The statement should not attempt to discredit the critic, that is, attack the competence, good faith, motives or associates of the critic;

(h) The statement should not provide evidence that the critic has hit a nerve, causing overreaction;

(i) The statement should not defend the indefensible;

(j) The committee should consider the cause of the criticism or controversy, which might not be immediately apparent.

4.   CONTENT OF THE RESPONSE. The following points may be included in a typical response:

(a) Identify the criticism and its source.

(b) We may frequently disagree with the decisions and actions of public officials, including judges. The federal and state constitutions protect our right to express that disagreement.

(c) We must remember that judges have no control over what cases come before them, but they must decide each and all of those cases. Judges must follow the law as established by higher courts. One side always loses in every lawsuit.

(d) Because of their position, judges are not wholly free to defend themselves and it is ordinarily not appropriate for them to personally answer charges made against them or their decisions (C.J.C. 2.A., 3, 3.B.7., 3.B.9., 4.A.1., 4.B.; C.P.R., EC 8-6).

(e) Lawyers, under the Code of Professional Responsibility and the Model Rules of Professional Conduct, have a duty to defend judges against unjust criticism (EC 8-6; Comment M.R. 8.2).

(f) Avoid taking a position on the merits of the controversy, since to do so will probably eliminate any educational benefit the balance of the points might have for those who agree with the criticism.

(g) The need for independent judges, who will not be influenced by criticism of them or their decisions, requires that the organized bar remind both lawyers and the public of these facts.

(h) The law has established appellate courts so that decisions of judges may be reviewed and, if appropriate, corrected. Our present judicial system provides for change in the law through legislative action or by constitutional revision.

5. RECOMMENDED EDUCATION PROGRAMS. An expanded public education program could be undertaken to familiarize the public with such fundamental concepts as:

(a) The rule of law;

(b) The need to preserve judicial independence and integrity;

(c) The organization and responsibilities of the judicial system; and

(d) The role of the lawyer in society.

Balancing Act

Legislative Power and Judicial Independence

THE REPORT OF THE CITIZENS FOR INDEPENDENT COURTS TASK FORCE ON THE ROLE OF THE LEGISLATURE IN SETTING THE POWER AND JURISDICTION OF THE COURTS

Members of the
Task Force*

Reporter

Erwin Chemerinksy, Sydney M. Irmas Professor of Public Interest Law, Legal Ethics, and Political Science, University of Southern California

Members

Pat Brady, Representative and former Director, League of Women Voters of the United States

Daan Braveman, Dean, Syracuse University College of Law

Jack E. Brown, Esq., Founder, Brown & Bain

The Honorable William F. Clinger, Senior Fellow, Johns Hopkins University; former Member of Congress (R-PA)

Jay Conison, Dean, Valparaiso University School of Law

Francis J. Conte, Dean, University of Dayton School of Law

---

* Affiliations of members listed for purposes of identification only. The views expressed in this report do not necessarily reflect the views of the institutions with which the members are affiliated.

Robert M. Cooper, Esq.

Barry Friedman, Professor of Law, Vanderbilt University Law School

Michael J. Gerhardt, Professor of Law, College of William and Mary, Marshall-Wythe School of Law; Dean Emeritus, Case Western Reserve University, Franklin T. Backus School of Law

The Honorable John J. Gibbons, former Chief Judge, U.S. Court of Appeals for the Third Circuit; Partner, Gibbons, Del Deo, Dolan, Griffinger & Vecchione

Howard O. Hunter, Dean, Emory University School of Law

Carolyn Jefferson-Jenkins, Ph.D., President, League of Women Voters of the United States

The Honorable Robert W. Kastenmeier, former Member of Congress (D-WI); former Chair, House Judiciary Subcommittee on Courts, Civil Liberties, and the Administration of Justice; former Chair, National Commission on Judicial Discipline and Removal

Stephan Kline, Director of Health Care Policy, United Jewish Communities; former Legislative Counsel, Alliance for Justice

Mark Frederick Kozlowski, Esq., Staff Attorney, Brennan Center for Justice

Richard A. Matasar, Dean and Levin, Mabie & Levin Professor of Law, Fredric A. Levin College of Law, University of Florida

Elliot M. Mincberg, Esq., Vice President, General Counsel, and Legal Director, People for the American Way Foundation

The Honorable William A. Norris, former Judge, U.S. Court of Appeals for the Ninth Circuit

Robert S. Peck, Esq., Senior Director for Legal Affairs and Policy Research, Association of Trial Lawyers of America

Henry H. Perritt, Jr., Dean, Chicago-Kent College of Law, Illinois Institute of Technology

Donald J. Polden, Dean, University of Memphis, Cecil C. Humphreys School of Law

Peter M. Shane, Professor and former Dean, University of Pittsburgh School of Law

Steven R. Shapiro, Legal Director, American Civil Liberties Union

Ronald H. Weich, Esq., Partner, Zuckerman, Spaeder, Goldstein, Taylor & Kolker, L.L.P.; former Chief Counsel to Senator Edward M. Kennedy, Senate Judiciary Committee

Task Force
Recommendations

1. Congress and state legislatures should heed constitutional limits when considering proposals to restrict the powers and jurisdiction of the courts.

2. Legislatures should refrain from restricting court jurisdiction in an effort to control substantive judicial decisions in a manner that violates separation of powers, due process, or other constitutional principles.

3. Legislatures should not attempt to control substantive judicial decisions by enacting legislation that restricts court jurisdiction over particular types of cases.

4. Legislatures should refrain from enacting laws that command a particular interpretation of federal or state constitutions.

5. Legislatures should not restrict remedies that courts may impose when the restrictions on remedies have the effect of leaving constitutional or other rights with inadequate redress.

6. Legislatures should ensure that courts have adequate resources and judges to perform their essential functions. Legislatures should recognize that resource limits in retaliation to specific substantive decisions are undesirable and may be unconstitutional.

7. Legislatures should refrain from restricting access to the courts
    and should take necessary affirmative steps to ensure adequate
    access to the courts for all Americans.

Report of the Task Force on the Role of the Legislature in Setting the Power and Jurisdiction of the Courts

Introduction

The judiciary, at the federal and state levels, is both independent of and interdependent on the other branches of government. At the federal level, for example, the assurances of life tenure and salary protection found in Article III of the Constitution are meant to provide federal judges a high degree of independence in deciding the cases that come before them. At the same time, Article III leaves for Congress to decide whether lower federal courts shall exist and accords it substantial control over the courts' jurisdiction. For instance, Congress has set an amount-in-controversy in diversity suits since the first judiciary act in 1789. Indeed, all three branches of government are assured by the federal and state constitutions a degree of independence in some realms and interdependence in other areas so as to create checks and balances.

Independence of the judiciary is vitally important. Alexander Hamilton, quoting Montesquieu, forcefully declared: "For I agree, that 'there is no liberty, if the power of judging be not separated from legislative and executive powers . . . . [T]he complete independence of the courts of justice is peculiarly essential in a limited constitution.'"[1] The Constitution's framers were acutely concerned about judicial independence because of their experience with judges in the colonies who served at the pleasure of the King and were widely distrusted.[2] It is not hyperbole to say that freedom and liberty depend on the existence of an independent judiciary.

The goal of this Task Force has been to identify basic principles as to when legislatures act unconstitutionally in setting the powers and jurisdiction of the courts. Not all legislative actions directed at the judiciary should be regarded as unconstitutional.[3] As described below, however, the Task Force is unanimous in its conclusion that some legislative acts restricting the powers and jurisdiction of the courts are unconstitutional. Additionally, the Task Force believes that some legislative actions, even if constitutional, are undesirable.

CONCLUSIONS AND RECOMMENDATIONS

1. The ability of Congress to restrict the powers and jurisdiction of the federal courts is limited by Article III of the Constitution, as well as by the separation of powers, due process of law, and other constitutional provisions. Similarly, the ability of state legislatures to restrict the powers and jurisdiction of state courts is limited by provisions in state constitutions as well as by the guarantee of due process of law in the United States Constitution.

Separation of powers protects judicial independence. At the federal level and in every state, the judiciary is a coequal branch of government. Justice Lewis F. Powell explained that the doctrine of separation of powers can be violated in two ways: "One branch may interfere impermissibly with the other's performance of its constitutionally assigned function. Alternatively, the doctrine may be violated when one branch assumes a function that more properly is entrusted to another."[4] In other words, legislative actions unconstitutionally violate separation of powers if they keep the judiciary from performing its duties or if the legislature takes over responsibilities assigned to the judiciary.

Second, due process of law is a basis for constitutional protection of judicial independence. For example, legislative actions that deny a meaningful hearing before a neutral decision-maker violate procedural due process. The Supreme Court long has declared that the very essence of due process of law is a fair hearing before an impartial decision-maker.[5] Over a century ago, the Supreme Court declared that due process "is a restraint on the legislative as well as on the executive and judicial powers of the government, and cannot be so construed as to leave congress free to make any 'due process of law,' by its mere will."[6] For instance, the Court has explained "that the Due Process Clauses protect civil litigants who seek recourse in the courts, either as defendants hoping to protect their property or as plaintiffs attempting to redress grievances."[7]

This is not to imply that these are the only constitutional limits on legislative control over the judiciary. Article I, section 9 of the Constitution directly limits Congress's authority over the federal courts in its declaration that "[t]he Privilege of the Writ of Habeas Corpus shall not be suspended, unless when in Cases of Rebellion or Invasion the public Safety may require it." Article III limits congressional authority to define the crime of treason by specifying that "[t]reason against the United States shall constitute only in levying War against them, or in adhering to their Enemies giving them aid and comfort."

Likewise, provisions of the Bill of Rights limit the legislature's control over the judiciary. The First Amendment's right "to petition the Government for a redress of grievances" can be violated by legislative actions denying availability of the judiciary. The Sixth and Seventh Amendments' guarantees of jury trials in criminal and civil cases also limits an area of legislative control over judicial procedures. For instance, an attempt by Congress to restrict the fact-finding power of juries, in common law or statutory cases, would run afoul of these constitutional protections.

State constitutions also mandate separation of powers and independently protect rights such as due process, a right to petition government for redress of grievances, and a right to a jury trial. In addition, thirty-eight states have constitutional provisions that require a right to a remedy for injuries and violations of rights. These provisions, too, limit the scope of legislative control over the judiciary.

Recommendation: Congress and state legislatures should heed constitutional limits when considering proposals to restrict the powers and jurisdiction of the courts.

2. Separation of powers, due process, and other constitutional provisions limit the ability of legislatures to restrict court jurisdiction in an effort to control substantive judicial decisions.

The Task Force also is unanimous in its view that there are some constitutional limits on the ability of a legislature to restrict court jurisdiction in an effort to control substantive judicial decisions. In response to controversial Supreme Court decisions, there have been proposals to curtail federal court jurisdiction to hear particular types of issues. For example, during the 1950s, the Supreme Court invalidated some loyalty oaths for government workers and attorneys.[8] In response, the Jennings-Butler Bill was introduced in the Senate to prevent review of State Board of Bar Examiners' decisions concerning who could practice law in a state.[9] During the 1960s, in response to the Supreme Court decisions ordering reapportionment of state legislatures,[10] proposals were made to preclude federal courts from hearing constitutional challenges to apportionment.

Altogether, between 1953 and 1968, over sixty bills were introduced into Congress to restrict federal court jurisdiction over particular topics.[11] During the 1980s, there were proposals in Congress to prevent federal courts from hearing cases involving challenges to state laws permitting school prayers or state laws restricting access to abortions.[12] Bills of this sort have continued to be introduced into Congress throughout the 1990s.

Similar proposals have been advanced at the state level. For example, after the New Hampshire Supreme Court ruled in 1997 that the state's system of funding public education was unconstitutional, the governor and state legislature drafted constitutional amendments restricting the supreme court's oversight of school funding.[13] A similar proposal to restrict the jurisdiction of Ohio courts was introduced after the Ohio Supreme Court declared the Ohio system for funding public schools unconstitutional.[14] In Washington, in 1997, a bill was introduced to amend the state constitution to allow the legislature to overrule decisions of the state supreme court on issues of constitutional interpretation.[15]

Task Force members have differing views about the scope and source of the constitutional limit on the legislature's power in this area. For instance, many, but not all, of the Task Force members believe that restrictions on jurisdiction become unconstitutional, as argued by Professor Henry Hart a half century ago, when "they destroy the essential role of the Supreme Court in the constitutional system."[16] Others rely on a reading of the Vesting Clause of Article III, which places judicial power—the power to decide cases—in the hands of the courts alone. Although Task Force members may disagree about the nature of the constitutional limit on a legislature's ability to restrict judicial jurisdiction, all believe that a constitutional limit exists.

Congressional limits on the ability of federal courts to review constitutional issues can undermine the federal judiciary's crucial role in the constitutional system. For example, the Constitution's structure would be compromised if Congress could enact a law and immunize that law from constitutional judicial review.

Task Force members believe that some legislative actions regulating jurisdiction would be clearly unconstitutional. For example, it is unconstitutional for a legislature to require that a court render a judgment for one party or another in a particular case. Also, it is unconstitutional for a legislature to dictate an unconstitutional result or decision. No court may render a decision that it believes violates the Constitution and a legislative command to do so is obviously unconstitutional.

Moreover, a legislature cannot vest jurisdiction in courts to deal with some issues in a matter and prohibit it from considering the constitutionality of the law that it is enforcing. For instance, it would be unconstitutional for a legislature to assign the courts with enforcing a criminal statute, but preclude them from deciding the constitutionality of this law.

Perhaps most important, legislation precluding court jurisdiction that prevents the judiciary from invalidating unconstitutional laws is impermissible. Neither Congress nor state legislatures may use their powers to keep courts from performing their essential function of upholding the Constitution.

These constitutional limits, of course, are not exhaustive of all the situations where jurisdictional restrictions are unconstitutional. The Task Force is unanimous in its conclusion that separation of powers and due process, as well as other constitutional principles, limit the ability of legislatures to restrict court jurisdiction in an effort to control substantive judicial decisions.

Recommendation: Legislatures should refrain from restricting court jurisdiction in an effort to control substantive judicial decisions in a manner that violates separation of powers, due process, or other constitutional principles.

3. Legislative acts stripping courts of jurisdiction to hear particular types of cases in an effort to control substantive judicial decisions are undesirable and inappropriate in a democratic system with coequal branches of government.

Apart from the constitutionality of laws restricting federal court jurisdiction, the Task Force is unanimous in its view that such legislative actions are undesirable. Legislative restriction of jurisdiction in response to particular substantive decisions unduly politicizes the judicial process. At the federal level, limits on Supreme Court review undermine desirable uniformity in the interpretation of federal law. At every level of government, attempts by legislatures to control substantive outcomes by curtailing judicial jurisdiction are inappropriate, even if some believe that they may be constitutional. Indeed, it is striking that members of Citizens for Independent Courts reflecting a broad ideological range—from, for example, Leonard Leo of the Federalist Society to Steven R. Shapiro of the American Civil Liberties Union—agree that restrictions on jurisdiction to achieve substantive changes in the law are unwise and undesirable policy. The Task Force is thus unanimous in urging self-restraint by legislatures in not restricting court jurisdiction in response to particular rulings.

Recommendation: Legislatures should not attempt to control substantive judicial decisions by enacting legislation that restricts court jurisdiction over particular types of cases.

4. Legislatures may not command a particular judicial interpretation of the Constitution; such legislation is undesirable and unconstitutional.

Judicial independence also is compromised by legislation that directs the courts to interpret the Constitution in a particular manner. Central to the judicial power, at both the federal and state levels, is the ability of judges to decide the meaning of the United States Constitution and state constitutions. Long ago, in *Marbury v. Madison*, the Court declared: "It is emphatically the province and duty of the judicial department to say what the law is."[17] Legislation commanding a particular interpretation of the Constitution is undesirable and unconstitutional.

In *United States v. Klein*, more than a century ago, the Supreme Court held that Congress cannot constitutionally direct particular substantive results.[18] The Court explained that legislation that directs the Court to decide cases in a particular manner "passe[s] the limit which separates the legislative power from the judicial power."[19]

For example, the House of Representatives recently passed H.R. 1501, a bill that directs the judiciary to interpret the First Amendment in a particular manner. The bill seeks to permit the posting of the Ten Commandments on government property.[20] The bill accomplishes this by declaring that the Tenth Amendment should be interpreted as leaving this choice to state governments: "The power to display the Ten Commandments on or within property owned or administered by the several States or political subdivisions thereof is hereby declared to be among the powers reserved to the States respectively."[21] Moreover, the bill directs the courts to interpret the Constitution to uphold the law. Section (c) of the bill declares: "The courts constituted, ordained, and established by the Congress shall exercise the judicial power in a manner consistent with the foregoing declarations."

The Task Force is unanimous in concluding that such legislative commands to the judiciary to interpret the Constitution in a particular manner are unwise and unconstitutional.[22]

Recommendation: Legislatures should refrain from enacting laws that command a particular interpretation of federal or state constitutions.

5. Restrictions on remedies are distinct from jurisdictional limitations; restrictions on remedies are generally undesirable and unconstitutional when they have the effect of leaving constitutional or other rights with inadequate redress.

In *Marbury v. Madison*, Chief Justice John Marshall declared that "[t]he very essence of civil liberty certainly consists in the right of every individual to claim the protection of the laws, whenever he receives an injury."[23] Although there are instances where the law does not fulfill this command, such as because of sovereign immunity, remedies are essential if rights are to have meaning and effect.

While Task Force members may disagree over the extent of a legislature's power to restrict remedies, the Task Force is unanimous that there are constitutional limits on the ability of legislatures to preclude remedies. At the federal level, where the Constitution is interpreted to vest individual rights, it is unconstitutional for Congress to preclude the courts from effectively remedying deprivations of those rights.

For instance, the Fourth Amendment's prohibition of unreasonable searches and seizures clearly was intended to create a remedy against unlawful police behavior. The Fifth Amendment's takings clause requires that just compensation be available when the government uses its power to take private property. Likewise, equal protection was denied by state laws mandating segregation and courts constitutionally had to have the authority to provide an effective remedy.

More generally, courts must have the authority to enjoin ongoing violations of constitutional rights. For example, legislatures cannot preclude courts from enjoining laws that violate the First Amendment's guarantee of freedom of speech.

Congressional action that precludes effective remedies in such situations is unconstitutional. Moreover, apart from constitutionality, such attempts by Congress to prevent federal courts from providing necessary remedies for constitutional violations are undesirable. The Task Force urges self-restraint by Congress in this regard.

Restrictions on remedies at the state level can violate state constitutions. Indeed, thirty-eight states have constitutional provisions that require a right to a remedy for injuries and violations of rights. Preclusion of effective remedies, for common law wrongs as well as for constitutional violations, violates these provisions.

Recommendation: Legislatures should not restrict remedies that courts may impose when the restrictions on remedies have the effect of leaving constitutional or other rights with inadequate redress.

6. Although legislatures have great latitude in determining the resources available to the judiciary, legislative actions that undermine the institutional functioning of the courts are undesirable and unconstitutional.

The judiciary depends on the legislature for necessities essential for its operation. The most obvious example is funding. If a legislature were to refuse funding of the judiciary, or to fund it inadequately, the judiciary would be compromised in its ability to function. Additionally, judicial independence would be further compromised if this were done in response to particular rulings. For example, the governor of New Hampshire recently proposed cutting the funding of the New Hampshire courts in response to the state supreme court's decision finding that the state's system for funding public schools violates the state's constitution.[24]

The Task Force recognizes the constitutional role for the legislature in determining the level of funding for the judiciary. Legislatures undoubtedly have great discretion in this regard. Moreover, there is an obvious need for judicial restraint in ordering legislatures to provide more resources for courts. However, the Task Force is unanimous in its conclusion that it is undesirable for the legislature to restrict funds for the judiciary in retaliation to specific court decisions. Moreover, at some point, where restrictions on funding are so great as to disable the judiciary from performing its basic tasks, the legislative action violates separation of powers.

Apart from the Constitution's requirements, the Task Force believes that legislatures should, as a matter of desirable public policy, ensure adequate funding for the judiciary so that it will be able to fulfill its duties. This includes a responsibility to ensure sufficient judges and sufficient resources so that the courts can deal with their caseloads in an effective and efficient manner. Moreover, at the federal level, restraint in adding additional work for the federal courts is desirable and any significant increases must be accompanied by necessary added resources and judges.

Recommendation: Legislatures should ensure that courts have adequate resources and judges to perform their essential functions. Legislatures should recognize that resource limits in retaliation to specific substantive decisions are undesirable and may be unconstitutional.

7. Legislation that restricts access to the courts and precludes individuals from using a judicial forum to vindicate rights is undesirable and unconstitutional.

Rights are meaningless without a forum in which they can be vindicated. Therefore, access to the courts at both the federal and state levels is essential in order for rights to have effect. Although Task Force members may disagree about the desirability of particular legislative actions, the Task Force is unanimous that access to the judiciary is crucial if the courts are to perform their constitutional role. Legislatures have the duty to ensure meaningful access to the courts and legislative actions that preclude this are undesirable and unconstitutional.

The Task Force believes, for example, that legislatures should ensure adequate funding for legal services so that all in society have access to the judiciary. Similarly, the Task Force has grave concerns about laws that have the effect of cutting off access to the courts.

For example, the Prison Litigation Reform Act of 1995 limits the authority of federal courts to order systemic relief in prison condition cases, provides for the termination of injunctions issued by federal courts as remedies, and restricts the ability of federal courts to issue relief in prisoner cases.[25] Legislation of this sort undermines needed access to the courts.

Recommendation: Legislatures should refrain from restricting access to the courts and should take necessary affirmative steps to ensure adequate access to the courts for all Americans.

CONCLUSION

Judicial independence, vital in a democratic society, is compromised by legislative actions restricting the powers and jurisdiction of the judiciary. The Task Force is unanimous in its conclusion that federal and state legislatures act unwisely and unconstitutionally when they attempt to control substantive judicial decisions by restricting jurisdiction, controlling remedies, or by mandating that courts interpret the Constitution in a particular manner. The Task Force urges legislatures to exercise restraint in this area and to ensure that courts can perform their essential role in our constitutional democracy. This requires that courts have sufficient resources and that all litigants have adequate access to the courts.

NOTES

1. Alexander Hamilton, *The Federalist* No. 78, Clinton Rossiter, ed. (New York: New American Library, 1961), p. 466, quoting Montesquieu, *Spirit of Laws*, vol. I, p. 186.

2. *See* Charles Gardner Geyh, "The Origins and History of Federal Judicial Independence," in *An Independent Judiciary: Report of the ABA Commission on Separation of Powers and Judicial Independence,* American Bar Association, Washington, D.C., 1997, Appendix A.

3. *See, e.g., Report of the National Commission on Judicial Discipline and Removal* (1993), p. 16 ("Although . . . the constitutional provisions pertaining to judicial tenure and the power of the courts may be understood in terms of their underlying purpose of judicial independence, this is not to say that everything that could interfere with the work of an Article III judge or court is unconstitutional").

4. *INS v. Chadha,* 462 U.S. 919, 963 (1983) (Powell, J., concurring).

5. *See, e.g., Gibson v. Berryhill,* 411 U.S. 564 (1973).

6. *Murray's Lessee v. Hoboken Land & Improv. Co.,* 59 U.S. (18 How.) 272, 276 (1856); *see also Hutardo v. California,* 110 U.S. 516, 531 (1884).

7. *Logan v. Zimmerman Brush Co.,* 455 U.S. 422, 429 (1982). The specific issue of the legislature's ability to restrict the availability of remedies is discussed in Recommendation 4 (see pp. 218–19).

8. *See, e.g., Schware v. Board of Bar Examiners,* 353 U.S. 232 (1957); *Konigsberg v. State Bar,* 353 U.S. 252 (1957).

9. S. 3386, 85th Cong., 2d Sess. (1958); *see also* Shelden D. Elliott, *Court-Curbing Proposals in Congress,* 33 Notre Dame Law. 597 (1958).

10. *See, e.g., Reynolds v. Sims,* 377 U.S. 533 (1964).

11. Paul M. Bator, Daniel J. Meltzer, Paul J. Mishkin, and David L. Shapiro, *Hart and Wechsler's The Federal Courts and the Federal System,* 3d ed. (New York: Foundation Press, 1988), p. 377.

12. *See, e.g.,* S. 158, 97th Cong., 1st Sess. (1981); H.R. 3225, 97th Cong., 1st Sess. (1981) (bills restricting federal court jurisdiction in abortion cases); S. 481, 97th Cong., 1st Sess. (1981); H.R. 4756, 97th Cong., 1st Sess. (1981) (bills restricting federal court jurisdiction over cases that involve voluntary school prayers).

13. *See, e.g.,* Ralph Jimenez, "Judges, Lawyers Decry the Virulence of Attacks on High Court," *Boston Globe,* October 4, 1998, New Hampshire Weekly, p. 1.

14. Catherine Candisky, "2 Senators Propose to Amend State Constitution School-Funding Debate," *Columbus Dispatch,* March 4, 1999, p. 1A; Randy Ludlow, "School Call: Skip Courts Lawmakers Want Funding Control," *Cincinnati Post,* March 4, 1999, p. 7A.

15. "Defeat this Poor Attempt to Curb the Judiciary," *Seattle Times,* March 7, 1997, p. B4; Peter Callaghan, "Legislature 1997: Bill Would Let Legislature Override the Courts; Some Lawmakers Want the Final Say in Interpreting the State Constitution," *News Tribune,* March 3, 1997, p. A1.

16. Henry Hart, *The Power of Congress to Limit Jurisdiction of Federal Courts: An Exercise in Dialectic,* 66 Harv. L. Rev. 1362, 1402 (1953).

17. 5 U.S. (1 Cranch) 137, 177 (1803).

18. 80 U.S. (13 Wall.) 128 (1872).

19. 80 U.S. at 146–47.

20. The Supreme Court has invalidated such posting in public schools as violating the establishment clause of the First Amendment. *See Stone v. Graham,* 449 U.S. 39 (1980).

21. H.R. 1501, "Rights to Religious Liberty," section (b).

22. Of course, legislatures possess the ability to create additional rights by statute, beyond those recognized by courts as being constitutionally protected. *See, e.g., Katzenbach v. Morgan,* 384 U.S. 641 (1966). In *City of Boerne v. Flores,* 519 U.S. 1088 (1997), the Court reaffirmed that Congress cannot use its powers under section five of the Fourteenth Amendment to reinterpret the Constitution, but it may use this authority to enhance protection for constitutional rights.

23. 5 U.S. (1 Cranch) 137, 163 (1803).

24. Shirley Elder, "As Shaheen Plans are Foiled, Some Judges Fall Out of Favor," *The Boston Globe,* May 2, 1999, New Hampshire Weekly, p. 7.

25. Pub. L. No. 104-131, 110 Stat. 1321 (1996).

Appendix:

Historical Background of the Role of the Legislature in Setting the Power and Jurisdiction of the Courts

Erwin Chemerinsky[*]

A crucial topic in considering judicial independence is the relationship between the legislatures and the courts. As the Task Force Report observes, courts at the federal and state levels are both independent and interdependent of the other branches of government. The Task Force set out to identify basic principles as to when legislatures act unconstitutionally in setting the powers and jurisdiction of the courts. This paper is meant to provide historical background for the Task Force's conclusions.

The Founding

The debate over the relationship between the courts and the other branches of government can be traced to the earliest days of American history. The Constitution's framers were acutely concerned about

[*] Reporter, Task Force on the Role of the Legislature in Setting the Power and Jurisdiction of the Courts; Sydney M. Irmas Professor of Public Interest Law, Legal Ethics, and Political Science, University of Southern California.

judicial independence because of their experience with judges in the colonies who served at the pleasure of the King and were widely distrusted.[1] There was great dissatisfaction with a court system beholden to the King and unresponsive to the needs of the colonists. The enumeration of grievances in the Declaration of Independence stated that the King "made judges dependent upon his will alone for the tenure of their offices and payment of their salaries."

The Constitutional Convention recognized the need for a federal judiciary and, in fact, unanimously approved Edmund Randolph's resolution "that a National Judiciary be established."[2] To ensure the independence of the federal judiciary, the framers voted to accord all federal judges life tenure, "during good Behaviour," and salaries that cannot be decreased during their time in office.

In fact, a crucial, lasting difference between federal and state court judges is the electoral accountability of the latter. In thirty-eight states, state court judges are subject to some form of electoral review.[3]

Article III vests the judicial power of the United States "in one supreme Court and in such inferior courts as Congress may from time to time ordain and establish." A major dispute at the Constitutional Convention was whether lower federal courts should exist. The Committee of the Whole, echoing resolutions offered by Randolph, proposed that there should be both a Supreme Court and inferior courts.[4] This proposal drew strong opposition from those who thought it was unnecessary and undesirable to create lower federal courts. Opponents of lower federal courts argued that they were unnecessary because state courts, subject to review by the Supreme Court, were sufficient to protect the interests of the national government. Furthermore, lower federal courts were perceived as an unnecessary expense and a likely intrusion on the sovereignty of the state governments. Farrand explains: "[Inferior courts] were regarded as an encroachment upon the rights of the individual states. It was claimed that the state courts were perfectly competent for the work required, and that it would be quite sufficient to grant an appeal from them to the national supreme court."[5]

But others expressed distrust in the ability and willingness of state courts to uphold federal law. James Madison stated, "Confidence cannot be put in the State Tribunals as guardians of the National authority and interests."[6] Madison argued that state judges were likely to be biased against federal law and could not be trusted, especially in instances where there were conflicting state and federal interests.[7]

Appeal to the Supreme Court was claimed to be inadequate to protect federal interests because the number of such appeals would exceed the Court's limited capacity to hear and decide cases.

The proposal to create lower federal courts was initially defeated, five votes to four, with two states divided.[8] Madison and James Wilson then proposed a compromise. They suggested that the Constitution mandate the existence of the Supreme Court, but leave it up to Congress whether to create inferior federal courts. They said that "there was a distinction between establishing such tribunals absolutely, and giving a discretion to the Legislature to establish or not establish them."[9] Their proposal was adopted by a vote of eight states to two, with one state divided.[10] Congress, in its first judiciary act, established lower federal courts and they have existed ever since.

This history is important to contemporary discussions of judicial independence in two ways. First, Congress's control over some aspects of federal courts is part of the very structure of the Constitution. Congress is given discretion as to whether to create lower federal courts. This inevitably raises issues as to the extent of Congress's authority to control their jurisdiction and when exercise of this power is a threat to judicial independence. Second, some of the framers—most notably James Madison—expressed concern about judicial independence at the state level from the earliest moments of American constitutional history.

Although Article III is based on a strong belief in the need for an independent judiciary, the framers also institutionalized an interdependent relationship between the federal courts and the other branches of government. Congress, for example, determines the salary of federal judges, so long as they are not decreased during the terms of office. Additionally, Article III provides that, except for a few instances in which the Supreme Court is granted original jurisdiction, the Supreme Court is granted appellate jurisdiction, both as to law and fact, subject to "such Exceptions and under such regulations as Congress shall make." This is express authority for some congressional control over Supreme Court jurisdiction, though the scope of this authority has never been resolved.

The same issues regarding judicial independence and interdependence arise at the state level. Many of those who wrote state constitutions were just as concerned about judicial independence as those who framed the United States Constitution. On the other hand, many of the states experimented in their initial constitutions with the establishment of all-powerful legislatures as a contrast to an all-powerful executive,[11] only to learn the truth of Thomas Jefferson's warning that "173 despots would surely be as oppressive as one."[12] By the middle of the nineteenth century, states were rewriting their constitutions to constrain legislative power and begin a march toward greater judicial independence.[13]

At the state level, just as much as for the federal government, legislative actions can threaten judicial independence. State legislatures, too, have some control over state court jurisdiction and judges' salaries; often they have greater control than exists at the federal level. Most states do not have provisions prohibiting decreases in judicial salaries during their tenure in office. Thus, the same basic issues arise at both the federal and state levels as to the appropriate legislative role in setting powers and jurisdiction of the courts.

HISTORICAL EXPERIENCE WITH LEGISLATIVE CONTROL OVER THE JUDICIARY

The Task Force premised its report on the conclusion that "the ability of Congress to restrict the powers and jurisdiction of the federal courts is limited by Article III of the Constitution, as well as by the separation of powers, due process of law, and other constitutional provisions. Similarly, the ability of state legislatures to restrict the powers and jurisdiction of state courts is limited by provisions in state constitutions as well as by the guarantee of due process of law in the United States Constitution." The Task Force was particularly concerned about legislative actions that attempted to control the judiciary by restricting court jurisdiction to control substantive decision-making, by limiting remedies that courts can impose, and by directing judicial interpretation of the Constitution.

There is surprisingly little guidance from history and prior decisions concerning the scope of Congress's powers in these areas. Because Congress rarely has attempted such jurisdiction stripping—and never in a manner that has been interpreted as precluding *all* Supreme Court review or *all* federal court review—the question of constitutionality is uncertain. The scholarly literature is rich with articles arguing both sides of whether, and when, Congress may restrict federal court jurisdiction.[14]

Distinct constitutional issues are raised concerning Congress's authority over the Supreme Court as compared to over the lower federal courts. Those who believe that Congress can limit Supreme Court jurisdiction to hear particular matters point to the language of Article III, section 2: "[T]he supreme Court shall have appellate Jurisdiction, both as to Law and Fact, with such Exceptions, and under such Regulations as the Congress shall make." Supporters of jurisdiction-stripping proposals argue that the Framers of the Constitution intended such congressional control as a check on the judiciary's power.[15]

Opponents of jurisdiction-stripping proposals—including the Task Force—take a very different view of the language of Article III. Some argue that the term "Exceptions" in Article III was intended to modify the word "Fact."[16] The contention is that the Framers were concerned about the Supreme Court's ability to overturn fact-finding by lower courts, especially when done by juries. Hence, Congress was given the authority to control the manner in which the Supreme Court reviews questions of fact. Under this view, Congress could create an exception to the Supreme Court's jurisdiction for review of matters of fact, but Congress could not eliminate the Court's appellate jurisdiction for issues of law.

Alternatively, it is argued that even though Congress is given authority to limit Supreme Court jurisdiction under the text of Article III, this power—like all congressional powers—cannot be used in a manner that violates the Constitution. Opponents of jurisdiction restriction contend that congressional preclusion of Supreme Court review of particular topics would violate other parts of the Constitution.[17]

The initial Supreme Court decision concerning congressional control over Supreme Court jurisdiction is *Ex parte McCardle*.[18] McCardle was a newspaper editor in Vicksburg, Mississippi, who was arrested by federal officials for writing a series of newspaper articles that were highly critical of Reconstruction and especially of the military rule of the South following the Civil War. McCardle filed a petition for a writ of habeas corpus pursuant to a statute adopted in 1867 that permitted federal courts to grant habeas corpus relief to anyone held in custody in violation of the Constitution or laws of the United States by either a state government or the federal government. Under the 1867 law, the Supreme Court was empowered to hear appeals from lower federal courts in habeas corpus cases. Before 1867, under the Judiciary Act of 1789, which was supplemented but not replaced by the 1867 law, federal courts could hear habeas petitions of only those who were held in federal custody.

McCardle contended that the Military Reconstruction Act was unconstitutional in that it provided for military trials for civilians. He also claimed that his prosecution violated specific Bill of Rights provisions, including the First, Fifth, and Sixth Amendments. The United States government argued that the federal courts lacked jurisdiction to grant habeas corpus to McCardle under the 1867 Act. The federal government read the 1867 statute, despite its language to the contrary, as providing federal court relief only for state prisoners. The Supreme Court rejected this contention and set the case for argument on the merits of McCardle's claim that the Military Reconstruction Act and his prosecution were unconstitutional.[19]

On March 9, 1868, the Supreme Court held oral arguments on McCardle's constitutional claims. Three days later, on March 12, 1868, Congress adopted a rider to an inconsequential tax bill that repealed that part of the 1867 statute that authorized Supreme Court appellate review of writs of habeas corpus. Members of Congress stated that their purpose was to remove the McCardle case from the Supreme Court's docket and thus prevent the Court from potentially invalidating Reconstruction. Representative Wilson declared that the "amendment [repealing Supreme Court authority under the 1867 Act is] aimed at striking at a branch of the jurisdiction of the Supreme Court . . . thereby sweeping the [McCardle] case from the docket by taking away the jurisdiction of the Court."[20]

On March 25, 1868, President Andrew Johnson vetoed the attempted repeal of Supreme Court jurisdiction. The Congress immediately overrode President Johnson's veto on March 27, 1868.

The Supreme Court then considered whether it had jurisdiction to hear McCardle's constitutional claims in light of the recently adopted statute denying it authority to hear appeals under the 1867 Act that was the basis for jurisdiction in McCardle's petition. The Court held that it could not decide McCardle's case because of Congress' authority to create exceptions and regulations to the Court's appellate jurisdiction.

Chief Justice Salmon P. Chase, writing for the Court, began by noting that the "first question necessarily is that of jurisdiction," and that the case had to be dismissed for want of jurisdiction if the 1868 Act repealed the Court's authority under the 1867 statute.[21] Chief Justice Chase then observed that although the Court's authority stems from the Constitution, it "is conferred 'with such exceptions and under such regulations as Congress shall make.'"[22] The

Court concluded that the 1868 Act was an unmistakable exception to the Court's appellate jurisdiction, thus mandating the dismissal of McCardle's appeal. The Court stated: "The provision of the Act of 1867, affirming the appellate jurisdiction of this court in cases of habeas corpus is expressly repealed. It is hardly possible to imagine a plainer instance of positive exception."[23] Accordingly, the Court dismissed the case for lack of jurisdiction.

It should be noted that *McCardle* is easily distinguished from contemporary attempts to prevent Supreme Court review of topics such as abortion and school prayer. In *McCardle*, even after the repeal of the 1867 Act, the Supreme Court still had authority to hear McCardle's claims under the 1789 Judiciary Act, which allowed federal courts to grant writs of habeas corpus to federal prisoners. In other words, in *McCardle*, the Supreme Court was considering the constitutionality of a statute that did not completely preclude Supreme Court review, but rather eliminated only one of two bases for its authority. The *McCardle* Court expressly indicated that it still had jurisdiction in habeas corpus cases notwithstanding the repeal of the 1867 Act. The Court, at the conclusion of its opinion, declared:

> Counsel seem to have supposed, if effect be given to the repealing act in question, that the whole appellate power of the court, in cases of habeas corpus, is denied. But this is an error. The act of 1868 does not except from that jurisdiction any cases but appeals from Circuit Courts under the act of 1867. It does not affect the jurisdiction which was previously exercised.[24]

In fact, a year after its decision in *McCardle*, the Supreme Court in *Ex parte Yerger* held that it had authority to review habeas corpus decisions of lower federal courts under the Judiciary Act of 1789.[25]

The Supreme Court's next consideration of the constitutionality of jurisdiction restrictions was in *United States v. Klein.*[26] *Klein*, like *McCardle*, arose during Reconstruction. In 1863, Congress adopted a statute providing that individuals whose property was seized during the Civil War could recover the property, or compensation for it, upon proof that they had not offered aid or comfort to the enemy during the war. The Supreme Court subsequently held that a presidential pardon fulfilled the statutory requirement of demonstrating that an individual was not a supporter of the rebellion.[27]

In response to this decision and frequent pardons issued by the president, Congress quickly adopted a statute providing that a pardon was inadmissible as evidence in a claim for return of seized property. Moreover, the statute provided that a pardon, without an express disclaimer of guilt, was proof that the person aided the rebellion and would deny the federal courts jurisdiction over the claims. The statute declared that upon "proof of such pardon . . . the jurisdiction of the court in the case shall cease, and the court shall forthwith dismiss the suit of such claimant."[28]

The Supreme Court held that the statute was unconstitutional. While acknowledging Congress' power to create exceptions and regulations to the Court's appellate jurisdiction, the Supreme Court said that Congress cannot direct the results in particular cases. The Court stated:

> It seems to us that this is not an exercise of the acknowledged power of Congress to make exceptions and prescribe regulations to the appellate power. . . . What is this but to prescribe a rule for the decision of a cause in a particular way? . . . Can we do so without allowing one party to the controversy to decide it in its own favor? Can we do so without allowing that the legislature may prescribe rules of decision to the Judicial Department of the government in cases pending before it? . . . We think not. . . . We must think that Congress has inadvertently passed the limit which separates the legislative from the judicial power.[29]

Thus, opponents of proposals to restrict Supreme Court jurisdiction argue that *Klein* establishes that Congress may not restrict Supreme Court jurisdiction in an attempt to dictate substantive outcomes. By analogy, it would be unconstitutional for Congress to restrict Supreme Court jurisdiction in an attempt to undermine the Court's protections in cases involving controversial social issues such as abortion and school prayer.

Apart from these decisions that are more than a century old, the Supreme Court has had very little occasion to consider congressional efforts to restrict its jurisdiction. Recently, in *Felker v. Turpin*, the Supreme Court considered a federal law that precluded Supreme Court review of some habeas corpus petitions.[30] Title I of the 1996 Antiterrorism and Effective Death Penalty Act prohibits state prisoners from bringing successive habeas corpus petitions unless approval is received from the United States Court of Appeals.[31] The law precluded United States Supreme Court review, by appeal or certiorari, of any decision by a court of appeals granting or denying authorization for a state prisoner to file a successive habeas corpus petition.[32]

In *Felker v. Turpin*, the Supreme Court unanimously upheld the constitutionality of this jurisdictional restriction.[33] Chief Justice William Rehnquist, writing for the Court, emphasized that the law did not preclude *all* Supreme Court review of petitions from individuals denied the ability to file successive ones; the law did not repeal the Court's authority to entertain original habeas petitions.[34] The Court explained: "But since it does not repeal our authority to entertain a petition for habeas corpus, there can be no plausible argument that the Act has deprived this Court of appellate jurisdiction in violation of Article III, section 2."[35]

The authority of Congress over lower federal court jurisdiction is no more settled by prior case law. Again, the debate in the scholarly literature has been heated and lengthy.[36]

The Supreme Court in many cases has held that Congress's discretion as to whether to create lower federal courts gives it authority to determine lower federal court jurisdiction.[37] Yet it also has been recognized throughout American history that there are limits on Congress in the exercise of this power. Justice Joseph Story, in *Martin v. Hunter's Lessee*,[38] stated that the full judicial power must be vested in some federal court. Justice Story argued that "[t]he language of the article throughout is manifestly designed to be mandatory upon the legislature. . . . The judicial power of the United States *shall be vested* (not may be vested). . . . If then, it is the duty of congress to vest the judicial power of the United States, it is a duty to vest the *whole judicial power*."[39] Justice Story stated, "[i]t would seem, therefore, to follow, that congress [is] bound to create some inferior courts, in which to vest all that jurisdiction which, under the constitution, is *exclusively* vested in the United States and of which the supreme court cannot take original cognizance."[40]

Indeed, the Supreme Court long has interpreted federal statutes to avoid complete preclusion of federal court jurisdiction. For example, in *Johnson v. Robison,* the Court refused to interpret a statute limiting review of Veterans Administration decisions in a manner that would have foreclosed all judicial review.[41] Robison, a conscientious objector who had performed alternative service, challenged a federal statute that provided educational benefits to veterans but excluded conscientious objectors. A federal law appeared to preclude federal court review of Robison's claim. The statute provided: "[T]he decisions of the Administrator on any question of law or fact under any law administered by the Veterans Administration providing benefits for veterans . . . shall be final and conclusive and no official or any court of the United States shall have power or jurisdiction to review any such decision."[42]

The Court observed that there would be "serious question" about the constitutionality of this provision if it precluded all review. The Court, however, narrowly interpreted the statute and said that it did not apply in this case because this was not an objection to a decision made by the Veterans Administration, but instead a challenge to a statute adopted by Congress. The Court said that the purposes for the limit on judicial review—deference to the agency in awarding benefits—would not be undermined by allowing jurisdiction to hear challenges to the statute.

Similarly, in *Oestereich v. Selective Service System Local Board No. 14*, the Court narrowly interpreted a provision limiting review of Selective Service decisions.[43] During the 1960s, the Selective Service Commission retaliated against students involved in anti-Vietnam War protests by revoking their student deferments and classifying them as ready for induction. After the federal courts held that this was impermissible and enjoined the Selective Service Commission, Congress responded by adopting a statute limiting judicial review. The act provided that "no judicial review shall be made of the classification or processing of any registrant . . . except as a defense to a criminal prosecution . . . after the registrant has responded affirmatively or negatively to an order to report for induction."[44] The statute appeared to limit challenges to its validity to two contexts: defenses to a criminal prosecution and habeas corpus.

Oestereich was a full-time student at a theological school preparing for the ministry and was therefore entitled to a draft exemption under federal statutes. But after he participated in an antiwar protest, he was reclassified as I-A, ready for induction. Despite the federal statute appearing to preclude jurisdiction, the Court held that Oestereich could bring a suit challenging the legality of his reclassification. The Court held that the law limiting judicial review was not meant to apply to a clearly lawless action by a draft board. Justice Harlan, in a concurring opinion, stated that it "is doubtful whether a person may be deprived of his personal liberty without the prior opportunity to be heard by some tribunal competent fully to adjudicate his claims."[45]

In many other cases as well, the Court has interpreted statutes to leave open federal jurisdiction—even in the face of language and legislative intent that seems to foreclose a federal judicial forum.[46] The Court's decisions support the view—strongly endorsed by the Task Force—that principles of separation of powers and due process limit Congress's authority over lower federal court jurisdiction.

State constitutions also mandate separation of powers, leading state courts to strike down legislative attempts to exercise judicial power. In 1846, the Tennessee Supreme Court struck down such a legislative action in a case in which an 1838 statute regulating the sale of liquor was repealed and the legislature attempted to absolve all prior offenders of the earlier statute. In a case involving a pending prosecution, the court found the statute an unconstitutional interference with the judicial function.[47] A similar result was reached by the Pennsylvania Supreme Court in 1850 after the state legislature attempted to grant a new trial to the losing party in a trespass case.[48]

State constitutions also independently protect rights such as due process, a right to petition government for redress of grievances, and a right to a jury trial. In addition, thirty-eight states have constitutional provisions that require a right to a remedy for injuries and violations of rights. These provisions, too, limit the scope of legislative control over the judiciary.

PRINCIPLES LIMITING LEGISLATIVE CONTROL OVER THE JUDICIARY

The Task Force unanimously concluded that basic constitutional principles, as well as over two hundred years of American history, support its conclusions as to the limits that exist on legislative control over judicial power and jurisdiction. The Task Force believes that restrictions on jurisdiction become unconstitutional, as argued by Professor Henry Hart a half century ago, when "they destroy the essential role of the Supreme Court in the constitutional system."[49] For example, the Constitution's structure would be compromised if Congress could enact a law and immunize it from constitutional judicial review. The

Task Force also believes that due process and other constitutional provisions limit Congress' control over federal court jurisdiction.

The Task Force thus unanimously concluded that legislative acts stripping courts of jurisdiction to hear particular types of cases in an effort to control substantive judicial decisions are undesirable and inappropriate in a democratic system with coequal branches of government. Likewise, legislatures may not command a particular judicial interpretation of the Constitution. The Task Force also was unanimous in its conclusion that restrictions on remedies are generally undesirable and unconstitutional when they have the effect of leaving constitutional or other rights with inadequate redress.

The Task Force also recognized other ways in which legislatures can undermine judicial independence. For example, although legislatures have great latitude in determining the resources available to the judiciary, legislative actions that undermine the institutional functioning of the courts are undesirable and unconstitutional. The Task Force is unanimous in its conclusion that it is undesirable for the legislature to restrict funds for the judiciary in retaliation for specific court decisions. Moreover, at some point, where restrictions on funding are so great as to disable the judiciary from performing its basic tasks, the legislative action violates separation of powers.

Additionally, judicial independence requires the availability of courts to redress grievances. The Task Force thus unanimously concluded that legislation that restricts access to the courts and precludes individuals from using a judicial forum to vindicate rights is undesirable and unconstitutional. Rights are meaningless without a forum in which they can be vindicated. Legislatures have the duty to ensure meaningful access to the courts, and legislative actions that preclude this are undesirable and unconstitutional. The Task Force believes, for example, that legislatures should ensure adequate funding for legal services so that all in society have access to the judiciary.

For decades the debate over congressional restrictions on federal court jurisdiction has been academic, as Congress did not adopt any of the court-stripping proposals. Since 1994, however, Congress has enacted several important restrictions on jurisdiction. Each of these raises important questions concerning judicial independence and whether Congress has impermissibly violated the Constitution. Although the constitutionality of many of these provisions is unresolved, so far the Supreme Court has upheld all that it has considered.

For example, there have been significant restrictions on the authority of the federal courts to hear certain immigration matters. Both the Antiterrorism and Effective Death Penalty Act[50] and the Illegal Immigration Reform and Immigrant Responsibility Act of 1996[51] significantly restrict federal court jurisdiction over certain immigration matters.[52] The Antiterrorism and Effective Death Penalty Act greatly restricts the ability of federal courts to review deportation orders. The Act provides: "Any final order of deportation against an alien who is deportable by means of having committed a criminal offense [within the listed category] shall not be subject to review by any court."[53] Additionally, the Act expressly deletes the prior provision in federal law that permitted habeas corpus review of claims by aliens who were held in custody pursuant to deportation orders.[54] The law thus appears to foreclose all judicial review of deportation orders.[55]

Congress further restricted judicial review in the Illegal Immigration Reform and Immigrant Responsibility Act of 1996. This law repealed a long-standing provision that authorized judicial review in the circuit courts of appeals and guaranteed habeas corpus upon detention. Additionally, the act limits review of removal orders directed at aliens by declaring that "all questions of law and fact . . . arising from any action taken or proceeding brought to remove an alien from the United States under this title . . . shall be available only in judicial review of a final order."[56] The act also limits court review of discretionary decisions by the attorney general, stating that no court has jurisdiction to review such rulings by the attorney general as cancellation of removal,[57] voluntary departure,[58] or adjustment of status.[59]

In 1999, in *Reno v. American-Arab Anti-Discrimination Committee*, the Supreme Court upheld the provisions limiting review of deportation orders.[60] The case involved a First Amendment challenge to a deportation order by a group of individuals who claimed that they were being deported solely for constitutionally protected speech activities. The group repeatedly had prevailed in the lower federal courts prior to the enactment of the new law, but the government then invoked it and claimed that it stripped the federal judiciary of discrimination to hear the matter. The Supreme Court reversed the U.S. Court of Appeals for the Ninth Circuit and held that the law limits judicial review to final deportation orders and that this is permissible.

The availability of federal habeas corpus relief is another area in which Congress has recently restricted judicial review. The Antiterrorism and Effective Death Penalty Act of 1996 limits federal habeas corpus relief, especially by precluding successive habeas corpus petitions without the express permission of the Court of Appeals.[61] In *Felker v. Turpin*, the Court upheld this provision's restriction on Supreme Court review of Court of Appeals decisions by concluding that there remained some opportunity for Supreme Court review: writs for habeas corpus filed directly in the Court.[62]

Yet another federal law that imposes substantial limits on federal jurisdiction is the Prison Litigation Reform Act of 1995.[63] Among other things, the law provides for the termination of prospective relief issued by federal courts in prisoner cases and limits the remedies that federal courts can impose in prison condition cases. The Court of Appeals for the Ninth Circuit recently held the law unconstitutional.[64] Other courts, however, have upheld the law.[65] This statute could well provide the opportunity for the Supreme Court to answer a question that long has been unresolved: When may Congress limit the authority of federal courts to impose remedies in constitutional cases?

CONCLUSION

The most important lesson to be drawn from this history is the almost constant recognition by Congress, for over two hundred years, as to the importance of judicial independence. Successful attempts by Congress to restrict Supreme Court jurisdiction or to preclude all federal jurisdiction have been almost nonexistent. Likewise, at the state level, successful legislative efforts to control courts and undermine judicial independence have been rare.

The Task Force unanimously urges continued legislative self-restraint in this regard. Judicial independence is vital in a democratic society and legislatures must refrain from actions that compromise the ability of the courts to serve their essential functions. If and when legislatures act improperly, it is the duty of the courts to invalidate such actions to ensure continued judicial independence.

NOTES

1. *See* Charles Gardner Geyh, "The Origins and History of Federal Judicial Independence," in *An Independent Judiciary: Report of the ABA Commission on Separation of Powers and Judicial Independence,* American Bar Association, Washington, D.C., 1997, Appendix A.

2. Max Farrand, *The Records of the Federal Convention* (New Haven: Yale University Press, 1913), pp. 20–23.

3. *See* Julian N. Eule, *Judicial Review of Direct Democracy,* 99 Yale L.J. 1503, 1589–1590 (1990); Larry Charles Berkson, Scott Beller, and Michele Grimaldi, *Judicial Selection in the United States: A Compendium of Provisions* (Chicago: American Judicature Society, 1981) (listing each state's method of judicial selection).

4. Farrand, *The Records of the Federal Convention,* pp. 104–5.

5. Ibid., pp. 79–80.

6. Ibid., p. 27.

7. Ibid.

8. Ibid., p. 125.

9. Ibid.

10. Ibid.

11. *See, e.g.,* Gordon S. Wood, *Foreword: State Constitution-Making in the American Revolution,* 24 Rutgers L.J. 911, 916–917 (1993).

12. Thomas Jefferson, *Notes on the State of Virginia,* William Peden, ed., (Chapel Hill: University of North Carolina Press, 1955 [1781]), p. 157.

13. *See, e.g.,* Ill. Const. (1848), Ohio Const. (1851), and Ind. Const. (1851).

14. Recent scholarship on the issue includes: Akhil Amar, *The Two-Tiered Structure of the Judiciary Act of 1789,* 138 U. Pa. L. Rev. 1499 (1990); Daniel J. Meltzer, *The History and Structure of Article III,* 138 U. Pa. L. Rev. 1569 (1990); Martin H. Redish, *Text, Structure, and Common Sense in Interpretation of Article III,* 138 U. Pa. L. Rev. 1633 (1990); Barry Friedman, *A Different Dialogue: The Supreme Court, Congress and Federal Jurisdiction,* 85 Nw. U.L. Rev. 1 (1991); Akhil Amar, *Taking Article III Seriously: A Reply to Professor Friedman,* 85 Nw. U.L. Rev. 442 (1991); Mark Tushnet, *The Law, Politics, and Theory of Federal Courts: A Comment,* 85 Nw U.L. Rev. 454 (1991); Michael Wells, *Congress' Paramount Role in Setting the Scope of Federal Jurisdiction,* 85 Nw. U.L. Rev. 465 (1991).

15. *See, e.g.,* Herbert Wechsler, *The Courts and the Constitution,* 65 Colum. L. Rev. 1001, 1005–1006 (1965).

16. *See* Raoul Berger, *Congress v. The Supreme Court* (Cambridge, Mass.: Harvard University Press, 1969), pp. 285–96.

17. *See, e.g.,* Leonard Ratner, *Congressional Power over the Appellate Jurisdiction of the Supreme Court,* 109 U. Pa. L. Rev. 157 (1960); Lawrence Gene Sager, *Foreword: Constitutional Limitations on Congress' Authority to Regulate the Jurisdiction of the Federal Courts,* 95 Harv. L. Rev. 17 (1981); Laurence Tribe, *Jurisdictional Gerrymandering: Zoning Disfavored Rights out of the Federal Courts,* 16 Harv. C.R.-C.L. L. Rev. 129 (1981).

18. 74 U.S. (7 Wall.) 506 (1869). For an excellent discussion of this case, *see* William Van Alstyne, *A Critical Guide to Ex parte McCardle,* 15 Ariz. L. Rev. 229 (1973).

19. *Ex parte McCardle,* 73 U.S. (6 Wall.) 318 (1868).

20. *Quoted in* Van Alstyne, *supra* note 18, at 239.

21. 74 U.S. at 512.

22. *Id.* at 513.

23. 74 U.S. at 514.

24. *Id.* at 515.

25. 75 U.S. (8 Wall.) 85 (1869).

26. 80 U.S. (13 Wall.) 128 (1872). For an excellent discussion of this case, *see* Gordon G. Young, *Congressional Regulations of Federal Courts' Jurisdiction and Processes: United States v. Klein Revisited,* 1981 Wis. L. Rev. 1189.

27. *United States v. Padelford,* 76 U.S. (9 Wall.) 531 (1869).

28. 92 Stat. 2076.

29. 80 U.S. at 146–47.

30. 518 U.S. 651 (1996).

31. Pub. L. 104-132, 110 Stat. 1217, §106(b).

32. §106(b)(3)(E).

33. 518 U.S. 651 (1996).

34. *Id.* at 658.

35. *Id.* at 661–62.

36. *See, e.g.,* Akhil Amar, *A Neo-Federalist View of Article III: Separating the Two Tiers of Federal Jurisdiction,* 65 B.U. L. Rev. 205 (1985); Robert Clinton, *A Mandatory View of Federal Court Jurisdiction: A Guided Quest for the Original Understanding of Article III,* 132 U. Pa. L. Rev. 741 (1984); Theodore Eisenberg, *Congressional Authority to Restrict Lower Federal Court Jurisdiction,* 83 Yale L.J. 498 (1974); Martin H. Redish and Curtis Woods, *Congressional Power to Control the Jurisdiction of Lower Federal Courts: A Critical Review and New Synthesis,* 124 U. Pa. L. Rev. 45 (1975).

37. *See, e.g., Sheldon v. Sill,* 49 U.S. (8 How.) 441 (1850); *Kline v. Burke Construction Co.,* 260 U.S. 226 (1922); *Lauf v. E. G. Shinner & Co.,* 303 U.S. 323 (1938); *Lockerty v. Phillips,* 319 U.S. 182 (1943); *Yakus v. United*

States, 321 U.S. 414 (1944).

38. 14 U.S. (1 Wheat.) 304, 328–331 (1816). *See* Michael G. Collins, *Article III Cases, State Court Duties, and the Madisonian Compromise,* 1995 Wis. L. Rev. 39 (1995) (arguing that history supports Justice Story's theory; that the framers thought that state courts would not adjudicate federal issues and that Congress was required to create lower federal courts to hear these claims).

39. *Id.* at 328–330 (emphasis in original).

40. *Id.* at 331 (emphasis in original).

41. 415 U.S. 361 (1974).

42. 38 U.S.C. §211(a) (1982).

43. 393 U.S. 233 (1968).

44. Military Selective Service Act of 1967, 50 U.S.C. §10(b)(3) (1982).

45. 393 U.S. at 243–244 n.6.

46. *United States v. Mendoza-Lopez,* 481 U.S. 828 (1987); *McNary v. Haitian Refugee Center, Inc.,* 498 U.S. 479 (1991); *Reno v. Catholic Social Services,* 509 U.S. 43 (1993).

47. *State v. Fleming,* 26 Tenn. 152 (1846).

48. *DeChastellux v. Fairchild,* 15 Pa. 18 (1850).

49. Henry Hart, *The Power of Congress to Limit Jurisdiction of Federal Courts: An Exercise in Dialectic,* 66 Harv. L. Rev. 1362, 1402 (1953).

50. Pub. L. No. 104-132, 110 Stat. 1214.

51. Pub. L. No. 104-208, 110 Stat. 3009, amended Pub. L. No. 104-302, 110 Stat. 3656 (Oct. 11, 1996).

52. For a discussion of these provisions and their constitutionality, *see* Lenni B. Benson, *Back to the Future: Congress Attacks the Right to Judicial Review of Immigration Proceedings,* 29 Conn. L. Rev. 1411 (1997); Note, *The Constitutional Requirement of Judicial Review for Administrative Deportation Decisions,* 110 Harv. L. Rev. 1850 (1997).

53. Antiterrorism and Effective Death Penalty Act §440(a).

54. Antiterrorism and Effective Death Penalty Act §401(e). The Act also provides that an alien convicted of an aggravated felony is to be "conclusively presumed" to be deportable. A petition for review or for habeas corpus on behalf of such an alien may challenge only whether the alien is in fact an alien. §242A(c).

55. Lower courts generally have upheld the constitutionality of the restrictions found in the Antiterrorism and Effective Death Penalty Act. *See, e.g., Mansour v. INS,* 123 F.3d 423 (6th Cir. 1997); *Chow v. INS,* 113 F.3d 659 (7th Cir. 1997); *Yang v. INS,* 109 F.3d 1185 (7th Cir. 1997).

56. §242.

57. §240(a).

58. §240(b).

59. §245.

60. 119 S.Ct. 936 (1999).

61. Pub.L. 104-132, 110 Stat. 1214 (Apr. 24, 1996) (amended 1996, 1997).

62. 518 U.S. 651 (1996).

63. Pub. L. No. 104-131, 110 Stat. 1213 (1996).

64. *Taylor v. United States,* 1998 WL 214578 (9th Cir. 1998).

65. *See, e.g., Hadix v. Johnson,* 133 F.3d 940, 942-43 (6th Cir. 1998); *Dougan v. Singletary,* 129 F.3d 1424, 1426 (11th Cir. 1997); *Benjamin v. Jacobson,* 124 F.3d 162, 170-73 (2d Cir. 1997).